LEARNING TO TEACH CITIZENSHIP IN THE SECONDARY SCHOOL

What is the role of citizenship? How can it be taught effectively?

The fully updated second edition of *Learning to Teach Citizenship in the Secondary School* is an essential text for students training to teach citizenship as a first or second subject, as well as for experienced teachers who have opted to take responsibility for this vital subject.

Written in a clear and practical way, yet underpinned by a sound theoretical background, it examines citizenship as a wide-ranging subject that can be taught in its own right or through other curriculum subjects and activities.

The new edition includes a range of brand new chapters covering key themes in citizenship education, including:

- historical origins and contemporary contexts;
- developing subject knowledge and skills of enquiry;
- effective lesson plans, Schemes of Work, and assessment;
- citizenship beyond the classroom: community-based work and learning outdoors;
- citizenship across the curriculum: history, English, drama, media, and religious education;
- research in citizenship.

With key objectives and tasks for each chapter, this book will help trainee and practising teachers improve their understanding of citizenship education and in turn, help their pupils understand their roles as citizens in today's society.

Liam Gearon is Professor of Lifelong Learning and Participative Pedagogy at the University of Plymouth, UK.

LEARNING TO TEACH SUBJECTS IN THE SECONDARY SCHOOL SERIES

Series Editors: Susan Capel, Marilyn Leask and Tony Turner

Designed for all students learning to teach in secondary schools, and particularly those on school-based initial teacher training courses, the books in this series complement *Learning to Teach in the Secondary School* and its companion, *Starting to Teach in the Secondary School*. Each book in the series applies underpinning theory and addresses practical issues to support student teachers in school and in the training institution in learning how to teach a particular subject.

Learning to Teach in the Secondary School, 5th edition
Edited by Susan Capel, Marilyn Leask and Tony Turner

Learning to Teach Art and Design in the Secondary School, 2nd edition
Edited by Nicholas Addison and Lesley Burgess

Learning to Teach Design and Technology in the Secondary School, 2nd edition
Edited by Gwyneth Owen-Jackson

Learning to Teach English in the Secondary School, 3rd edition
Edited by Jon Davison and Jane Dowson

Learning to Teach Geography in the Secondary School
David Lambert and David Balderstone

Learning to Teach History in the Secondary School, 3rd edition
Edited by Terry Haydn, James Arthur, Martin Hunt and Alison Stephen

Learning to Teach ICT in the Secondary School
Edited by Steve Kennewell, John Parkinson and Howard Tanner

Learning to Teach Mathematics in the Secondary School, 2nd edition
Edited by Sue Johnston-Wilder, Peter Johnston-Wilder, David Pimm and John Westwell

Learning to Teach Modern Foreign Languages in the Secondary School, 3rd edition
Norbert Pachler, Ann Barnes and Kit Field

Learning to Teach Music in the Secondary School, 2nd edition
Edited by Chris Philpott and Gary Spruce

Learning to Teach Physical Education in the Secondary School, 2nd edition
Edited by Susan Capel

Learning to Teach Religious Education in the Secondary School, 2nd edition
Edited by L. Philip Barnes, Andrew Wright and Ann-Marie Brandom

Learning to Teach Science in the Secondary School, 2nd edition
Edited by Jenny Frost and Tony Turner

Learning to Teach Using ICT in the Secondary School, 2nd edition
Edited by Marilyn Leask and Norbert Pachler

Starting to Teach in the Secondary School, 2nd edition
Edited by Susan Capel, Ruth Heilbronn, Marilyn Leask and Tony Turner

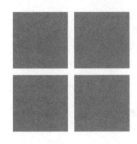

LEARNING TO TEACH CITIZENSHIP IN THE SECONDARY SCHOOL

A companion to school experience

2nd Edition

Edited by

Liam Gearon

Routledge
Taylor & Francis Group

LONDON AND NEW YORK

First published 2010
by Routledge
2 Park Square, Milton Park, Abingdon, Oxon OX14 4RN

Simultaneously published in the USA and Canada
by Routledge
270 Madison Avenue, New York, NY 10016

Routledge is an imprint of the Taylor & Francis Group, an informa business

© 2010 Liam Gearon for editorial material and selection.
Individual contributors, their contribution.

Typeset in Times and Helvetica
by Florence Production Ltd, Stoodleigh, Devon
Printed and bound in Great Britain by
TJ International Ltd, Padstow, Cornwall

British Library Cataloguing in Publication Data
A catalogue record for this book is available from the British Library

Library of Congress Cataloging in Publication Data
Learning to teach citizenship in the secondary school: a companion
to school experience/edited by Liam Gearon.—2nd ed.
      p. cm.
   Includes bibliographical references and index.
   1. Citizenship—Study and teaching (Secondary)—Great Britain.
   2. Civics—Study and teaching (Secondary)—Great Britain.
   I. Gearon, Liam.
   LC1091.L34 2009
   320.4071'241—dc22   2009001285

ISBN 10: 0–415–49905–4 (hbk)
ISBN 10: 0–415–48029–9 (pbk)
ISBN 10: 0–203–87456–0 (ebk)

ISBN 13: 978–0–415–49905–7 (hbk)
ISBN 13: 978–0–415–48029–1 (pbk)
ISBN 13: 978–0–203–87456–1 (ebk)

CONTENTS

ILLUSTRATIONS

TASKS

CONTRIBUTORS

Marcus Bhargava is Course Leader for PGCE Citizenship at the Department of Education, London Metropolitan University.

Liz Craft is Curriculum Adviser at the Qualifications and Curriculum Authority in England.

Hilary Cremin is Senior Lecturer in Young People's Social and Emotional Well-being at the Faculty of Education, University of Cambridge.

Ian Davies is Chair of the Board of Educational Studies and Course Director of the MA programme in Citizenship and Global Education at the University of York.

Liam Gearon is Professor of Lifelong Learning and Participative Pedagogy at the University of Plymouth.

Jeremy Hayward is Lecturer in Citizenship at the Faculty of Culture and Pedagogy, Institute of Education, University of London.

Derek Heater is former Dean of the Faculty of Social and Cultural studies at the then Brighton Polytechnic, and co-founder of the Politics Association.

John Keast is former Principal Manager for RE, Citizenship and PSHE at the Qualifications and Curriculum Authority (QCA). He is currently an advisor on Religious Education at the Department of Education and Skills.

David Kerr is Principal Research Officer, Director of the Citizenship Education Longitudinal Study and Associate Director IEA International Civic and Citizenship Education Study (ICCS) at the National Foundation for Educational Research, Birkbeck Institute for Lifelong Learning, University of London.

Sandie Llewellin is Senior Teaching Fellow and Subject Leader for PGCE Citizenship at University of Bristol.

John Moss is Dean of Education at the Faculty of Education, Canterbury Christ Church University.

Audrey Osler is Professor of Education and founding director of the Centre for Citizenship and Human Rights Education at the University of Leeds.

Andrew Peterson is Senior Lecturer at the Faculty of Education, Canterbury Christ Church University.

Tony Rea is Lecturer at the Department of Curriculum, Pedagogy and Educational Change, University of Plymouth.

Hugh Starkey is Reader in Education at the Faculty of Culture and Pedagogy, Institute of Education, University of London

Paul Warwick is Lecturer in Educational Reform at the University of Leicester.

Liz West is PGCE Secondary History and Citizenship Course Co-ordinator, University of Cumbria.

INTRODUCTION TO THE SERIES

Learning to Teach Citizenship in the Secondary School is one of a series of books entitled *Learning to Teach Subjects in the Secondary School* covering most subjects in the secondary school curriculum. The books in this series support and complement *Learning to Teach in the Secondary School: A Companion to School Experience, 5th edition* (Capel, Leask and Turner, 2009), which addresses issues relevant to all secondary teachers. These books are designed for student teachers learning to teach on different types of initial teacher education courses and in different places. It is hoped that they are equally useful to tutors and mentors in their work with student teachers. In 2004, the second edition of a complementary book was published entitled *Starting to Teach in the Secondary School: A Companion for the Newly Qualified Teacher* (Capel, Heilbronn, Leask and Turner). This book is designed to support newly qualified teachers in their first post and covers aspects of teaching which are likely to be of concern in the first year of teaching.

The information in the subject books does not repeat that in *Learning to Teach*; rather, the content of that book is adapted and extended to address the needs of student teachers learning to teach a specific subject. In each of the subject books, therefore, reference is made to *Learning to Teach*, where appropriate. It is recommended that you have both books so that you can cross-reference when needed.

The positive feedback on *Learning to Teach*, particularly the way it has supported the learning of student teachers in their development into effective, reflective teachers, has encouraged us to retain the main features of that book in the subject series. Thus, the subject books are designed so that elements of appropriate theory introduce each element of the teaching and learning process. Recent research into teaching and learning is incorporated into the discussion. The material is interwoven with tasks designed to help you identify key features of the behaviour or issue and apply them to your practice.

Although the basic content of each subject book is shared, each book is designed to address the unique nature of each subject. The knowledge and understanding that young people have about their duties and rights as a citizen is critical to the well-being of our society. Therefore you will find many different groups have an interest in citizenship education and so are interested in how to approach teaching citizenship and the contribution citizenship education makes to the ethos in the secondary school through its curriculum content and teaching methods.

We hope that, whatever the type of initial teacher education course you are following and wherever you may be following that course, you find this book useful and supportive of your development into an effective, reflective teacher. Above all, we hope that you enjoy teaching citizenship and that your pupils understand their role in society.

Susan Capel, Marilyn Leask and Tony Turner
July 2009

INTRODUCTION

Liam Gearon

Dating back to the role of the individual in the Greek city state – with ideas of rights, of duties to society, of equality of privileged citizens before the law, of the responsibilities of political office, of the processes of democracy and governance – citizenship retains a conceptual resonance today that would be recognisable to the Greeks. Though citizenship has a place in the ancient as well as modern history of ideas (Heater 2004), the contemporary world in which citizenship is debated would be far less than familiar to the Greeks (Morgan 2005). Paramount here would be the notion that human beings were inherently equal, a notion at odds with the kinds of philosophy of citizenship we find in Plato's *Republic* or Aristotle's *Politics*. Yet even in antiquity, tensions existed between whether citizenship applied to a narrow city state (the *polis*) or a wider notion of citizenship across states, the universal state (*cosmopolis*, from which we derive cosmopolitan), a more unifying definition, stressing what human beings share rather than geopolitical differences in culture, language and religion. Today, challenged in contexts where national identity is uncertain, and in global terms, where religious traditions encourage transnational allegiances, where cosmological and theological identity are more important than relations with earthly states, citizenship lacks consensus in both definition and sociopolitical application. Citizenship thus retains some of its characteristics from antiquity in contemporary context and, as it was in ancient times, it remains a contested concept. That in part is what gives the subject its educational, sociocultural, philosophical and political vitality. *Learning to Teach Citizenship in the Secondary School* engages with the theoretical and practical elements of a theoretical multidisciplinary subject, providing expert perspectives and pedagogical guidance for student teachers on how to engage children and young people with ancient notions of citizenship in contemporary context.

Heater's (2004) major study of citizenship is a history of the subject, and his chapter in this volume provides a helpful and concise synthesis of this history in Britain. An accessible overview of the *contemporary* context of citizenship education can be found in a report by the *House of Commons Education and Skills Committee* (2007). Acknowledged in this report is the late Sir Bernard Crick's influence on National Curriculum Citizenship in England (Crick 1998; DfEE 1999).

Crick also usefully outlined some parameters for defining citizenship at four often interrelated levels:

Firstly, it can refer simply to a subject's rights and duties to be recognised as a legally permanent inhabitant of a state – irrespective of the system of government of that state; but the principles behind such recognition can vary greatly, especially in relation to migrants.

Secondly, it can refer to the more specific belief (often called 'civic republicanism' . . .) that countries that enjoy constitutional government, representative government or democracy depend upon a high degree of active participation by inhabitants who themselves are active citizens, not simply good subjects.

Thirdly, it can refer to an ideal (once held by the Stoics of antiquity, now often called 'global citizenship') that we should all act as citizens of one world: that for the sake of peace, justice and human rights there must be limitations of international law on the sovereignty and power of individual states' powers.

And fourthly, 'citizenship' can refer to an educational process; learning and teaching in schools and colleges show how to improve or achieve the aims inherent in the second and third meanings.

(Crick 2004: 2)

Learning to Teach Citizenship in the Secondary School's distinguished group of teacher educators and researchers deal largely with the fourth of these elements. Thus, Jeremy Hayward reflects on what it is like actually starting to teach citizenship (Chapter 4), Liz West looks at the processes of developing subject knowledge (Chapter 5), Hilary Cremin and Paul Warwick examine the development skills of enquiry (Chapter 6) while Sandie Llwellin provides guidance on how to develop lesson plans and Schemes of Work in citizenship (Chapter 7). Marcus Bhargava deals with assessing and examining citizenship in Chapter 8. Because citizenship education, by its very nature, extends learning beyond the classroom, this practical emphasis develops strategies for both school- and community-based work. Three chapters deal with this aspect of citizenship: Liam Gearon (Chapter 9), Ralph Leighton (Chapter 10) and Tony Rea (Chapter 11).

Throughout, *Learning to Teach Citizenship in the Secondary School* also provides practical approaches to dealing with the legislative and related contexts you will face as a teacher of citizenship, especially official guidance on the National Curriculum provided by the Department for Children, Schools and Families (DCSF) and the Qualifications and Curriculum Authority (QCA). Thus the QCA and the DCSF provide outline Schemes of Work and a useful *Teacher's Guide for Citizenship*, including information on:

- what whole-school issues need to be considered when planning the citizenship curriculum;
- deciding how best to combine the different ways of delivering citizenship;

- links between citizenship and the non-statutory guidelines for PSHE, the other national curriculum subjects and religious education (RE), as well as literacy, key skills and thinking skills;
- how citizenship relates to issues of inclusion and diversity;
- how to assess pupils and involve them in reviewing their own progress;
- different approaches to teaching and learning, including ideas for developing active citizenship skills, such as participation and communication;
- how to use and combine units to ensure that the requirements of the Key Stage 3 Programme of Study for citizenship are addressed; and
- dealing with sensitive and controversial issues.

(DCSF, especially the Standards Site (www.dfes.gov.uk and follow links; www.qca.org.uk and follow links)

Learning to Teach Citizenship in the Secondary School's expert contributors address here, though, the wider philosophical, political, pedagogical and related contexts that permeate the practicalities of teaching citizenship, demonstrating the theoretical richness of the subject. Thus, as stated, Derek Heater provides an outline history of citizenship in Britain (Chapter 1), Ian Davies provides analysis of how we can define citizenship (Chapter 2), while John Keast and Liz Craft specifically examine the development and current context of National Curriculum Citizenship in England (Chapter 3). Since citizenship is taught both as a distinctive subject and across the curriculum, *Learning to Teach Citizenship in the Secondary School* also includes a sample of cross-disciplinary links: John Moss dealing with links between citizenship and English, drama and media education (Chapter 12), Andrew Peterson with those between citizenship and history (Chapter 13), and Liam Gearon those between citizenship and religious education (Chapter 14).

Learning to Teach Citizenship in the Secondary School closes with some of the leading researchers in citizenship: with Audrey Osler and Hugh Starkey (Chapter 15) 'Learning for cosmopolitan citizenship'; and analysis from David Kerr (Chapter 16) on 'Research in citizenship'.

Further, *Learning to Teach Citizenship in the Secondary School* includes two useful appendices:

Appendix 1: Useful websites and organisational links
Appendix 2: Citizenship and special educational needs: key resources and guidance

The book can be used as a source of historical and contemporary perspectives on citizenship, as an introduction to research in citizenship in national and international contexts and as a resource for the research-informed practicalities of learning to teach citizenship in secondary schools.

CITIZENSHIP

Historical origins and contemporary contexts

A HISTORY OF CITIZENSHIP IN BRITAIN

Derek Heater

INTRODUCTION

Understanding what is meant by the concept and practice of citizenship and providing learning and encouragement to take this social status seriously in the present are complicated and difficult enough; so why should we concern ourselves about the past?

There is room here for only the thinnest of outline answers to this kind of question about the purpose of history, an issue that has exercised the minds of innumerable historians, philosophers of history and educationists.

One of the most basic responses is to posit the following case. It is the necessity to comprehend the relationship between the present and the past. This understanding is necessary because knowledge of each illuminates the other; and the accuracy and profundity of the understanding of the two perspectives can well have significant effects. As the distinguished nineteenth-century English historian H.T. Buckle declared in his *History of Civilization in England*, 'There will always be a connection between the way in which men contemplate the past and the way they contemplate the present' (quoted Marwick 1970: 244).

A few words, therefore, about the negative dangers attendant upon a faulty understanding or ignorance of history and the positive benefits of a sturdy knowledge.

At worst, lacking a firm command of history or depending on a twisted collection of 'facts' can lead to prejudice and hatred, even violence. Think of some ethnic English people's hostility to, in chronological order, Jewish, Irish, Caribbean and Islamic immigrants being accorded the same civic rights as the host community. And think of some of those new resident people's unwillingness to assimilate the host community's traditions and life-style. Furthermore, think of how sound historical comprehension of the circumstances and reasons for this demographic mingling could have helped mitigate the tensions.

Turning to more intellectual issues, misunderstandings can occur if one reads the past development of citizenship anachronistically or as 'Whig' history. Citizens should be conscious, for instance, that current civil, political and social rights have by no means always been enjoyed; that their achievement is a story of intermittent struggles, not smooth progress; and that their ancestors' successes should be prized and vigilantly guarded. The story of the Chartist movement and the immediate failure to obtain their Six Points is a well-known example.

On the other hand, the valuable experiences of the past should not be dismissed or forgotten. Not everything that is present-day is new. And not everything introduced as fresh is necessarily novel: reinventing the wheel is an awful waste of time in politics as well as mechanical engineering. A clear example, for readers of this book, of simply reviving, as opposed to onerously reinventing, ideas of an earlier vintage is the presence in the Crick Report in 1998 of the work he had undertaken on Political Literacy and Key Concepts in the 1970s (see Crick and Porter 1978, and Crick 2000: ix, 59–96).

This warning and recommendation brings us to the positive advantages that can accrue from a sound grasp of the history of citizenship: to prize the benefits we now enjoy. First, we have the obvious argument that, because of pressures and concessions, progress has been made over the centuries. Without backtracking very far, the case-study of the development of women's rights is a clear lesson.

Second, with some judicious awareness of comparative history, it is possible to appreciate that Britain has developed its own characteristic style of citizenship. To present just a few differences from one example: the American form. Compared with the USA, Britain has no vivid revolutionary tradition; it has no written Constitution; (leaving aside recent devolution) it has no customary federal structure; it has a strong history of Imperialism, though not of internal slavery. The current attitudes towards, and meanings and practices of, citizenship in the two countries differ at least to some degree because of their different histories. A realisation of these dissimilarities can throw into sharp relief the specifically British tradition.

This brings us to a third advantage of historical knowledge, namely, recognising the complexity of citizenship. In Britain, its meaning and practice have constantly changed over time; studying its history renders this statement a platitude. Accordingly, some acquaintance with the historical processes of variation will make it easier to accept that the present condition should not be assumed to have been, nor will it continue to be, static.

The fourth consideration is that the very process of thinking historically while pondering about citizenship provides a depth of understanding of which one would otherwise be bereft. History offers a chronological context; it offers a narrative of pertinent events; it offers causative connections.

Moreover, and finally, we must notice the value for the especially interested British citizens of being introduced to the history of political theory. As a consequence, studying the great British thinkers such as the Levellers, Hobbes, Locke, J.S. Mill, T.H. Green and T.H. Marshall and their contributions to the concepts of citizenly rights, responsibilities and activities in everyday civic life sheds fascinating illumination onto our subject.

OBJECTIVES

At the end of this chapter you should be able to:

■   understand key aspects of the history of citizenship;
■   understand some of the ways in which this history of citizenship relates to citizenship in education.

PROBLEMS RELATING TO BRITISH HISTORY

But, what is this history of British citizenship that it is so essential to learn and understand? As with any facet of history as a subject to read and study, there is too much to digest. So what should be the principles of selection? This has been a particularly acute problem in English schools since the 1960s. Furthermore, the debates, sometimes acrimonious that started then, about what, when and how to teach the subject are still unresolved. Perhaps the widest agreement among the teaching profession, the news media, politicians and the public at large is the deep ignorance that abounds. At a teachers' conference in May 2008, for instance, the headmaster of the private Brighton College announced that, in the words of a journalist, 'he felt impelled to introduce a basic history course for 11- to 13-year-olds because so few had even a basic grasp of British history' (Cairns 2008). Even so: how much will they have remembered when they leave school; and what about the demands of the National Curriculum for state schools?

The issue of selection faces the writer also. I have but a few thousand words for this chapter. I hope that I have chosen material that will allow the reader to comprehend the main features of the lengthy and complex story and to recognise the background to the present pattern.

The history of citizenship is in general a confusing, complex story, and the British tale, for all its distinctiveness, and in some ways because of it, shares that character. It is possible to say, for example, that the status of citizen has existed for most of the past two millennia. However, what the status, even the word, meant was very different in, say, Roman, medieval, Tudor, Victorian or twentieth-century times.

A simple etymological examination of the word and its relatives is itself educational. We start with the Latin word '*civis*', meaning citizen. From this came the word '*civilis*', meaning civic. But, also, 'civil' in the sense of polite. By the early sixteenth century the English words 'civil/civility' had indeed extended, like the Latin antecedents, from their original political meaning to the behavioural connotation. A citizen was courteous, socially well-mannered.

To return to the political usage. 'Citizen' derives from Latin and Norman-French words that had strong allusions to an urban connection. Thus the English word 'city' emerged in the thirteenth century from the Latin '*civitas*', itself deriving from '*civis*' and diversifying into a portmanteau word meaning 'city', 'state', 'citizenship'. The post-Conquest word for a person identified with a city was '*citesein*'.

Two especially interesting points follow. One is that the first Britons to carry the status of citizen were accorded that title by the Romans – they were *cives Romani*, the earliest, as far as we know, being residents of Verulanium, now called St Albans. The second comment is that, for centuries, the terms 'citizen' and 'citizenship' were, in fact, confined to cities. Some pedants maintained that sole usage even to a century ago. And, of course, that usage has not died: it survives alongside the word's state/national meaning. As a British national I am a citizen of the United Kingdom; as a resident in a ward within the bounds of Brighton and Hove I am a citizen of that city.

THE MEDIEVAL AND RENAISSANCE AGES

The reality of citizenship (even though not by title) in a medieval municipality – whether a city or mere borough – indicated a status, held by those members who had the franchise. This provided sets of activities, rights and responsibilities as defined in the municipality's royal charter.

By this system, which was strongly sustained throughout the Middle Ages, the citizens elected and stood for the various local offices, engaged in and oversaw general administrative needs, justice (including the jury system), policing and the management of the economy and environment. It was citizenship in a very real and active, albeit somewhat elite, sense. The following very brief excerpt from Lincoln's city charter is indicative of the use of the term 'citizen' and the tight detail of the regulations: 'four men worthy of trust shall be elected from amongst the citizens . . . to keep an account of outgoings, tallages, and arrears belonging to the city, and that they shall have one chest and four keys' (Bagley 1965: 76).

Towns with the lower rank of borough were organised by similar arrangements, though the title of 'citizen' was denied, the equivalent being 'burgess'. Any expansion of the use of the term was, in fact, inhibited in both medieval and modern times by several factors. One was that the country had thoroughly rooted Anglo-Saxon and feudal traditions, which had no need of the wide concept of citizenship as developed by the Romans. Another, in modern times, was the continuation of the monarchy, which ensured that the British people were considered legally and constitutionally as subjects of the sovereign, not citizens of the state.

Nevertheless, during the Middle Ages and, more so, at the time of the Renaissance, knowledge of classical literature burgeoned. Many of these works contained information and discussions about the principles of citizenship, especially civic virtue, which so coloured ancient Greek and republican Roman political thinking and practice. These ideas were absorbed and expressed in a British context by scholars known as the Humanists. True, in developing their civic proposals their vocabulary rarely contained the word 'citizenship'. Even so, as most wrote in Latin, the temptation to think of citizenship in state terms was surely there.

Let us take one of the most distinguished sixteenth-century scholars, the Scotsman, George Buchanan. He argued that good citizens (notice the qualifying adjective) should participate in national government. An English translation of one of his key sentences, defining citizens in this sense, runs thus: 'Those who obey the laws, who maintain human society, who would rather undergo every hardship and every peril for the well-being of their fellow countrymen, than, through cowardice, grow old in dishonourable ease' (Burns 1951: 64).

THE CIVIL WAR

But leap forward the traditional human life-span of three score years and ten to the period of the Civil War and we reach a recognisably modern discussion about citizenship, notably through the penetrating arguments of the radical group called the Levellers.

From the thirteenth century the endowment of the franchise existed in a meaningful, though again elitist, sense through the parliamentary as well as the municipal system. When antagonism between king and parliament intensified during the reign of Charles I, and to the horrific extent of civil war, dethronement and regicide, the issues of constitutional change and the legal and political rights of 'freeborn Englishmen' (to use the current widely used term) became urgent practical, not just theoretical, matters. The most distinguished campaigner for radical reform was John Lilburne, whose activities and publications earned him popularity, imprisonment and the sobriquet 'Freeborn John'.

By 1647 the army had become a considerable, politically conscious, force. In that year representatives gathered for discussion at St Mary's Church in the Surrey village of Putney. Their recorded Debates are a crucial turning-point in the evolution of citizenship in this country. The key document for discussion was *The Agreement of the People*, based in large measure on the views of Lilburne. The central, controversial issue was the right to the parliamentary vote. Should the national franchise be democratically defined or confined to the relatively wealthy? Colonel Rainsborough pronounced the democratic case, summed up in the following words:

> I think it's clear, that every man that is to live under a government ought first by his own consent to put himself under that government; and I do think that the poorest man in England is not at all bound in a strict sense to that government that he has not had a voice to put himself under.
>
> (Wootton 1986: 38)

Now, although the word 'citizen' in the modern, national sense was not used in these Debates, it is implied; and there is evidence that it was at about this time that the broader meaning was coming into vogue, beyond the absorption of its scholarly, classical rendering.

HOBBES AND LOCKE

However, during the 40 years from 1649 to 1689 – from the creation of the republican Commonwealth to the Bill of Rights – although there were constitutional innovations aplenty, they contained little alteration to the political status of citizenship.

On the other hand, it was during this period that Britain's most renowned political theorists wrote their major works pertinent to our interest here. Thomas

Hobbes published the main edition of his *De Cive* (*On the Citizen*) in 1647 and *Leviathan* in 1651. John Locke published the Latin version of *A Letter Concerning Toleration* in 1689 and the *Two Treatises on Civil Government* in 1690.

Both were writing in the context of social contract theory. Famously, Hobbes has been categorised as formulating a conservative interpretation and Locke, a liberal one, though both, especially Locke, were more subtle and complex in their arguments than this dichotomy suggests. True, Hobbes stressed citizens' duties and Locke, citizens' rights.

For our purposes Hobbes' use of the Latin word for citizen as the very title of his essay is significant. Yet his case that, by virtue of the social contract, the citizen owes strict obedience to the sovereign is made quite clear. In the English translation, for example, he states, 'Each of the *citizens* . . . is called a SUBJECT of him who holds sovereign power' (Hobbes 1998: 74). And notice his emphases. Citizens are responsible for sustaining political stability, even though, he concedes, they by no means all have the will or competence to be trusted to do so. However, it is only later, in *Leviathan*, that Hobbes tackles this problem by advocating adult civic education.

Locke's fame as a political theorist rests on his assertion of man's rights of life, liberty and property. In principle, therefore, all, irrespective of social status, should be able to enjoy them, equally. Moreover, no monarch could infringe them. However, the issue of property was so dear to Locke's heart that he found it difficult to allow the suffrage to all irrespective of the size of property-ownership. Citizenship still has an elitist character: a matter of considerable recent intellectual discourse on his writings.

Much modern academic study of citizenship, though criticised for being over simplistic, has also made the distinction between the 'republican' style, rooted in the ancient classical world and emphasising citizenly virtue, on the one hand; and the modern 'liberal' style, emphasising citizenly rights, on the other. Locke, because of his influence on eighteenth-century thinking and reform outside Britain, has been considered the father of the latter.

Nevertheless, even if Locke's message about political citizenship is, on reflection, a little ambivalent, his influence on civil, that is legal, rights is less equivocal. He was keenly interested in the right of liberty and the rule of law. For example, Locke was a personal friend of the Earl of Shaftesbury, who successfully introduced the Habeas Corpus Amendment Act of 1679; and his work on religious toleration was reflected in the Toleration Act of 1689.

THE EIGHTEENTH CENTURY AND CONTEXTS

Arriving at the eighteenth century, we can provide an easy structure for our analysis by focusing on two themes. These are: the quality and representativeness of the parliamentary system and the feelings of patriotism and nationhood.

At the beginning of the century, in 1707, the Scottish and English parliaments were amalgamated. This is a cue to admit that much of the above material relates mainly to England. So, a few words here about the nature of citizenship north of the border prior to the Act (Treaty in Scottish terminology) of Union. The Scottish parliamentary and local government systems were roughly similar to the English, though they developed more slowly; indeed there was less enthusiasm among the Scots to participate. Even so, the fourteenth and sixteenth centuries were periods of increasing civic consciousness.

The earlier of those two centuries witnessed an efflorescence of patriotic and national consciousness. Notable dates include Wallace's uprising against English intrusion in 1297, Robert Bruce's victory at Bannockburn over the English in 1314 and the Declaration of Arbroath in1320. These events in the struggle to sustain Scotland's independence revealed a sense of nationhood – for example, the Declaration, written in Latin, refers to the *natio Scottorum*. And the widespread support for military resistance against the English provides a clear echo of the ancient classical tradition of civic duty and virtue in the form of army service.

Both the Renaissance and the Reformation had strong influences in Scotland. The fissiparous effects of the Reformation, added to the traditional inter-clan hostilities, initially rendered the sixteenth century an age of the undermining of the earlier unifying national consciousness. As a reaction, the need for civic leadership by the aristocracy to prevent the country's disintegration became accepted. In addition, with the accession of James VI as King of England in 1603, a few civically thoughtful people were now pondering on a new, integrated British nationhood and patriotism.

The equation of nationality and citizenship has become increasingly accepted in modern years. The validity of, and the difficulties attending this habit will be discussed below. Here we need to explain how the two terms were understood and accepted in Britain in the eighteenth century. 'Citizenship' was regularly used in the early and late decades in political debates (*c.*1690–1740 and *c.*1760–1815); the consciousness of nationhood throughout the century was more vague.

Linda Colley has argued powerfully in her *Britons: Forging the Nation 1707–1837* that, during this period, a national consciousness was welded mainly by an acceptance of the English–Scottish amalgamation, universal hostility to the ancient enemy, France, and commitment to the Protestant faith.

Popular patriotic/national feeling came to be expressed from the 1740s by the singing of *Rule Britannia* and *God Save the King*. Although Britain was at war with France continually from 1689 to 1815, it was the almost continuous conflict with Revolutionary and Napoleonic France that really intensified Britain's Francophobe sense of national identity. Hatred and fear of the Terror and the threat of invasion were the main adhesives. It was then that John Bull became the anti-French symbol of British nationhood. Nonetheless, whether a sense of Britishness in this age extended very much beyond the English upper classes has been questioned.

However, in its early years, the Revolution consolidated France as the very epitome of the citizenly state, a determination unambiguously expressed in its first Constitution and Declaration of the Rights of Man and the Citizen, and, for a while later, the proud adoption of the titles of *citoyen* and *citoyenne*. In 1789 Britons of a reforming and radical turn of mind became envious. As Wordsworth later wrote: 'Bliss was it in that dawn to be alive.'

For Britain still had a corrupt, aristocratic political system, against which the advocates of civic virtue and of a democratic franchise, respectively, campaigned during the two chronological patches already mentioned. In the first of these periods, commentators were looking back to the ideal of the past classical age of republican virtue; in the second, to a future ideal of radical reform.

First, then, the half-century from roughly 1690, was the age of the tussle between the ideal principle of virtue and the real practice of political corruption. Robert Walpole became famous for being the first prime minister, thus strengthening parliament against the power of the monarch, and notorious for entrenching avarice and bribery for himself and his friends, as a means of maintaining their own power. The disease of corruption spread. Even as early as the reign of William III a popular essayist, Charles Davenant, wrote: 'The little publick spirit that remained among us, is in a manner quite extinguished. Every one is upon the scrape for himself, without any regard to his country' (quoted Dickinson 1977: 110).

This was the very antithesis of citizenly behaviour. Men of conscience sought to rectify the condition. The most renowned campaigners for civic virtue as a means of counteracting the corrupt practices, that is, achieving an efflorescence of a righteous mood of citizenship, were Viscount Bolinbroke, most notably, and two men who wrote under the combined *nom de plume* of 'Cato', harking back to that personification of Roman republican virtue.

Bolingbroke became utterly committed to combating the evil of Walpole's corrupt government. Particularly through the medium of his successful journal *The Craftsman*, he publicised the sharp contrast between the vices of Whig England and the virtues of republican Rome. He also suggested that good British citizens were those who supported his anti-Walpole campaign, which would be a public form of civic virtue.

The other organ publicising civic virtue at this time was *Cato's Letters*, the publishers of which were more pessimistic about the existence among Britons of the public-spirited altruism that Bolingbroke's case required. In contrast, Cato appealed for a private civic virtue. The argument was that the British citizen's freedom and property were endangered by the current corruption, so a combined effort was needed; that is, the success of a selfish, privately motivated campaign depended on a publicly organised onslaught against the threat.

These publishing operations emanated from London. Meanwhile, Scotland, with its more scholarly environment and home of the vigorous Scottish Enlightenment, was, therefore unsurprisingly, the birthplace of a different idea. This was that intellectuals should provide leadership and advice in the move for more and better civic consciousness.

Interesting as these illustrations of thinking about citizenship are for those of us who are taken up today with the study of the subject, the influence of such work proved to be evanescent. Of greater and more persistent strength were the writings and activities demanding reform of the parliamentary franchise.

Although there was much to be criticised about the British political and social systems before the reforming programmes got under way from *c.*1832, the country was the envy of many continentals. Voltaire's *Letters on England* provide famous evidence. Even so, historians have been warned recently not to draw too complacent a picture of the eighteenth century, especially by J.C.D. Clark's *English Society 1688–1832: ideology, social structure and political practice during the ancien regime*. Notice the telling use of the pre-revolutionary French term to reduce the supposed distinction between the two major European powers.

It is therefore no coincidence that demands for parliamentary reform burgeoned in Britain at the time of the age of the Atlantic revolutions from the American Revolution onwards and, particularly, during the French Revolution, the most dramatic of them all.

We can identify three main themes. These are: the relationship between the electorate and parliament; how far property ownership should define the franchise; and the nature of citizenship rights.

The right to select one's representative in the legislature is a basic indicator of citizenship. In the eighteenth century, even Britons who by law had the right to vote by the suffrage arrangements were denied that power in fact because of the atmosphere and practice of corruption. For example, in 1793 a reform body called the Society of the Friends of the People estimated that of the 513 MPs representing English and Welsh constituencies, 303 obtained their seats by patronage or nomination. So much for the electoral process! And consequently discontent could rarely be channelled through MPs. Hence demonstrations occurred as outlets of demands. We shall return to this topic later.

But even if the franchise was fairly administered, the question that we have seen was raised by the Levellers – who should be eligible – remained a divisive issue: property qualification or, to use the accepted term, universal manhood suffrage? From *c.*1760 to 1780 a radical movement grew in strength and breadth of demands for parliamentary reform. Metropolitan and regional organisations flourished, most famously the Society for Constitutional Information, the London Corresponding Society and the Yorkshire Association. Members varied in their characters and radicalism, some of the most advanced in their views being considered a tad eccentric: Major Cartwright and the Duke of Richmond, for instance. The latter even introduced a Bill in the House of Lords in 1780 for annual elections, equal electoral districts, secret ballot, abolition of property qualifications for MPs, payment of MPs and universal manhood suffrage. Few of their Lordships were very keen on these ideas!

By the end of the eighteenth century the Lockean concept of natural rights was entering the vocabulary of political discourse. Of particular fame were the French Declaration of the Rights of Man and the Citizen of 1789 and the American Bill of Rights of 1791. These ideas were echoed in England by Thomas Paine's two-volume *The Rights of Man* (1791–92) and Mary Wollstonecraft's *Vindication of the Rights of Woman* (1792). Whereas the traditional concept of citizenship had stressed the political rights and duties of men of that status, these two works were landmarks for canvassing arguments for what has more recently been called social citizenship; Paine detailing a kind of welfare state system and Wollstonecraft, of course, highlighting the unjust plight in society of the female half of the population.

Pressure for increasing membership of the citizenly status, advances in acceptance that reform was needed, legislation to facilitate progressive changes and identification of the nature of citizenship, characterise British citizenship during the period from about the 1820s to the present day.

Focus on the extension of the franchise

Taking stock in the 1820s and comparing that age with the enjoyment of citizens' rights today, we may list the following restrictions in the earlier time. Women were denied many legal as well as almost all political rights, the age of majority was set at 21, membership of trade unions was effectively illegal, Roman Catholics were denied the franchise and Protestants who were not members of the Church of England had limited rights.

What of the milestones of progress from then? In 1829 Catholics were allowed the vote; by Acts of Parliament in 1918 and 1928 women were given that right; in 1969 the age of majority was lowered to 18. A start was made in 1824 to provide trade unions with rights and in 1828 Non-Conformists were relieved of their social disabilities.

The three Reform Acts of the nineteenth century gradually modernising parliament were due to the initiatives of key politicians, namely, Lord Grey and Lord John Russell (1832), Disraeli and Lord Derby (1867) and Gladstone (1884).

But there are two questions of greater historical and political interest. One is, how far has public pressure led to such reforms? The other is, how far can movements and demonstrations for these ends, whether successful or not, be regarded as citizenly actions even if undertaken by people denied effective citizenly rights? Put more bluntly, how does one distinguish between a justifiable civic assembly from a dangerous riotous mob when their motives and objectives are the same – the pursuit of civic rights?

To take a few notable examples, though there is no space here for vivid detail. To cover this issue effectively we must backtrack to the eighteenth century. From 1768 to 1774 the colourful personality John Wilkes was elected as MP for Middlesex several times and denied his seat by the House of Commons because of his shady character. By what right did parliament thwart the will of the enfranchised citizens? Demonstrations, some disorderly, took place in London and Middlesex until, in 1774, parliament succumbed.

After the Napoleonic War came to an end in 1815, popular demand for parliamentary reform revived. Notoriously, a perfectly peaceful meeting in St Peter's Field, Manchester, in 1819 was bloodily dispersed by the yeomanry – it was dubbed the Peterloo Massacre by analogy with the recent Battle of Waterloo. For a number of years in the nineteenth century an organisation known as the Chartists existed, demanding parliamentary reform, listing six points in their Charter – the same as the Duke of Richmond's two generations before. Their biggest gathering took place in 1848 at Kennington Common, south London. Strong policing had been prepared, but was not necessary. Unlike the bitter revolutionary activity on the continent, including the French capital in the same year, the Chartists dispersed. As a French observer commented: the British will never have a revolution because the weather is too bad. The Chartists were, at least partly, deterred by the heavy rain that day!

These events have become more famous than those surrounding the passage of the Second Reform Bill in 1867. Yet they raise interesting questions for us. The year 1866 brought popular discontent and worries. Economic troubles were epitomised by the collapse of a leading London financial house and serious difficulties on the Stock Exchange. (At the start of the financial crisis in 2008, some historically literate journalists referred back to this precedent.) Expectations of a new Reform Bill seemed to be threatened by the hesitation of the new Conservative government. A gathering in London became the most serious outburst of protest: the crowd tore down the railings of Hyde Park, which had been closed by the authorities to prevent the meeting. The shutting off of this traditional place of popular gathering in London especially infuriated the assembled throng. Indeed, the Home Secretary himself actually burst into tears when he heard of this action by local officialdom.

Meanwhile the politicians were struggling to devise an acceptable compromise between universal suffrage and property qualification. 'Fancy franchises' were suggested by many. A particularly bizarre proposal was offered by the famous radical John Bright: that rat-catchers who owned two dogs should be enfranchised! A number of politicians were horrified at the prospect of enlarging the electorate, yet as a result of the confused debates, what emerged was more radical than intended. It is estimated that it more than doubled.

By this date, the distinguished political philosopher, John Stuart Mill, had become an MP. Moreover, he was thoroughly convinced that women should be enfranchised; though his amendment to the Bill providing for this measure was defeated. Nonetheless, a respectable number of MPs did support him. Less than half a century later, militant women, led by the Pankhursts and called 'suffragettes', were organising demonstrations that could by no means be ignored. After a few years, women's very evident performance of distinguished civic duties during the changed circumstances from peace to wartime conditions with the start and exacerbation of the First World War undermined the arguments against their enfranchisement.

THE WELFARE STATE

We have now arrived in the twentieth century, a period in which concern about the need for improvement in social rather than political citizenship was coming to the forefront; what came to be called 'the Welfare State'.

The intellectual grounding for these reforms was laid in the late nineteenth century by the philosophers known as the 'British Idealists', under the influence of the Oxford scholar T.H. Green. The two periods of legislation were 1908–11 and 1944–48. It is of note that the prime ministers in both these periods, namely, Asquith and Attlee, were influenced by Green's thinking.

The 1940s reforms both improved on and expanded the range of the earlier Acts by adding education reform and the creation of the National Health Service to more generous social insurance arrangements. The inspiration for these foundations of current social rights of citizenship was a pamphlet published in 1942, in advance of the end of the Second World War and which became eponymously referred to as the Beveridge Report. William Beveridge was also influenced by the Idealist philosophy. His message, almost a catch-phrase, was that five giants had to be attacked on the road to post-war reconstruction: Want, Disease, Ignorance, Squalor and Idleness.

T.H. MARSHALL

The interpretation that citizenship is not solely a political matter was significantly argued by the British sociologist T.H. Marshall in a series of lectures, published in 1950 in enlarged book form as *Citizenship and Social Class*. Although some features of his thesis have been criticised, three main lessons can be learned from Marshall. We can do no better than quote his own words. One is the famous tripartite analysis of the constituents of citizenship:

> [Civil:] rights necessary for individual freedom – liberty of the person, freedom of speech, thought and faith, the right to own property and to conclude valid contracts, and the right to justice . . . . [Political:] right to participate in the exercise of political power, as a member of a body invested with political authority or as an elector of the members of such a body . . . . [Social:] the whole range from the right to share to the full in the social heritage and to live the life of a civilised being according to the standards prevailing in the society.
>
> (Marshall and Bottomore 1992: 8)

The second lesson, and most controversial, is his argument that the rights developed in sequence: very roughly, civil rights in the eighteenth century, political in the nineteenth, and social in the twentieth.

The third lesson is his assertion that 'the inequality of the social class system may be acceptable provided the equality of citizenship is recognised'.

DEVELOPMENT OF CURRENT INTEREST

Although intellectuals before Marshall had used the term 'citizenship', particularly those such as J.S. Mill, with a firm classical education, it did not sit comfortably in British political and social discourse; not until more than a generation after Marshall's lectures. Then, in 1988, the renowned journalist Hugo Young famously described the astonishing lexical alert in the following assertion:

> Something is rotten in the state of Britain, and all the parties know it . . . . The buzz-word emerging as the salve for this distress is something called citizenship. . . . Somewhere out there there is an immense unsatisfied demand for it to mean something. But it needs to become much more than a word.
>
> (Young 1988)

Notice the phrase 'something called', an indicator of its hitherto unfamiliarity.

By this time academics had found the topic a fertile field for investigation. For a few years politicians thought it beneficial to associate themselves with the theme. The Conservative Party tried to popularise the concept of active citizenship, namely, individuals' acceptance and practice of their civic responsibilities. And all three main parties published their 'citizens' charters'. However, not until the turn of the century, during the Labour administrations of Blair and Brown, was the issue of citizenship publicly taken seriously.

This chapter was written in the middle of 2008, after the publication of the Home Office green paper *The Path to Citizenship* and the 'citizenship review' by the former Attorney General Lord Goldsmith, which, in turn, followed a decade of discussion and legislation and with even more promised.

What is clear from all this mental activity is that the subject has been, and continues to be, drenched in confusion. From an historian's perspective we can usefully ask how this muddle has derived from our political, legal and social inheritances. There are two crucial linguistic clues in the current flood of commentary. One is the unquestioned assumption that citizenship and nationhood are synonymous. The other is that the felt need for clarification and legislation has been triggered by intensive immigration. Each will be examined in turn.

Although we have the authority of international law since the early nineteenth century that the words 'citizenship' and 'nationality' are interchangeable – a British passport reveals one's identity as 'National status/nationalité: British Citizen' – this universal legal practice is both relatively modern and equivocal. One example of the resultant confusion has been expressed by the British constitutional lawyer, Dawn Oliver: 'English law generally prefers the word "citizen" to "national", but it also employs the term "subject"' (Oliver and Heater 1994: 53).

Only *c.*1800 did the two concepts merge as a result of the burgeoning of the ideology of nationalism. Prior to that, 'citizenship' described a sociopolitical identity, 'nationality', a cultural identity.

The word 'identity' is crucial because it means a sense of belonging as well as legal status. Moreover, in new arguments in Britain, the term 'Britishness' (a word my ageing spell-check does not recognise!) has been bandied about, often meaning British identity as acceptance of being a member of the British cultural nation.

To illustrate the distinction: a person can be politically/legally a British citizen, but feel culturally Scottish, Muslim or Filipino, for instance, or an amalgam – hyphenated Britons, to copy the American practice. It is most unfortunate that, just at the time in British history when it is vital to understand the distinction between citizenship and ethnicity, we persist in linguistically melding the two concepts by utilising the word 'nationality' for both. The reason for recognising the two meanings is closely related to the constant present-day appearance of the word 'immigration' in the context of citizenship. Because of the recent increased influx of foreign peoples, arrangements have been required to incorporate them legally and socially as loyal and compatible citizens. Of course, acceptance that 'nationality' in both its etymological meanings is identical with 'citizenship' has been, consciously or subconsciously, a convenient device for achieving these ends. But danger lurks in the resultant dilution of national cultural identity, antagonising both British nationalists and ethnic minorities.

Here, again, historical reasons for the 'mongrelisation' of Britain in recent years (let alone over millennia) should be appreciated. They are the results of the country's membership of the British Empire and Commonwealth and of the European Union.

It is sometimes said that, just as Britons colonised the Caribbean, southern Asia and parts of Africa in past centuries, so, during the past half-century, Britain has been colonised by peoples from those lands. How have the processes of colonisation and counter-colonisation related to citizenship?

By the early twentieth century the idea emerged that the Empire could be consolidated by the creation of the status of a supra-state 'citizenship of the Empire'. After all, some individuals felt in their bones that they already had that identity. For instance, in 1937, the relatively young scholar Keith Hancock, already recognised as an experienced authority on the subject – an Australian, a former Rhodes scholar and an Englishman by country of adoption – called 'maintaining . . . effective . . . common citizenship . . . one of the principal non-fundamental conventions of the Commonwealth' (Hancock and Latham 1937: 584).

Yet, it was not until the introduction of an inordinate number of British Nationality and Commonwealth Immigration Acts from 1948 to 1981 that increasingly confusing clarifications of different peoples' legal positions were undertaken. At any rate, by means of these enactments, the word 'citizen' crept increasingly into our official vocabulary. Two examples: the 1948 British Nationality Act contains the phrase, 'British nationality by virtue of citizenship'; the 1981 measure of the same title divided people of the Commonwealth into five categories, including British citizens, citizens of British dependent territories and British overseas citizens. Even lawyers have found this assistance baffling.

By that year, Britain was also part of another multinational organisation, the European Community, membership of which was coming to entail some sense of European citizenship. This status was confirmed in international law in 1993 by the Maastricht Treaty, which formulated the title of 'citizen of the European Union' for all citizens of member-states.

A consequence of British involvement in these two geographically different international bodies has been a considerable increase in immigrants' access to British state citizenship, albeit, of late, by means of a ceremony and tests. The tests involve knowledge of the British political system, history and way of life. Yet, the acquisition of such information even by native schoolchildren has been decidedly weak.

Task 1.1 UNDERSTANDING HISTORY IN ORDER TO UNDERSTAND CITIZENSHIP

After reading through this chapter, reflect on whether you agree with the premise presented about the importance of understanding history in order to understand citizenship. In small groups if possible, within your teacher education context, interrogate critically how the role of history in citizenship might be enhanced.

Assign a chair and a reporter/notetaker to record the findings of each group and report back for further discussion and reflection.

To support your reflections and discussions, you might use one of many historical resources on line, for example, the Centre for Contemporary British History (CCBH) is one of the three research centres of the Institute of Historical Research, School of Advanced Study, University of London. Go to www.ccbh.ac.uk/home.php, and follow links to other relevant sites.

SUMMARY AND KEY POINTS

The history of citizenship education in Britain is, in truth, a thin story. Arrangements were made by the episcopacy in the reign of Elizabeth I for extracts from *De Proeliis Anglorum*, a schoolbook about England's military successes, to be read in churches: pulpit patriotism. But, not until the Victorian era was the matter taken seriously. Again, we must refer to the Second Reform Act. Now that some of the 'rude working class' were enfranchised, the most vocally bitter opponent of that extension of the franchise, Robert Lowe, asserted in a phrase that was adapted to 'Now we must educate our masters'. Three years later, the Forster Education Act started the process of publicly funded education. This, as Lowe intended, was for basic literacy. Although the following introduction of the secret ballot provided voters with the ability to place a cross on the ballot papers, it was widely considered that they should be more than able to substitute the illiterates' cross for their written name.

From *c*.1880 specific social and political subject matter was introduced into school curricula. Nevertheless, for the following century or so, acceptance of, and interest in, these Civics lessons, as they were often called, and the quality of the manner in which they were supported and purveyed, were intermittent and questionable. Bodies such as the Association for Education in Citizenship, the Council for Education in World Citizenship and the Politics Association, for instance, were predecessors of the Association for Citizenship Teaching. Government publications until the end of the twentieth century were exceedingly weak on the topic. Indeed, of the key 1963 document the distinguished Political Scientist, W. A. Robson, wrote, 'The Newsom Report's treatment of education for democracy is pedestrian, narrow and unimaginative' (Robson 1967: 36). Not until the initiative of David Blunkett and the deep commitment of Bernard Crick from 1997 did real progress get under way. But, readers of this book are well aware of that.

FURTHER READING

Crick, B. (1998) *Education for Citizenship and the Teaching of Democracy in Schools: Final report of the Advisory Group on Citizenship*, London: QCA.
   This is essential reading, forming as it does the basis for the introduction of citizenship into the National Curriculum in England.

Crick, B. (2000) *Essays on Citizenship*, London: Continuum.
   A politically informed overview of citizenship and education.

CHAPTER 2

DEFINING CITIZENSHIP EDUCATION

Ian Davies

INTRODUCTION

The central ideas and practices of citizenship are controversial and contested so it comes as no surprise that citizenship education is the subject of fierce debate. When you teach citizenship education you will, of course, need to be alert to many complex ideas and issues from several academic disciplines and policy contexts and lived experience. But you will not be treading on unfamiliar territory. Although, to state the obvious, citizenship education in its current form is new, teaching and learning about contemporary society to develop understanding, encourage action and reflection on action and to explore and promote democratic dispositions has a very long and respectable history. It is also something that in one way is very easy to define. I agree with the authors of the 2008 National Curriculum for citizenship in England: 'Education for citizenship equips young people with the knowledge, skills and understanding to play an effective role in public life.' There is nothing that I would wish to see as complicated or controversial about that.

However, there are, of course, significant complexities that lie close to the surface of that definition and this chapter will explore some of those challenges. I do not wish to suggest that citizenship education has always been (or must always be) aligned with democratic societies but, of course, that is what I am – and all professional student teachers are – concerned to promote. The definition given above from the National Curriculum documentation does not in itself make that distinction clear (although in the detail of what is specified in the National Curriculum it is clear that democratic citizenship is favoured). There are other very significant challenges that must be faced if you are to understand what citizenship education is about. Following a formal statement of the objectives for this chapter that are designed to help you meet at least some of the standards for qualifying to teach, I will explore key ideas about how we might define or characterise citizenship education. In doing so I will emphasise what, in my view, teachers should do as they promote citizenship education. My definition of citizenship in relation to teaching and learning is that there will be contemporary content; Schemes of Work will be based on those concepts that are centrally relevant to citizenship (allowing for forms of understanding and action that are essential to citizenship education); there will be a commitment to exploring and promoting social justice; the structure and process of teaching and learning are congruent with the aims of citizenship education; and the whole will be, in appropriate ways, assessed. This is my working definition or characterisation of citizenship education.

OBJECTIVES

At the end of this chapter you should be able to:

■ understand fundamental aspects of citizenship education;
■ understand several of the ways in which citizenship education is contested;
■ establish your own particular understanding of citizenship in a way that helps you in your teaching and/or your research.

DEFINING AND CHARACTERISING CITIZENSHIP EDUCATION

The aim of this part of the chapter is to introduce you to some of the many controversies that surround citizenship education and to propose my view on how citizenship education is or should be defined.

Although there are debates and dilemmas in citizenship education it is not necessarily less coherent than other fields. Historians are always interested in the question of 'what is history'; the nature of scientific truth is always under examination; philosophers would never want to claim that no further discussion was needed about their central concerns. I also do not want to suggest that there is some simple way of clarifying issues – citizenship is about understanding and participating in a democratic society and that should always be occasion for lively debate. But I would want to argue that there are points about which we can agree and to encourage you to develop the sorts of educational activities in and beyond schools that make a real contribution to the lives of learners. Principally this involves being able to identify what counts as citizenship education.

If someone came into your classroom to see you teach how would they know that you were involved in citizenship education? This is not as obvious as it might at first sound. I have seen many lessons that were supposed to be about a particular subject but were actually about something else. For example, some teachers have told me that in the lesson I had just observed they were promoting historical understanding whereas they were actually providing opportunities for pupils to be creative ('draw a picture of a battle'; 'write a poem about the First World War'; 'write a story about Robin Hood'); or helping pupils in a very general way to improve their memories ('learn for a test 20 important things about the Industrial Revolution'). I wish to make very clear that I am not opposed to creative activities or to requiring pupils to remember information. But I do wish learning to be appropriate for specific areas of understanding and action and not a distraction that is comforting or which achieves a high level of demand only in terms of 'busy' work.

I will highlight several (of the many) key issues in citizenship education, and suggest that within the definition of citizenship education as given in the 2008 version of the National Curriculum there is scope for some hard thinking and some exploratory action. If I observed a lesson in which the following areas were present I would be reasonably confident that citizenship education was occurring.

CONTEMPORARY CONTENT

Citizenship education is about understanding and participating in contemporary society. As such it seems obvious that the bulk of any work taking place must focus on contemporary matters. Simply, citizenship education is about today. Of course, there is a much more to be said about what sort of content is appropriate for illuminating the present. Just because contemporary content is used it does not mean that citizenship education will always be taking place. Two related arguments can be made: first, that certain sorts of contemporary content (what I will refer to as the constitutional and the issues-based curriculum) are inadequate in themselves as the basis of the citizenship education curriculum; and, second, that history education is intimately connected with, but not in itself a substitute for, citizenship education.

Prior to the establishment in 1969 of the Politics Association, and before the work of the Programme for Political Education in the 1970s the few examples of explicit and professionally established citizenship education consisted of British Constitution for the middle class (who needed to know something about the system that they would later manage) and civics for the working class (who were thought to need guidance on how to follow the 'rules'). In the face of political socialisation research, which showed that young people could understand political messages, a growing concern for the democratisation of schools through, for example, the comprehensive school movement, awareness of low levels of political understanding and a lowering of the age at which one could vote to 18, led to a rejection of former approaches. Instead it was accepted that British Constitution was, in the words of Ian Lister, 'all Brit and mainly a con'. It was narrowly focused on the nation state, pushing irrelevant and misleading facts (the system does not actually work as it is supposed to but instead relies on shifting alliances of power brokers) and – perhaps worst of all – boring. It might have been contemporary and it might have taught some people some things and helped them gain qualifications, but it was not a good example of citizenship education.

An alternative approach to the fact-laden British Constitution or civics courses was to rely on an issues-driven curriculum. In this scenario the content was always contemporary and strongly connected to what was appearing in news media. The rationale seemed to be that these stories would be informative, engaging and help young people develop a real insight into the workings of contemporary society. Pupils would, hopefully, be inspired to get involved. Content would not be forgotten but there would be a shift to explore issues in order to promote political literacy as promoted in the 1970s by Crick and colleagues. It is important to stress that political literacy was much more than issue-based teaching (there were real attempts, for example, to develop a meaningful conceptual base, and attention was given to procedural values) but, in the retreat from British Constitution style of course, issues were highlighted, as can be seen in the following quotation:

> A politically literate person will know what the main political disputes are clearly about; what beliefs the main contestants have of them; how they are likely to affect him, and he [*sic*] will have a predisposition to try to do something about it in a manner at once effective and respectful of the sincerity of others.
>
> (Crick 1978: 33)

However, the issues-based approach has a number of weaknesses. If pupils are faced only with a constantly shifting terrain there is the negative potential for fragmented understanding to be achieved. News editors are not, principally, educators and stories are often told merely for the purpose of increasing circulation. There is the possibility that young people can feel alienated by a constant diet of crisis. The major controversial issues of war, famine and injustice cannot be solved by pupils and they might feel as if they are being invited merely to identify their own impotence. I am not advocating excluding contemporary controversial issues – far from it – but it is vital that they are not seen as the principal means of establishing a curriculum.

Thus far the case has been made for contemporary content but, of course, of a sort that is not irrelevant, misleading or educationally incoherent. But, as I have emphasised so strongly the need for contemporary content, I want to include something here, briefly, about the contribution that could be made by history educators in the development of citizenship education. Curiously, focusing on contemporary content does not mean ignoring history. History education is important for citizenship and I have written about this at length with others (see Arthur *et al.* 2001). Indeed, it is almost axiomatic that history education is very close to citizenship education. The meanings and purposes ascribed to the teaching and learning of citizenship and history are very similar. Dewey (1966: 93) in his key work of *Democracy and Education* believed that education utilises 'the past for a resource in a developing future'. Many relate citizenship particularly to politics and there are some commentators who have stressed the importance of seeing, consequently, a particular link with history. Oakshott (1956: 16) defined political education as 'knowledge as profound as we can make it of our tradition of political behaviour'. Heater (1974: 1) even went so far as to say that history and politics are 'virtually identical subjects'. History has the enormous advantage of allowing pupils the space to develop critical distance, which could help in the development of understanding about political institutions, concepts and issues.

However, I also feel very strongly that we must be wary of some types of work in history education. There are several significant obstacles: history as an optional National Curriculum subject is not taken by all and so cannot be used exclusively as the means by which a school establishes its citizenship education programme; the critical distance to which I referred positively above could actually serve to confuse pupils (simply, the past is not a good illustration of what happens today); indeed, mining history for events that illuminate today is possibly an ahistorical approach to studying the past; pupils often in cross-curricular approaches do not realise what they are learning if it is not given in the title of the lesson; and, teachers may be using the rhetoric of citizenship to justify their own specialist area of work (such as history). Some of these criticisms of the supposed link between history education and citizenship education apply similarly to other subjects that claim such a connection, such as science (for example, Davies 2005). Nevertheless one of the great attractions of the claim for connections between a well-established school subject and citizenship education is the way in which claims are made on the basis of conceptual overlap. History has something to offer in that it shows generally that a conceptual framework allows for content to be selected meaningfully and many historical concepts are relevant to understanding and action in contemporary society and so there is, potentially, a strong connection with citizenship education. The nature of concepts that, in my view, actually reflect citizenship education will be explored in the next section of this chapter.

Task 2.1 **USING CONTEMPORARY AND HISTORICAL KNOWLEDGE IN CITIZENSHIP EDUCATION**

The argument has been made for certain sorts of contemporary content to be used in citizenship education. It has been emphasised that simply drawing material from today's news stories would not be enough and that a history lesson could be a useful part of a citizenship education programme. You have two tasks:

1   Make a list of lessons that include contemporary content and explain why they are or they are not potentially useful for citizenship education.
2   Observe three history lessons and judge the extent to which they do – or could with some changes – contribute to citizenship education.

HIGHLIGHTING APPROPRIATE CONCEPTUAL UNDERSTANDING

The 2008 version of the National Curriculum for citizenship highlights Key Concepts in a very valuable manner. These concepts are: 'Democracy and justice', 'Rights and responsibilities' and 'Identity and diversity: living together in the UK'. Citizenship education, in my view, depends fundamentally on a conceptual base and, as such, it is very important to consider the meaning of these concepts. By focusing on concepts, a very significant shift has already been made away from both content and context. Although, as above, content is important, it is 'merely' the raw material on which lessons are based. Content provides illumination and exemplification but, as I demonstrated above when criticising the issues-based approach, it is not in itself sufficient to define citizenship education. Similarly, context is not enough. By this I mean that if one were able, for example, to identify the importance of economic contexts as well as those that are political we would be better able to justify the selection of content but we would still not have provided a rationale for, or definition of, citizenship education. Concepts are the fundamental building blocks of how we make sense of the world and it is on them that a curriculum needs to be based.

Now that I have asserted the significance of concepts I need to go further by explaining their nature. Concepts come in different forms. A rather basic distinction can be made between substantive and procedural concepts. Procedural (or second-order) concepts (such as evidence and interpretation) are distinct from substantive concepts that relate more narrowly to the study of particular issues (such as government or war). In short, substantive concepts readily involve learning *about* something, whereas procedural concepts allow for explicit consideration of how things are learned and suggest something of what is needed as people put that learning into action. The ambitious position would be to assert that by identifying procedural concepts it would be possible to invite pupils not just to think about citizenship but to think as citizens. As such, teachers and others will be encouraged to move away from citizenship as 'merely' a goal and allow for the possibility of a clearer identification of what pupils need to do and how they should think in order to demonstrate effective learning. We need to identify what it is that we expect pupils to be doing as they learn. Pupils need to be rational as they reflect on social and political realities; they need to participate as they consider their rights and responsibilities, and they need to be tolerant in the context of a pluralistic democracy. This has been stated in such a way as to emphasise that learning for and through citizenship requires a clear connection between the processes of learning with the substantive concepts of citizenship. This balancing act between the substantive and the procedural allows for pupils not just to participate but to participate in a citizenship activity; not just to be good to others but to be good citizens; not simply to learn about society but to become more rational about matters that concern a citizen.

A COMMITMENT TO SOCIAL JUSTICE

Throughout all of the above (and everything that I write) I wish to emphasise the centrality of learning. Citizenship education is not a party political programme or the latest fad or fashion that will satisfy those who have climbed aboard a newsworthy bandwagon. Citizenship educators are concerned with education above all else. But, and it is a very large 'but', it is obviously the case that education is not a neutral process. We do not have to be acolytes of Freire in order to know that we always educate for something. Education is never neutral: it is either for domestication or liberation. This does not, however, mean that citizenship educators need to know 'the answer' any more than a history teacher, for example, can explain without any fear of disagreement what really led to the Russian Revolution. But skilled and knowledgeable teachers of citizenship know what they think about the key issues in the definition of citizenship and can help others – in a way appropriate to their age experience and ability – to find a route through these difficult areas. Of these many complex areas I will refer only to three about which the teacher should be expected to feel confident, and in this way I am highlighting the way in which we need to approach the substantive concepts of citizenship.

1   The centrality of the two traditions – rights and duties

It is vital that citizenship education allows pupils to understand their rights and responsibilities in a democratic society and that they have the skills and dispositions and opportunities to participate. This is one of the ways in which citizenship education is defined, and one of the ways that we see that it is not neutral.

Focusing on rights and responsibilities shows immediately that defining citizenship education is complex. However, there has been, at times, too much unnecessary uncertainty. I am very keen not to set up a false generalised position of rights being more important than responsibilities (or vice versa) just for the sake of generating an artificial controversy. There are significant issues to discuss in relation to fundamental aspects of citizenship education but when those issues are discussed in terms of simple dualities we need to move to a more reasoned position. We do not have a simple exclusive choice between whether citizenship is about rights or duties. In some ways, the differences between rights and duties may break down fairly readily. I agree with Derek Heater that: 'by being a virtuous, community-conscious participant in civic affairs (a republican requirement), a citizen benefits by enhancing his or her own individual development (a liberal objective). Citizenship does not involve an either/or choice' (Heater 1999: 177).

And yet, if teachers are to define citizenship education for themselves and for their pupils it is important to be able to probe these matters a little more. Heater refers in the above quotation to 'a republican requirement' and a 'liberal objective'. Broadly, this relates to the two key traditions that exist within citizenship. In the civic republican tradition emphasis is placed on people carrying out their responsibilities in the public context. In the liberal tradition there is a greater emphasis on rights for private individuals. The debates about these matters can rapidly become very demanding (intellectually and politically).

The perspective and purpose of rights and duties need to be considered. Simplistically, an emphasis on rights (liberal tradition) is at times thought to be intrinsically left wing while an expectation of the fulfilment of responsibilities (civic republican tradition) is somehow right wing. But, of course, it is not so easy. If rights are the expression of a private individual's desire to be left alone by government it is easy to see a connection with free market liberalism seems more relevant rather than civic republicanism. When during the 1980s President Reagan used the slogan 'get government off our backs' to emphasise the importance of rights for US citizens, no one imagined him to be left wing. Indeed, Reagan's membership of the Republican Party did not mean that he would necessarily promote civic republicanism.

Peterson (2008) has very usefully shown that within (as well as between) these traditions there are key distinctions and it might not be helpful in the future to present citizenship as if it involved only two traditions. I am suggesting that citizenship education can be defined, generally, without artificial dualism but that there is a need to go further in an education process to create a definition through reflection on complex matters. The definition that is created in relation to key aspects such as rights and responsibilities, by individuals and groups, will be a refinement of, but not a completely different position from, the underlying position.

2   Identity and diversity

Citizenship has boundaries that help us define it. But these limits are, rightly, in need of discussion and, perhaps, constant readjustment. This section of the chapter, by strongly emphasising the need for a definition of citizenship education to encompass identity and diversity, focuses on two related matters: the private and the personal; and the ways in which perspectives or contexts are highlighted.

I am very strongly in favour of ensuring that issues about power in personal contexts can find a place in citizenship education. Feminism, for example, is entirely relevant to citizenship and certainly does not always fit with the traditional view of politics in public contexts (Arnot 2008). The celebration, exploration and further development of an ethnically diverse society are absolutely central parts of citizenship education. But what, in my view, is not acceptable is for all issues to do with interpersonal and individual identity and actions to be seen as relevant to citizenship education. Advising a pupil that smoking is not good for their health, for example, may be useful and necessary but it is not citizenship education unless one explores issues about rationality, participation and toleration in public contexts as discussed above. Smoking could be used as a case study for citizenship work but an explicit attempt for a particular type of work is needed by the teacher. Furthermore, we need to consider whether we are dealing 'merely' with contexts in which a definition of citizenship education is enacted or with something more fundamental in which a perspective is adopted that is, in itself, a definition. Are we looking, for example, at feminism as a context in which particular issues are played out, or is feminism something that in itself defines citizenship? If it is then does this mean that a wide ranging definition in which we commit ourselves to justice is not enough but, instead, we have to explore and develop more precise thinking in relation to groups of people who identify themselves as belonging to one or more groups?

More work is needed on this topic before it will become something about which teachers and pupils feel very comfortable. As with other school subjects there are various characterisations that are possible and we must not close down debate. Recent shifts in this area can be seen in Crick's work (2007) as he now writes much more explicitly about a diverse society than he did in the original Crick Report. There must be confidence in the development of that debate within the simple and obviously necessary commitment to the vital significance of identity and diversity.

3   The state and citizenship

One of the strengths of citizenship is its capacity to allow for concrete expression. Turner (1993) has rightly suggested that unless there is a concern with what actually happens, then we will be open to the problems of citizenship being seen as just so much empty rhetoric. If, however, we concern ourselves primarily with the concrete expression of citizenship, we are closer to emphasising what until now has been seen as the preserve of national institutional politics. National systems guarantee (and can abuse) rights and currently there are few transnational organisations that hold as much power (although flows of capital are international, and recent economic crises have seen the rise of more advanced international collaboration). There is a variety of forms of citizenship that exist beyond the nation state but it will be seen from Heater's work (see the tables below) that the global is placed, for some controversially, towards the 'vague' end of the spectrum. Another, more positive characterisation of global citizenship is to suggest that it is expansive, holistic and concerned at least in part with the affective as well as the cognitive and with achievement in concrete terms of justice. Again, there is little merit in suggesting that we should focus either on national or global citizenship. There is a problem for teachers in such an exclusive approach. But there is a problem if the different forms of citizenship are not recognised. Clarity of understanding in which fundamental issues are recognised and considered will lead to meaningful consensus in which difference of perception and characterisation will be possible. Heater (1997) has outlined those forms of citizenship that exist beyond the nation state:

Legally defined	Dual – citizenship of two states held simultaneously
	Layer – in federal constitutions; and in a few multinational communities
Mainly attitude: limited legal definition	Below state level – municipal, local allegiance/sense of identity
	Above state level – world citizenship

Heater goes on to explain (1997: 36–8) that there is a range of meanings that can be applied to global citizenship. He has outlined four main meanings that can be placed on a spectrum, the opposite ends of which are 'vague' and 'precise'.

The meanings of world citizenship

Vague . . . . **Precise**

Member of the human race	Responsible for the condition of the planet	Individual subject to moral law	Promotion of world government

Teachers and learners are not involved in a political project in which certain precisely formulated goals must be achieved. It is not the job of teachers to promote specific forms of national or global citizenship. But it is vital for teachers to be able to understand and explain these matters in ways that are appropriate for learners who need to come to terms with, and make choices about, the ways in which the good society can be achieved.

Task 2.2 **WHAT IS INDOCTRINATION?**

Teachers have at times been worried about the possibility of being accused of attempting to indoctrinate their pupils. What is meant by indoctrination? Is it acceptable to insist that young people accept that democracy is the best system of government?

DEFINING CITIZENSHIP EDUCATION THROUGH PEDAGOGY

The means by which citizenship education is developed by teachers and learners is part of its definition. The means need to be consistent with the ends. This has three aspects.

First, we need to ensure that our definition of citizenship education is sufficiently focused to help us avoid seeing it everywhere. I have always found the following quotation by Audigier (1998: 3) to be useful in providing a warning to teachers:

> Since the citizen is an informed and responsible person, capable of taking part in public debate and making choices, nothing of what is human should be unfamiliar to him [*sic*], nothing of what is experienced in society should be foreign to democratic citizenship.
>
> (p. 13)

Citizenship education is wide ranging and it would be wrong to discount the relevance of any issue in contemporary society but to suggest that everything is citizenship and, by extension, to make teachers responsible for everything, is a recipe for disaster. Audigier is warning us to be aware of the need for expansive, dynamic and focused understanding.

Second, and more particularly, there is a need to consider what sorts of structure are used as a distinction is made between the personal and the public. The whole school is a necessary arena for the citizenship education as mock elections and school councils, for example, can contribute to the development of understanding and involvement. Similarly, individual subject areas such as history have a role to play. All these areas involve investigation into public and private contexts. But Crick has been very clear about the distinction between citizenship education and personal and social education. Specifically, he has provided a useful distinction for citizenship by clarifying its boundaries and relationships with other important areas: 'PS-E, RE, moral education, whatever we call education specifically for values, are necessary but not sufficient conditions for good citizenship and good behaviour' (Crick 2000: 129).

Third, the ways in which interactions occur between teachers and learners matter a great deal. A distinction should be made between teachers who are authoritative and those who are authoritarian. Discussions need to be focused. Anything does not 'go'. Some opinions are not welcome. Some arguments are not as well expressed as others. In Crick's telling phrase we must avoid the 'postmodernism of the streets' in which a perverted form of democracy is seen to require acceptance of any position, however badly considered and politically inappropriate. The days of the Humanities Curriculum Project of the 1960s in which the teacher's role was restricted to that of a 'neutral chair' are over. But there is, of course, an overwhelming need for mutual respect, decency and dignity in and beyond schools.

> ## Task 2.3 **DISCUSSING CONTROVERSIAL ISSUES**
>
> Devise the ground rules for discussing controversial topics with a class of pupils aged 14 years. What is allowed? What is encouraged? What is forbidden?

ASSESSMENT

Teachers have an entirely legitimate (and necessary and unavoidable) interest in knowing what pupils are learning. Learners have a need and a right to know how much progress they are making. Therefore, the question of assessment must be tackled. Assessment is not the same as testing, and all forms of assessment do not lead negatively to unwieldy bureaucracy and the judging of success in terms of league table position. Some teachers (for example, Jerome 2008) are experimenting with investigations into learners' understandings in citizenship education that are diagnostic and evaluative and which will enhance future pedagogical intervention.

In order to make progress in assessment a number of issues need to be addressed. Fundamentally, a distinction must be made between the assessment of citizenship and citizenship education. In other words, teachers and learners are not in the business of assessing whether someone is or is not a citizen. Rather, we are very interested in making sense of what is being learned in relation to the knowledge, skills and dispositions of citizenship. The types of conceptual understanding and practice that teachers and learners should, in my view, focus on are discussed above. The form that the assessment takes is very important. Although knowledge is important, citizenship education will not be assessed appropriately if we rely too heavily on something like multiple choice tests designed to identify whether information has been retained. Rather, pupils should be given an opportunity to think and act and to provide feedback. Discussion is one of the key ways in which assessment can occur and there is some very useful material that can be consulted (QCA 2006; Hess and Avery 2008).

> ## Task 2.4 **ASSESSING CITIZENSHIP**
>
> Watch the DVD available at www.post16citizenship.org/makeithappen/index.htm. Discuss with a colleague whether this approach to assessing citizenship education is valuable.

SUMMARY AND KEY POINTS

Citizenship education can be defined, or perhaps more accurately, 'characterised'. I would not be so bold as to assert that there is or will be widespread agreement about my characterisation. Continuing debate and controversy is necessary if we are to continue to celebrate and develop education that is a reflection of, and a means of achieving, a democratic society. But we will know when citizenship education is taking place if it deals with contemporary situations, is conceptually based, is wedded to social justice, is taught and learned appropriately with a proper concern for knowing what is being achieved.

Citizenship educators should not be too ambitious. Claiming too much will result only in disappointment. But teachers and learners of citizenship education are engaged in an extremely significant undertaking. A clear understanding of the nature of that undertaking – its definition or characterisation – is a vital part of its likely achievement.

FURTHER READING

Arthur, J., Davies, I. and Hahn, C. (eds) (2008) *The SAGE Handbook of Education for Citizenship and Democracy*, London: SAGE.
This book has 42 chapters so it covers a wealth of themes. There are sections on key ideas underlying citizenship education, examples from many countries, perspectives on citizenship education and examples from evaluation studies and practical projects.

Heater, D. (1999) *What is Citizenship?*, Cambridge: Polity Press.
In this book, Heater gives a very clear overview of the key fundamental issues about citizenship. His informed even-handed approach is intelligent and very useful for those involved in citizenship education.

Huddleston, T. (2004) *Citizens and Society: Political literacy teacher resource pack*, London: Hodder & Stoughton.
This is a practical book for teachers. It provides many interesting and useful activities for teachers and learners. But it also very usefully provides an introduction in which some key ideas about political literacy are explored. The use of political information and issues are considered very carefully in an argument for the promotion of political literacy that is based on political concepts.

Kiwan, D. (2008) *Education for Inclusive Citizenship*, London: Routledge.
This book emerged from Dina Kiwan's excellent PhD thesis in which she explored key principles about citizenship education with reflections on interviews with some of the people who were responsible for the introduction of citizenship education into the National Curriculum in England. She argues for the promotion of an inclusive citizenship in practice (and Crick's glowing foreword shows interesting issues about the extent to which an explicit emphasis would be placed on diversity in citizenship education debates).

CHAPTER 3

CITIZENSHIP IN THE NATIONAL CURRICULUM

John Keast and
Liz Craft

INTRODUCTION

This chapter describes, first, how citizenship came into the secondary school curriculum and, second, how it continues to have a central role in the revised secondary National Curriculum for England. The development of the citizenship curriculum is in part linked with the development of personal, social, health education (PSHE). Questions about the nature and purpose of both these areas in the school curriculum arose. How they were resolved has shaped the content and support for the citizenship curriculum in recent years and today.

OBJECTIVES

By the end of this chapter you should be able to:

■ understand the background to the development of citizenship in the National Curriculum, and appreciate its complexity and links to other parts of the curriculum;

■ understand how citizenship plays a central role in the revised National Curriculum of 2008 and beyond and appreciate its importance for all young people and for society.

BACKGROUND

The subject-based National Curriculum (NC) with extensive assessment arrangements was introduced from 1989. Non-statutory cross-curricular themes were introduced in 1990 to help schools deal with important matters that were not specifically the concern of any one subject. These were health education, citizenship, economic and industrial understanding, careers education and guidance, and environmental education. By the mid-1990s it was apparent to many that the NC was too large and unmanageable to survive. Sir Ron (now Lord) Dearing was appointed to 'slim down' the curriculum and its assessment. A revised NC emerged in 1995. The reduced subject requirements did not, of course, add references to the cross-curricular themes from 1990, and many commentators felt that the material discarded by the slimmer curriculum were those very parts that helped subjects to promote more explicitly the wider purpose of the curriculum. This was set out in the 1988 Education Reform Act and is summarised as 'to promote pupils' spiritual, moral, social and cultural development' and 'prepare them for the opportunities, responsibilities and experiences of adult life'.

In the mid-1990s there was much public concern about the values young people were growing up with. This was highlighted by two specific tragedies – the murder of James Bulger in Merseyside by two other youngsters, and the murder of Philip Lawrence, a head teacher in London, while carrying out his duties. These incidents provoked and reflected an anxiety that schools were paying insufficient attention to teaching pupils about right and wrong. One of the responses to this anxiety was the establishment of the Forum on Values in Education and the Community, by Dr Nicholas Tate, Chief Executive of the School Curriculum and Assessment Authority (SCAA). The Values Forum, as it came to be known, consisted of about 150 people from many walks of life and was asked to produce a set of values that were commonly held by most people. This was an attempt to nail a lie – that schools could not successfully promote values because there was no agreement on what they should be. A Statement of Values was produced in 1997, and was appended to the NC Handbooks published in 2000. The number of dissenting voices was small, mainly because the values held in common were very general ones. A MORI poll and various focus groups also indicated high levels of assent to nearly all elements of the statement. The most controversial elements were to do with marriage and the family.

The Statement was then used by SCAA (which became part of the QCA in 1997) as the basis for a set of guidance for schools on how they might promote more effectively the spiritual, moral, social and cultural development of pupils. A pilot of the guidance during 1998 produced a disappointing result from the schools involved. It was felt to be too large, complex and inappropriate in tone. Schools felt burdened by the literacy and numeracy frameworks then being introduced, by the newly elected Labour government with its social inclusion agenda. This was to take the work on values in a very different direction.

NEW LABOUR'S APPROACH IN 1997

David Blunkett published a White Paper, 'Excellence in Schools' in July 1997. As a consequence, advisory groups were established for Education for Citizenship and the Teaching of Democracy (led by Professor Bernard Crick, David Blunkett's former tutor at Birkbeck College), and PSHE (chaired jointly by the ministers of state for Education and Health, Estelle Morris and Tessa Jowell, though, in practice, led by Jane Jenks, a national figure in PSHE). In addition, groups on Creativity and Culture (led by Professor Ken Robinson) and Education for Sustainable Development were also established in part to consider the role of these areas in the curriculum. At this time the impending review of the NC was due to be carried out by the QCA for implementation in schools from 2000. It is worth noting that education in all of these areas had risen in importance as relevant government departments realised their significance, one example being the *Health of the Nation* initiative by the Department of Health.

The first of these groups was the most powerful, significant and successful. The group that Professor Crick led had cross-party support and members included Lord Baker, former Conservative Education Secretary, Michael Brunson from ITN, and Judge Stephen Tumin, Chief Inspector of Prisons. The group reported in the summer of 1998 (QCA 1998), recommending that citizenship be introduced into the NC and given 5 per cent of curriculum time. Citizenship was deemed to comprise social and moral responsibility, community involvement and political literacy. Key concepts, skills, attitudes and dispositions, as well as knowledge and understanding, were identified for each key stage. Much of the credit for this work goes to David Kerr from NFER, who has specialised in researching citizenship for some years in this country and abroad. The group had steered a path between several extremes, balancing rights and responsibilities, the importance of individuals with that of communities, politics and government with wider areas of study, skills with knowledge, and study with practical activity. The importance of this report was immense, as illustrated by this quotation: 'We aim at no less than a change in the political culture of this country . . . for people to think of themselves as active citizens, willing, able and equipped to have an influence in public life' (QCA 1998: 7).

The PSHE group was slower to get off the ground, and had some complex issues to deal with, notably the interface between health and education, which involved sensitive areas such as sex and drugs education. PSHE has always been beset by difficulties of definition. Although draft reports became available, the final report was not published until 1999. The work of Ken Robinson's group took even longer and was published in *All Our Futures: Creativity, culture and education* in 2000. The ESD panel produced a series of recommendations over a wide range of fronts, such as the workplace and further education (FE).

The curriculum had already been modified in 1998 with the suspension of the curriculum orders for non-core subjects in primary schools to make room for the literacy and numeracy frameworks. Concerns about overload, complexity and prescription were already high among teachers' associations, with whom the government was simultaneously in discussion over performance-related pay and other matters. In the autumn of 1998, therefore, the QCA established a working group to analyse the various developments and consider 'a single set of sensible suggestions' (to use a phrase of Dr Tate).

The Preparation for Adult Life (PAL) group was intended to bring people together from each of the four initiatives and make recommendations to the QCA on how each should impact on the review of the NC, which was then getting under way. The PAL group consisted of the chairs (or their representatives) of the advisory groups, Chris Woodhead HMCI, Anthea Millett of the TTA, David Hargreaves (later to become Chief Executive of the QCA), head teachers and officials from the DfEE and QCA. Content was contentious not only in the obvious sense when dealing with politics and

health, but also regarding how much there should be, and for what ages. What w..
right balance of skills and knowledge, and what skills at what level? What values anɑ
beliefs were to be assumed? Should all the desired new content be put into one area
of the curriculum and, if so, what should it be called? Should it be made statutory, either
through the NC or, like careers education and guidance, outside it?

Ministers eventually decided what should be done, and in May 1999 draft
proposals for revising the NC were published for consultation.

NATIONAL CURRICULUM FOR CITIZENSHIP

What emerged was a proposal for changes in the NC from September 2000 including:

- a joint non-statutory framework for PSHE and citizenship at Key Stages 1
  and 2;
- a non-statutory framework for PSHE at Key Stages 3 and 4;
- a new NC foundation subject for citizenship at Key Stages 3 and 4 with
  implementation delayed until 2002.

Aspects of these areas would be flagged in other NC subjects. A statement of the values,
aims and purposes of the school curriculum would accompany all this as a preamble
in the NC Handbooks for all schools. All this would be additional to careers education
and guidance, religious education and, in secondary schools, sex education.

The non-statutory joint framework for PSHE and citizenship in primary schools
contained four strands – personal development, citizenship, health and safety, and
relationships. All strands went through to the non-statutory framework for PSHE in
secondary schools, except citizenship, which became the basis for the NC citizenship
curriculum order. This had three elements – knowledge and understanding about
becoming informed citizens, skill of enquiry and communication (of citizenship and
related issues), and skill of participation and taking responsible action. The last of these
was the most innovative and was intended to ensure that citizenship did not become
civics, politics or other social studies, but was active citizenship where pupils learnt
the knowledge citizens need through taking part in activities that generate it. Through
investigating and articulating issues pupils develop some responsibility for getting
involved in them and taking action to help resolve them. When citizenship for post-
16 pupils was being developed later, this was characterised as 'Get involved – make
a difference!'. In this way, citizenship was a subject, with knowledge, understanding
and skills like other subjects, but more than a subject for it was a vehicle for engaging
young people in local, national and international issues.

An attainment target (citizenship) with end of key stage descriptions (rather than
levels of attainment) was attached to the Programme of Study. These were ambitious
on reading but were the inevitable corollary of the contents.

The decision to bifurcate citizenship and PSHE in the secondary school was a
fundamental one, which has had its consequences ever since. These are seen in the
different forms of curriculum development that have taken place for each area since,
and which include a current proposal to make PSHE part of the National Curriculum.

Once published, the curriculum proposals gradually gained awareness, then assent. They set out for the first time nationally a continuous and progressive programme for these areas of the curriculum. Although separated by their different structures and purposes, they were accompanied by some real innovation, especially in citizenship. However, publication was far from the end of the story. There was much preparation to do to enable the new curriculum to be understood and embedded in schools' provision. Key messages about citizenship (and PSHE) were developed and initial guidance for schools had to be published. The DFEE established a ministerial working party for citizenship and another one for PSHE. The QCA played a key role in both.

INITIAL GUIDANCE

While the story of the development of the curriculum has been told in some detail above, on the grounds that knowing how the curriculum developed adds to understanding of what it means, the story of the guidance will be told more briefly. Much of this guidance has now disappeared from sight though it was necessary and important at the time, since schools were teaching for the first time a new NC subject and quasi-national curriculum for PSHE. Schools needed to be clearer about issues of progression, expectations, planning processes, teaching and learning methods, resources, issues that might arise, and so on. For PSHE, in particular, where there was no overall subject structure as with the NC, clarity on rational and good practice was needed. With citizenship, QCA felt schools would appreciate help in understanding the new statutory order, and value guidance on how to prepare for teaching it.

Identifying the key messages was not always easy, nor was establishing the structure of the guidance. After much negotiation, some of which was difficult, it was decided to offer separate guidance on PSHE and citizenship for secondary schools and joint guidance on citizenship and PSHE for primary schools. A tension between the citizenship and PSHE camps was very real and was evidenced in the parallel work of the Passport Project. Published at about the same time as the NC publication, the Passport Project was another PSHE project organised by the Gulbenkian Foundation, and which involved many of the same people as the development of the PSHE frameworks. It had the potential, if not made coherent with government developments, to derail some of the work done on PSHE and citizenship. Much of the tension was defused by the Chairs of the two pieces of work, Professors Bernard Crick and John Tomlinson, respectively; and some of relevant correspondence is included in the Crick Report of 1998.

Among the questions that the guidance had to deal with were the following. How prescriptive and how 'light touch' should schools regard the PSHE frameworks and citizenship? (The answer was 'light touch', flexible and non-prescriptive.) How discrete should provision for citizenship and PSHE be in the curriculum? (The answer is that citizenship could be taught in a variety of ways, perhaps in combination, discretely, across the curriculum, through tutorial time, active involvement in running the school, and through special school activities.) What links should be made with other subjects? (This was particularly important to the RE community, many of whom feared that citizenship would be the thin end of the wedge that levered them out of the curriculum. Many links were made.) What should be said about careers education and financial capability? What was the role of form tutors? What teaching methods might teachers find helpful? How could teachers deal with issues of bias, imbalance and controversy? How could schools be helped to develop active citizenship? What place might there be for material supplied by other organisations and initiatives? (This was particularly important with health education, given the parallel introduction of the National Healthy Schools Standard at the same time, which had eight dimensions including both citizenship and PSHE.) Despite difficulties, guidance was published by the QCA in the spring of 2000. The DfES working party went on to other matters including assessing and reporting progress in citizenship, other forms of support, developing a website, stimulating community involvement, and teacher training.

Task 3.1 THE ORIGINS OF CITIZENSHIP

Discuss the origins and factors that influenced how citizenship came to be in the National Curriculum in 2000. What do they say about the nature of the citizenship curriculum? What issues arise regarding PSHE?

ASSESSMENT AND ACCREDITATION

A sub-group of the ministerial working party was established to look specifically at these matters, and it had to consider, again, the distinctive nature of citizenship in the NC. As an NC subject, citizenship had common characteristics of such subjects, such as an attainment target and statutory Programmes of Study. But as it was more than a subject, it lacked an eight-level scale of attainment and involved aspects that were not at all amenable to normal forms of assessment, such as promoting moral responsibility, stimulating community involvement (local to global) and dealing with contemporary issues that nobody, by definition, knew were coming up. Not only was the question 'Could this subject be assessed?' raised but so also was '*Should* this subject be assessed?'. One of the underlying concerns of the citizenship enthusiasts was that if no assessment and accreditation regime was attached to this new NC subject, then schools would too easily be able to ignore or devalue the subject, despite its status. After all, RE had been statutory since 1944 but many schools had ceased to take it seriously until the GCSE (short course) was introduced in 1996. The culture of many secondary schools had been greatly influenced by performance tables, so unless there was a GCSE that could allow schools to gain performance table points they would be reluctant to give the subject time and resources. However, the appropriateness of a GCSE in citizenship for all pupils was clearly an important issue. What about pupils for whom that approach was not appropriate? How could a written GCSE examination deal with active citizenship, and reflect the third strand of the Programme of Study? Would a GCSE stifle the very thing that citizenship was introduced into the curriculum to do, that is involve pupils in the process of decision making in school and society, and turn it into yet another academic subject? More importantly, what message would be sent to young people themselves and to our society at large if pupils were shown to get only a grade G or even be ungraded in citizenship? Would those who 'failed' citizenship be regarded as second-class citizens? The sub-group recommended the development of a GCSE (short course) in Citizenship Studies and entry level qualifications of the same name. These would provide accreditation for nearly the whole ability range and offer credibility for the new subject in terms of performance. The title 'Citizenship Studies' would signal that it was not the pupils' citizenship (or status as citizens) that was being assessed, but only their ability to study citizenship. Remember that the name of the subject was simply citizenship. This paralleled a similar distinction between religious education (the curriculum subject) and religious studies (the qualification title) that already existed. To deal with active citizenship the sub-group recommended that internal assessment (popularly known as coursework) would be obligatory and of a higher proportion than other subjects. Students could use their community involvement as evidence for this part of the assessment. A further development was that all other GCSEs had to show what their contribution to students' citizenship might be.

SCHEMES OF WORK 2001–02

QCA set its hand to the preparation of Schemes of Work, which was no easy task, given the nature of the key messages concerning citizenship, and the fact that schools were encouraged to develop what they were already doing rather than start everything afresh. Difficult decisions about content, flexibility, skill development rather than knowledge overload, and so on, had to be made. For Key Stage 3 the scheme was organised under three headings: rights and responsibilities, government and democracy, and communities and identity. It became clear that the scheme could not assume x minutes per week of discrete teaching and had to exemplify the variety of types of provision that were being encouraged, including ideas for community involvement. The Scheme of Work for Key Stage 3 was published in 2001 and that for Key Stage 4 in 2002, as well as schemes for Key Stages 1 and 2.

Much has happened since this initial work on citizenship in 1999–2002, but without that fundamental curriculum development and guidance it would have been impossible for the citizenship curriculum to have progressed alongside curriculum and other changes since then.

Task 3.2 **REVOLVING ISSUES AROUND ASSESSMENT IN CITIZENSHIP**

Discuss the issues first raised regarding the assessment of citizenship in the National Curriculum in 2000. How successfully have they been resolved?

TEN YEARS ON FROM THE CRICK REPORT: A NEW CONTEXT FOR CITIZENSHIP

In the ten years since Crick, the context for citizenship education has changed and the need for it is, arguably, now even greater. Two developments are particularly significant. The publication of 'Every Child Matters' following the Victoria Climbié inquiry in Hackney led to widespread change in the organisation and management of education and children's services in local authorities. 'Every Child Matters' has shaped a new understanding of the school curriculum. The events of 9/11 and 7/7 have had implications for society in general and schools in particular that impact on citizenship in the curriculum. The events led to a review and the Ajegbo Report, *Diversity and Citizenship Curriculum Review*, in 2007 for the Department of Children, Schools and Families. The report offered a new context for promoting diversity and equalities in the national curriculum and strengthened the role of citizenship education. Most recently, the new duty on schools to promote community cohesion has had an impact on the role of citizenship in the curriculum, as has the initiative to prevent violent extremism.

A NEW SECONDARY CURRICULUM

A revised secondary curriculum was introduced in September 2008 with a clear ambition to enable schools to design a better curriculum, to raise standards and help all learners meet the challenges of life in the twenty-first century in our fast changing world.

The national curriculum needed to change to prepare children and young people more fully for the challenges and the opportunities they face in the future. Citizenship has a key role to play in this.

The new curriculum aims to develop young people who are successful learners, confident individuals and responsible citizens who make a positive contribution to society. Citizenship is therefore at the heart of these curriculum aims. Citizenship also makes a significant contribution to 'Every Child Matters', personal development and the personal, learning and thinking skills.

The first set of NC teaching requirements for the subject have now been replaced with revised Programmes of Study at Key Stages 3 and 4 and the introduction of level descriptions that set out the national standards for the subject in a new attainment target.

The Year 7 pupils who began their classes in autumn 2008 were the first to experience the new Programmes of Study in all subjects, including citizenship. This cohort will also be the first pupils to be assessed using the new attainment target, in 2011. The new Programmes of Study for Key Stage 4 are implemented from September 2009 and new full course GCSE Citizenship Studies will be available for first teaching.

The revised NC has been developed with the whole child in mind. It is designed around three aims for the whole curriculum and the 'Every Child Matters' outcomes. The three aims are that all learners should become:

- *successful learners* who enjoy learning, make progress and achieve;
- *confident individuals* who are able to live safe, healthy and fulfilling lives; and
- *responsible citizens* who make a positive contribution to society.

For the first time, the aims of the NC have become statutory and are inspected by Ofsted.

THE BIGGER PICTURE

When considering how the curriculum needs to be developed and designed, schools are encouraged to use three questions to help them plan an inspiring, engaging and motivating curriculum for their pupils:

1 What are we trying to achieve for our learners?
2 How can we organise learning?
3 How will we know if we are achieving our aims?

These three questions form the basis of QCA's *Bigger Picture of the Curriculum*, a tool to help schools discuss, consider and develop a broad, balanced and motivating curriculum for their learners.

Schools are also encouraged to focus on the impact of the curriculum for learners and society – the bottom line. High standards of attainment and achievement for all are a given. But accountability should include a wider range of measures, such as healthy lifestyle decisions, participation in civic society as active citizens and more young people remaining in education or training for longer so they have the best chance of achieving their full potential.

The *Bigger Picture* challenges teachers to consider the best ways of organising resources, including curriculum time, to develop an engaging and inspiring curriculum for all, that meets the whole curriculum aims. Regimented timetable slots can be as unhelpful to citizenship as they are to many other subjects in the curriculum. Different kinds of learning outcomes need different kinds of learning experiences and differently organised amounts of curriculum time and resources. Learners need to experience both deep and immersive learning activities that might take several half days over a six-week stretch, and short and compelling learning activities that might take 45 minutes each week, depending on what each activity is trying to achieve. Pupils should participate in different kinds of citizenship learning: through independent research, investigations or enquiries; handling real evidence or data they have collected and researched themselves; by working collectively in teams, with their peers, experts or members of the wider community; learning within and beyond the classroom; participating in debates, decision making and courses of action on issues that matter to them; as well as learning through the events, routines and life of the school and the school community.

The *Bigger Picture of the Curriculum* provides a clear context for planning and developing citizenship and links well with the three Cs for planning citizenship learning. Created by Pete Pattisson, formerly of Deptford Green School in Lewisham, the three Cs help schools consider what needs to be included for an effective approach to citizenship at three levels – in the *curriculum*, the *culture* and *community* of the school.

- *curriculum* – what must be taught and learned, how the curriculum for citizenship is organised into teaching and learning activities and how learning is assessed;
- *school culture* – citizenship learning through the context of the school as a community with values, ethos and a culture, including the voice and involvement of students in the decision making, running and organisation of the school and school life;
- *community* – citizenship learning through opportunities for pupils to participate in purposeful, community-based citizenship actions and for schools to develop links and engage with community partners on a range of political and social issues of concern.

Task 3.3 **CITIZENSHIP IN THE TWENTY-FIRST CENTURY**

Discuss the changed context of citizenship at the end of the first decade of the twenty-first century. How different is it, and what is its likely impact on the teaching and learning of citizenship in schools?

THE SUBJECT MOVES ON – THE SECOND CITIZENSHIP CURRICULUM

The revised Programmes of Study for citizenship share a common format with the other NC subjects. For the first time, the NC includes Key Concepts for each subject, something advocated by the Crick Report in 1998 for citizenship, and essential learning experiences as well as skills and content. These changes help to give citizenship a sharper focus, a clearer definition and greater clarity about its unique contribution to the whole curriculum and the overarching curriculum aims.

The revised curriculum for citizenship also aims to ensure the original principles from the Crick Report remain the bedrock of effective citizenship education. The new curriculum is designed to develop young people's political literacy, social and moral responsibility and engage them actively in different kinds of community participation.

The new curriculum for citizenship is organised into an importance statement, Key Concepts, Key Processes, Range and Content, and Curriculum Opportunities. Alongside each is a set of explanatory notes that provide additional guidance to teachers about particular aspects.

The **importance statement** describes the essential aspects of citizenship, explains what learners can expect to gain from studying the subject and identifies how it links with, and contributes to, the aims of the whole curriculum:

Citizenship equips pupils with the knowledge and skills needed for effective and democratic participation. It helps them become informed, critical, active citizens who have the confidence and conviction to work collaboratively, take action and try to make a difference in their communities and the wider world.

(Extract from the *Importance Statement for Citizenship, National Curriculum*, 2007)

Key Concepts identify the key ideas that learners need to understand in order to deepen and broaden their knowledge, skills and understanding in the subject. There are numerous concepts that are applicable to learning in citizenship and many can be difficult to define and contested in their nature. The Crick Report identified several citizenship concepts. The revised curriculum defines the essential and Key Concepts of citizenship as being: 'Democracy and justice', 'Rights and responsibilities', 'Identities and diversity: living together in the UK'. The concepts provide a focus for planning teaching and learning and help teachers identify the key aspects of under-standing in the subject that learners should develop. If teaching is not developing understanding in one or more of these Key Concepts then what is being taught is unlikely to be citizenship. And to ensure the breadth of learning in the subject pupils need to develop understanding of each.

Key Processes identify the essential skills and processes that pupils need to learn in order to make progress in the subject. Critical thinking and enquiry, advocacy and representation, taking informed and responsible action are the essential processes in citizenship. Together they provide the basis for active learning and participation in active citizenship. Wherever possible, action should be informed by research and investigation of issues that learners are motivated and inspired to try to do some-thing about. This might involve young people presenting a case or concern to others; conducting a consultation, vote or election; organising a meeting, event or debate; reviewing a local policy; lobbying and campaigning via a website, podcast or display; setting up an action group or forum; training others in democratic skills.

Range and Content outlines the breadth of the subject matter that teachers should address when teaching Key Concepts and Processes. For citizenship this includes:

- political, legal and human rights and freedoms;
- role and operation of law and the justice system;
- operation of parliamentary democracy in the UK and other forms of government beyond the UK;
- central and local government, public services, voluntary sector;
- actions citizens can take through democratic and electoral processes to influence decisions;
- the economy in relation to citizenship including decisions about resources and the use of public money;
- consumer and employer/employee rights and responsibilities;
- origins and implications of diversity and the changing nature of society in the UK including values, identities and the impact of migration;

- the UK's role in the world including Europe, the EU, the commonwealth and the UN;
- challenges facing the global community including international disagreements and conflict, debates about equality and inequality, sustainability and the use of the world's resources.

Citizenship is an active and contemporary subject that requires teachers to use topical and controversial issues and real contexts for learning and action to develop young people's subject knowledge, understanding and skills and to keep the subject up to date and engaging.

Curriculum opportunities identify the essential experiences that enhance learner engagement with the subject. These include taking action with a range of community partners, participation in collective as well as individual forms of action, participating in debates on controversial issues, using different media and ICT to communicate and share ideas.

The full Programmes of Study for citizenship at Key Stages 3 and 4, together with further guidance, case studies, films of citizenship in action and the level descriptions that describe standards of pupil attainment can be viewed at the NC website (www.qca.org.uk).

PLANNING USING KEY CONCEPTS AND PROCESSES

In the first national curriculum for citizenship, one of the most overlooked statements was, arguably, one of the most important. 'Citizenship knowledge and understanding should be acquired and applied whilst using and developing citizenship skills.' This brings together knowledge, understanding and skills through the teaching and learning activities and ensures knowledge is developed through and alongside skills, and that skills are developed and used while acquiring useful knowledge. The new curriculum for citizenship relies on teachers using the Key Concepts and Processes in a similar way. Teaching needs to be planned with the Key Concepts and Processes in mind. The first question in the big picture is a useful starting point. What are we trying to achieve for learners? What understandings do we want learners to acquire? (concepts); what skills do we want learners to develop? (processes); which issues, topics or themes are we focusing on? (Range and Content); what kind of experiences do we want them to participate in? (Curriculum Opportunities).

For children and young people to become informed, responsible and active citizens, a citizenship curriculum full of high-quality teaching and learning activities needs to be planned. The curriculum should enable pupils to develop a clear knowledge and understanding of the Key Concepts, give them practical experiences of applying their knowledge and understanding to a range of issues, and provide different opportunities for working with others to make decisions and take action to address concerns. It is through informed, active and practical experiences of working together that young people develop a sense of engagement with their communities, a willingness to take actions to benefit others and a commitment to participate fully in democratic society.

45 ■

ASSESSING PUPIL PROGRESS IN CITIZENSHIP

Assessment in citizenship (as in other subjects) needs to be planned as part of effective teaching and learning. Assessment is most effective when used as a tool to help learners understand what they do well and what they can do next to improve progress and move forward. Level descriptions help teachers develop a clearer framework of standards and progression in the subject.

Level descriptions for citizenship

Since 2002, teachers have used the end of Key Stages 3 and 4 descriptions to assess pupils' attainment in citizenship. These describe the types and range of performance the majority of pupils should demonstrate by the end of the key stage. Pupils' attainment has frequently been described in terms of 'working at, working towards or working beyond' what is expected.

Alongside the revised NC for citizenship, there are new arrangements for assessing attainment. The attainment target for citizenship is set out as a series of level descriptions – levels 1 to 8 and exceptional performance, which replace the end of key stage descriptions. Schools will assess each pupil's attainment at the end of Key Stage 3, using a range of evidence to decide which level description is the best fit. The first statutory teacher assessment using level descriptions will take place in the summer of 2011, when the first cohort of pupils who have been taught the revised curriculum complete Key Stage 3.

The introduction of level descriptions for citizenship brings the subject into line with the assessment arrangements for other NC foundation subjects. They set out the national standards for the subject and allow teachers to assess how well pupils are doing and what they need to do to improve. The levels provide a climbing frame for progression and should help to promote consistency in teacher assessment.

Task 3.4 FORMS OF CITIZENSHIP EDUCATION

Compare the nature of the second citizenship curriculum with the first. How well do you think the second curriculum builds on the first?

Preparation

Schools should start to develop their approach to assessment now, in preparation for the changes to end of Key Stage 3 assessment. Teachers need to:

- be familiar with the levels in order to understand the standards;
- plan teaching and learning activities to ensure pupils have opportunities to demonstrate what they know and understand, and what they can do in the subject;

- develop learning outcomes or success criteria for tasks, and share expectations with pupils;
- establish a baseline of what pupils know, understand and can do at the start of the key stage;
- begin to collect evidence of learning to build a full picture of pupil progress and attainment.

QCA's principles of assessment

Assessment is an essential part of teaching and learning in all subjects. The Qualifications and Curriculum Authority (QCA) has four principles that should underpin successful assessment practice. The principles help schools take a fresh look at their approach to assessment and encourage them to think about how learners view the experience:

- *The learner is at the heart of assessment.* Effective assessment helps develop successful learners, clearly identifies ways for them to progress, and encourages them to take a central role in their own assessment.
- *Assessment provides a view of the whole learner.* It values a range of skills, dispositions and attitudes as well as knowledge and understanding, and draws on a broad range of evidence, including beyond the school, and involving peers, parents and members of the wider community in recognising progress.
- *Assessment is integral to teaching and learning.* It is embedded in what is taught and learned, teachers can recognise learning and progress as it is happening, and evidence of day-to-day learning is used when making assessments.
- *Assessment includes reliable judgements about how learners are doing, where appropriate, related to national standards.* This involves developing school assessment systems that support teachers and help them develop confidence and expertise in assessment through discussion and comparing judgements with colleagues.

Assessing pupils' progress materials

Working with schools to develop manageable and effective approaches to assessment and develop teachers' confidence and expertise is key to moving assessment forward. Assessing pupils' progress (APP) is the new national approach to assessment that equips teachers to make periodic judgements on pupils' progress, fine-tune their understanding of learners' needs and tailor teaching accordingly.

APP guidelines for foundation subjects, including citizenship, will include:

- guidelines for assessing pupils' work related to NC levels;
- standards files that offer an annotated collection of pupils' day-to-day work to exemplify national standards;
- a handbook to help teachers use the materials and implement the approach.

Recognising achievement through qualifications and awards

National qualifications in Citizenship Studies in the form of GCSE short courses and entry level for learners below qualification level 1 have been available since 2002. Citizenship Studies qualifications are offered by the three awarding bodies: AQA, Edexcel and OCR. The GCSE short course in Citizenship Studies has already been taken by more than 300,000 pupils since its introduction. The qualification successfully provides young people with a publicly recognised qualification that blends intellectual challenge and practical action in the subject. Following an extensive review of this new qualification in 2005–06 and in the light of the need to ensure GCSEs were in line with the new NC for secondary schools, full course GCSEs in Citizenship Studies are also available, with first teaching in 2009. The new GCSEs include a rigorous approach to controlled assessment, which replaces internal assessment (or coursework) and involves candidates in an active citizenship process involving skills of research, action, analysis and evaluation chosen from a range of citizenship themes. Candidates are encouraged to develop a range of evidence and teachers are provided with assessment criteria for assessing citizenship skills and understanding demonstrated. Short course GCSEs also remain available.

An A-level qualification in Citizenship Studies has been available through the awarding body AQA since September 2008. Opportunities for citizenship have been signalled in the new Diploma qualifications and in the AS Extended Project qualification.

Task 3.5 **NEW APPROACHES TO ASSESSING AND ACCREDITING CITIZENSHIP**

Discuss the new approaches to assessing and accrediting achievement in citizenship. What impact will these have on teaching and learning citizenship in schools?

Beyond the national curriculum

Many schools, colleges, youth and community learning providers agree there is great value in continuing citizenship education beyond the NC. The Learning and Skills Network is managing a support programme for post-16 citizenship with learners in schools, colleges, and training and workplace settings. National guidance about post-16 citizenship was developed by QCA in 2004 (*Play Your Part: Post-16 citizenship*). The guidance includes a framework of learning outcomes to support providers in planning and designing citizenship learning activities. The framework can be used flexibly and regardless of whether learning activities are part of a citizenship qualification or free-standing citizenship course, as part of personal development programmes or in combination with teaching other qualification subjects including diplomas.

OPPORTUNITIES

The new curriculum provides an entitlement for all learners across the country. Each school now has the task of designing and building its own curriculum to match the ethos of the school, the needs of the community and its learners.

As well as providing the impetus for high-quality citizenship teaching and learning, the new curriculum has potential to stimulate interdisciplinary learning across the curriculum. Citizenship is best where schools have a model that includes discrete learning in citizenship lessons, learning through explicit and planned opportunities in other subjects, learning beyond the classroom through activities and events, and learning through the life and organisation of the school. Citizenship is well placed then to take advantage of the links and connections between subjects and the coherence the new curriculum offers.

THE IMPACT

During the first ten years of citizenship there have been many inspirational examples of children and young people learning, doing and acting together for real change in communities. The process of citizenship is key to the health and wellbeing of our democratic society. Where schools provide rich and compelling citizenship learning experiences children become increasingly:

- *politically literate*, equipped with knowledge and skills to play an active part in public life and democratic processes;
- *critical, curious and questioning* about political, social and moral issues of the day;
- *skilled in debating controversial and sensitive issues* and able to argue and defend their point of view and advocate the views of others;
- *appreciative of the benefits of diversity in society*, why and how society is changing and their role in shaping it for a sustainable future;
- *confident about what being a citizen in the UK means*, informed about the rights and the obligations that we have to one another as we live together in communities;
- *equipped to take informed and responsible action* with conviction, to challenge injustice, promote change or resist unwanted change and try to make a difference in their communities;
- ready for work and life as independent thinkers, problem solvers and as informed, engaged and active citizens.

Task 3.6 CITIZENSHIP: FUTURE IMPACT?

What impact has the introduction of citizenship into the school curriculum had, and how is that likely to change in the future?

SUMMARY AND KEY POINTS

This chapter not only tells some of the history of the development of citizenship in the NC but also describes its nature and place in the revised secondary curriculum of 2008 and beyond. Among the issues covered are the aims and purposes of the NC and of citizenship in schools, the various ways in which citizenship can be provided in the curriculum, wider school life and community involvement, and how learners' attainment may be assessed and their achievement recognised. The chapter demonstrates how important citizenship is not only in helping to promote high achievement for individual learners but also how it plays a vital role in engaging and motivating learners, promoting community cohesion and in developing young people who are successful learners, confident individuals, and informed, critical and responsible citizens who make a positive contribution to society.

FURTHER READING

Ajegbo, K., Kiwan, D. and Sharma, S. (2007) *Diversity and Citizenship Curriculum Review*, London: DfES.

QCA (1998) 'Education for citizenship and the teaching of democracy in schools' (the Crick Report). Available online at www.qca.org.uk/citizenship.

QCA (2007) *The National Curriculum. Statutory Requirements for Key Stages 3 and 4.* Available online at www.qca.org.uk/curriculum.

QCA (undated) *Assessing Pupil Progress*. Available online at www.qca.org.uk/assessment.

PART

II

LEARNING TO TEACH CITIZENSHIP

CHAPTER 4

BEGINNING TO TEACH CITIZENSHIP

Jeremy Hayward

INTRODUCTION

Beginning to teach any subject presents a range of opportunities and challenges. Many of these will be fairly universal; however, each curriculum area will contain a unique set of issues and citizenship education is no exception. This chapter will focus on two aspects of beginning to teach: a short discussion on the emotions of teaching, linking to a discussion on the ethos of teaching citizenship.

There is very little existing literature on this topic so, to help illustrate the discussion, 20 student teachers of citizenship were invited to answer four questions about their initial experiences. The students were all undertaking an initial teacher education course (a PGCE) at a London Institute of Higher Education in 2008–09 and were (mostly) teaching in London schools. The survey was conducted after about four weeks of practical teaching experience. The students provided short written answers to the following questions: What are your thoughts on the challenges and opportunities of beginning to teach? What emotions have you experienced during this time? What have been the high points of beginning teaching? What are your thoughts on the challenges and opportunities of beginning to teach *citizenship* specifically? This survey makes no claims to be rigorous or scientific and the answers will only be used to illustrate findings from literature.

Beginning to teach

Taking the idea of 'teaching' in its broadest sense, we are all experienced teachers. Teaching is an everyday occurrence and, it could be argued, a part of the human condition. Much of what we know we have learnt from others and most days we informally impart new information or ideas. However, this is different from having experience of teaching in the formal setting of a school, although even in this realm no one is a complete novice. We have all experienced, first hand, many years of an education system and have forged our own ideas about what works. To some extent we are all 'experts in education' and come prepared with a range of opinions and ideas about how schools and teaching could be improved (Powell 2007: 24). Most people, it seems, know quite a lot about teaching and many are willing share their thoughts on the matter. As we are all 'experts', you will also have some established ideas about the sort of teacher you *want* to be and will encounter myriad opinions about the sort of teacher you *should* be, from lecturers, text books, fellow student teachers, official government advice, staff and pupils in schools, friends and parents:

> You cannot smile for the first several weeks of school, or until Christmas, or for the entire 1st year. Don't eat lunch in the cafeteria. Don't let them walk all over you. Don't let them see you sweat. You can't be too friendly – don't get attached to any of them.
>
> (Ayers 2006: 269)

Forging your own teaching identity against this 'cacophony' of advice is one of the key opportunities and challenges facing any student teacher (Stanulis *et al.* 2002: 46, Ayers 2006: 270).

OBJECTIVES

This chapter, although inevitably adding to this 'cacophony of advice', aims to encourage you to reflect on your emotions and ethos in the early stages of teaching. At the end of this chapter you should be able to:

■ catalogue and reflect on some of the emotions experienced in the early stages of teaching citizenship;
■ explore the idea of a teaching ethos for your citizenship classroom.

THE EMOTIONS OF TEACHING

Schools, colleges and universities are usually viewed as seats of learning – domains devoted to the development of the rational mind. Teacher education, likewise, is devoted primarily to the cognitive development of the student teacher's mind, typically focusing on areas such as subject knowledge, lesson planning, assessment, pedagogy and differentiation. Indeed, many of these processes are explored in the subsequent chapters of this book. However, teaching is not only a cognitive experience, it can also be seen as an 'emotional practice' (Hargreaves 1998) and for student teachers the affective domain, as much as the cognitive, is likely to be called upon in their initial experiences (Hayes 2003).

The role of the emotions in teaching, though, until recently, has received little academic attention (Hargreaves 1998; Sutton and Wheatley 2003; Zembylas 2004). In part this might be because the emotional side of teaching is viewed as a private and individual affair and so it is difficult to make generalisations. It could also be because emotions are difficult to measure and study (Zembylas 2004: 345; Ria *et al.* 2003: 219). These reasons provide a caveat for what follows. It is clear from the survey of student citizenship teachers that there was a wide range of different emotions experienced (only tiredness was almost universally mentioned!). Every teacher has a different social and environmental history and so has a distinct set of emotional responses and interpretations. Further, each school also represents a different social, cultural and environmental setting that will also impact on the experiences of the student teacher. What follows, then, can only be an indicative outline of some of the emotions that a student citizenship teacher might experience.

The emotions listed by the student teachers in the survey included: anxiety, apprehension, angst, despair, disappointment, enjoyment, elation, euphoria, excitement, frustration, happiness, humility, inadequacy, jubilation, misery, overwhelmedness, pride, relief, sadness, satisfaction, tiredness and warmth. Positive and negative emotions were mentioned in roughly equal amounts although the listing did not give an indication of the quantity of emotion experienced. The survey also did not give an indication of what the emotions were responses *to*. Goldie (2000), following Brentano (1995), sees emotions as intentional, that is they have an *object* about which they are directed. For example, a person may be angry with a *friend*, annoyed at a *pen* leaking, or elated at a *football team* winning. In each case the italicised object gives the emotion its focus. Feelings without objects are often classified as moods and it may well be the case that some feelings, such as a nervous apprehension prior to starting teaching, have no clear object and so could be classified as moods. However, the majority of feelings will be emotions with a clear object of focus such as:

- *standing in front of a class* – fear, excitement, exhilaration, tension;
- *pupils* – care, anger, laughter, irritation, pride;
- *yourself* – anxiety, surprise, doubt, pride;
- *lesson plans* – frustration, curiosity, enthusiasm, worry, happiness;
- *your school tutor* – relief, comfort, irritation, inspiration.

Emotions, of course, are a natural part of everyday existence, to the extent that Hume suggested reason itself was their slave (2000: 413). As if to illustrate this point Hargreaves points out how many supposed cognitive processes of teaching have emotions at their core (1998: 849). Consider lesson planning. A teacher might choose what activities to include not necessarily on cognitive or educational grounds but on the basis of what animated or bored the pupils, or what she enjoyed teaching. So emotions play a big part in teaching, as they do in life, and beginning teaching, as with beginning anything, is a time when emotions tend to be writ large.

That teaching is emotional should not be viewed as a negative; indeed the majority of teachers cite 'physic rewards' as the key reason for continuing in the profession (Hayes 2003; Kyriacou and Kunc 2007). Experiences such as the pleasure of helping others, pride in seeing pupils achieve and personal fulfilment tend to feature over factors such as financial reward or career progression. It can be argued that it is the range of emotions experienced on a daily basis that makes teaching such an interesting and varied profession.

What makes teaching emotional?

Nias suggests three main reasons why teachers have an emotional relationship with their work. First, teaching involves interaction with people and so is 'inevitably' emotional (1996: 296). This is, of course, true of many jobs however few involve such intense interaction with others (pupils, parents, other teachers) in such crowded conditions, nor might the interaction involve a duty of care as it does with teaching. Second, teaching is a domain in which self-identity is affected; from the development of a 'professional identity' to feelings of success, self-fulfilment or failure. Good experiences can lead to a sense of competency, excitement and exhilaration, negative experiences to feelings of frustration, anxiety and guilt. Third, teaching involves a great deal of investment of time and energy and so is naturally a place where high and low emotions will be experienced as various plans and intentions end in fruition or frustration. These feelings can be further heightened as this investment of effort is often carried out for broadly ethical reasons, such as a belief in the importance of education or wanting to raise the esteem of pupils.

Beginning to teach is a particularly emotional time (Hayes 2003; Ria *et al.* 2003) and these causal factors may help to explain why. In regard to working with people, some of the strongest emotions of experienced teachers are reserved for the process of being observed and judged during official inspections (Jeffrey and Woods 1996). For the student teacher, this is a daily occurrence. Receiving feedback and advice from others is a vital part of developing teaching; however, it is also an emotional experience. The pupils, too, are an unknown to begin with and getting to know them will involve a range of emotions. In regard to the second and third factors, choosing to enter a new profession involves considerable personal (and financial) investment, and many of the anticipatory thoughts and initial emotions will be related to the emerging identity that accompanies this decision. Can I teach? Have I made the right decision? What sort of a teacher will I be? Will the pupils like me?

Self-awareness

An established paradigm of teacher development suggests that in the early stages teachers pay a lot of attention to their own performance, focusing their concern on the 'self as teacher'. Over time the focus on the self decreases and issues of pupil performance start to take centre stage (Burn *et al.* 2000; Lundeen 2004). This transition is easily understood. The student teacher is usually being observed in the classroom and is also highly concerned about their performance. These factors will naturally cause a shift toward self-consciousness making student teachers 'acutely aware of themselves' in each action they take (Burn *et al.* 2000: 273). So the self could be a major concern while, at the same time, the student teacher might not know the pupils well, making it much harder to understand and consider their individual progress.

This will have an impact on the emotional experiences of teaching. Emotions bound up with self-esteem, such as pride and fear of failure, may be more prominent early on. Some of the longer term emotions associated with working with pupils, such as feeling proud of their achievements, might not be experienced so much to begin with.

In the words of a student teacher: 'In a sense being a BT [Beginning Teacher] gives you many of the frustrations of teaching without some of the rewards that come from developing a relationship with pupils over along period of time' (Student Teacher A).

This focus on the self might also have an impact on how classroom situations are perceived. Sutton and Wheatley give an example of how a pupil swearing at a teacher could provoke different emotional reactions (2003: 330). They suggest that whereas one teacher might feel anger – perceiving this as an offence to themselves, another teacher might feel sad – perceiving this as a symptom of parental neglect. It could be the case that a student teacher, being more concerned with their own performance, might tend to take the matter more personally. Teachers (sometimes because of cultural difference) can misconstrue pupils' emotions, for example, mistaking 'exuberance for hostility . . . embarrassment for stubbornness, and silent respect for stubborn resistance' (Hargreaves 1998: 839). The student teacher's focus on self and lack of initial awareness of pupils can also add to these difficulties.

Not being so attuned to the pupils and their performance can also have emotional consequences. As noted by Student teacher A, it can deny the teacher a major source of positive emotions, but it can also mean that the focus of attention strays elsewhere. For example, Ria *et al.* found that the lesson plan itself became an object of intense emotions for student teachers (which is not surprising given how long they can take to write). They noted a high level of anxiety if the plan was deviated from and, as a result, found that student teachers 'experience less satisfaction in seeing their students at work than in being able to carry out their lesson plans' (2003: 228).

Professional distance

If teaching is an emotional experience then how much emotion should the student teacher show? On this point Hargreaves (2001: 1069) notes a tension in the teaching 'profession'. On the one hand, teaching involves caring about pupils and so requires emotional interactions, yet, on the other hand, the 'professionalism' expected of teachers, as classically defined, requires they maintain a level of detachment by masking or moderating their emotional responses.

Sutton and Wheatley describe how teachers overcome their natural 'action tendencies', so enabling a regulation or moderation of their emotional reactions (2003: 331). For example, by saying 'well done' rather than shouting for joy, or overcoming the urge to shout at a pupil and asking them to leave instead. They also note that this might not always be possible. So the professionalism of teaching requires that some emotions are toned down in the classroom. On the other hand, it is important that all teachers are enthusiastic about their subjects. This would seem to be especially true of citizenship, which the Crick Report recommended partly as a reaction to measures of political alienation and apathy among young people (Crick 1998). It is important to teach with enthusiasm, even if you do not feel enthusiastic yourself, so sometimes emotions might need 'toning up' or acting out. Finding the appropriate emotional voice in the classroom is another of the important opportunities and challenges in beginning to teach citizenship.

Of course, it is not always possible, or even desirable, to tone up or down emotions. It might be good if sometimes the teacher engages in genuine dialogue with pupils over important issues, without having to constantly act out or disguise their thoughts and feelings. However, caution can be required as citizenship can involve very powerful feelings. For example, you might watch a film about the Rwandan genocide, with highly moving content. In such instances, it is sometimes best to allow quiet talk in pairs first before any whole-class discussion. This enables pupils to express their feelings or thoughts in a safe environment while allowing time for the teacher to reach an emotional equilibrium, if needed.

Reality shock

Another experience of some student teachers is that of the 'reality shock' (Veenman 1984: 143 cited in Lundeen 2004: 551 and Bezzina 2006: 417). Veenman describes this as 'The collapse of missionary ideals formed during teacher training by the harsh and rude reality of classroom life' (Bezzina 2006: 417). Students come to teaching with ideas about the profession and an image of the 'ideal' teacher. However, the reality of the classroom might mean that this ideal is not so easily achieved (Arnon and Reichel 2007). This naturally can be a low period. It might even be the case that this is felt more keenly by citizenship teachers who, because of the nature of the subject, might have developed a keen sense of political or ethical purpose in entering the profession and so have developed a more zealous 'missionary ideal'.

This 'reality shock' arrives from a disparity between ideals and actual school practice. Other related disparities might also be experienced at this time. There could even be frustration stemming from a perceived gulf between what is taught by lecturers and what happens in schools (Stanulis *et al.* 2002). As citizenship education in England is a fairly recent curriculum subject there is, as yet, no strong consensus on its aims among schools (HMI 2006). This can also be a potential source of conflict for the student teacher who, perhaps, might not share in the placement school's vision for citizenship (or lack of it). Strong and often negative emotions can occur in such instances when there is a moral distance between teachers which, in turn, can lead to a loss or undermining of purpose (Hargreaves 1998). 'Lack of specialists in the subject makes training difficult because they do not understand the ethos of the subject' (Student teacher B).

In reaction to the disparity between ideals and practice, Hayes (2003: 166) found that student teachers can adopt what Lacey terms 'strategic compliance', described as conforming to the school's or school tutor's practices while privately holding reservations (1977: 72). This might lead to approval from the school tutor, but at the cost of inner turmoil to the student teacher. Leighton (2004) notes the same of citizenship student teachers – highlighting the power differential in relationships with school tutors who, for example, often act as the referee for job applications. Such compliance, strategic or otherwise, is not necessarily bad as the experience and knowledge of school tutors and schools are crucial aids in developing as a teacher. However, it might be best placed within the broader context of developing your *own* teaching ethos.

Task 4.1 **KEEPING A DIARY OF EMOTIONS**

For one week keep a brief record of the emotions that you experience each day.

How many of these relate to:

- Working with other people?
- Your sense of self identity and esteem?
- Your goals and the investment of effort?
  It may be useful to compare your experiences with another student teacher.

Questions to discuss:

- How do you think your emotional experiences compare to those of a more experienced teacher?
- How many of your experiences are related to teaching citizenship specifically?

Repeat this activity later on in the course. Are there any changes in the pattern of your emotions?

Of course, it is perfectly normal to feel a range of different emotions at this time and the experiencing of intense emotions is not necessarily negative, unless it starts to become overly pervasive or debilitating. Being aware of some possible causes may help to place the emotions in a wider context to the extent that they can be more easily managed:

> So far it has been very up and down, although I have now begun to actively level out my emotions. By not tying my self-esteem/ego to the success or not of the lessons I have been able to deal much more effectively with starting to teach.
>
> (Student teacher C)

THE CITIZENSHIP CLASSROOM

Beyond emotions, beginning to teach citizenship raises its own specific challenges and opportunities, some of which we have noted already. Regarding challenges, as a contested subject is the understanding of citizenship shared by the school? As an emerging subject does it have status in the eyes of the pupils? As a topical subject are you able to draw upon existing curriculum or published material, or is this outdated? As a subject that deals with controversial issues, how do you cope with difficult and strong opinions (including your own)? Some of the challenges of teaching citizenship noted by the student teachers included:

- 'lack of status';
- 'being seen as the expert straight away';
- 'keeping abreast of contemporary issues';
- 'lack of understanding about the subject';

- 'convincing people of the merits of the subject';
- 'lack of specialists';
- 'overcoming apathy'.

Many of the reasons noted above can also be presented as opportunities. As a contested subject there is considerable scope for developing the subject in a particular way. As an emerging subject there is the possibility of helping shape its future (and the possibility of quick career progression). As a topical subject you are able to teach about the big issues of the day. As a subject that deals with controversial issues you are able to engage pupils in important discussions. Some of the opportunities listed by the student teachers included:

- 'greater freedom with planning than BTs in other subjects';
- 'opportunity to develop the subject and do something a bit different';
- 'having leeway on what I teach in my classes';
- 'you get to teach a subject that will make a difference to future society';
- 'opportunity to learn fantastic skills and strategies';
- 'being able to engage with contemporary issues as they occur';
- 'learning new subject material'.

A common theme in both the challenges and opportunities centres around the seemingly less-prescriptive nature of the subject which, on the one hand, allows for greater teaching freedom but may also be a contributing factor in the wider lack of understanding in pupils and other teachers. This 'looseness' of citizenship might also mean that the student teacher has both the need and opportunity to forge their own sense of purpose and direction regarding the subject. Doing so can be beneficial for other reasons. Earlier it was noted that the 'reality shock' experienced by many student teachers involves the 'collapse of missionary ideals'. If so then the early stages of teaching is a good time to revisit these ideals, re-examining your reasons for teaching, and develop your own classroom ethos. Further, thinking about your own ethos might also help to overcome some of the downsides of the 'strategic compliance' outlined above, as having a clearer idea of where you want to end up can help steer a path through the 'cacophony of advice' experienced during this time.

The idea of a teaching or even a school ethos is a little-explored notion, although it has recently gained momentum (McLaughlin 2005). In terms of the classroom it can roughly be defined as the 'characteristic, tone spirit or sentiment' informing teaching and pupil interaction (adapted from McLaughlin 2005: 311). An ethos can exist in the formal curriculum but is also encapsulated in the way in which a teacher goes about teaching; from tone of voice to use of humour, to the set up of tables and the look of the classroom. Every teacher will have a different teaching ethos whether consciously or unconsciously constructed and this difference is an important feature of a pupil's education. Indeed, the encounter with difference is at the heart of human experience and should be positively embraced in schools (Figueroa 2000). However, while acknowledging the importance of difference it could be asked whether there are certain qualities, tendencies, attitudes, teaching styles or methods that are more conducive to good citizenship education.

The 'hidden curriculum' and citizenship

Learning in schools not only takes place through the formal curriculum but through the 'hidden curriculum'. This refers to the manner in which schools and classrooms, often unintentionally, operate to socialise pupils into ways of thinking about the world, which can often be at odds with what is taught. This presents an interesting challenge for the citizenship teacher as the subject has a large potential for disparity between what is taught in the formal curriculum and what is 'caught' in the hidden curriculum (Hayward 2007). For example, you might spend several lessons on the importance of democratic decision making, yet not carry this through to any decision making in the classroom. Or a teacher might be a passionate advocate of freedom of expression while not constructing the class in a way that meaningfully allows pupils to voice their opinions. If we are genuine about promoting key citizenship skills and dispositions then it is important that we model them clearly ourselves, otherwise some of the learning will be undermined. Other potential disparities between the hidden and taught curricula include:

- Teaching about the importance of active citizenship, yet promoting passive learning.
- Promoting gender equality, yet letting male pupils dominate the teaching and learning agenda.
- Emphasising the importance of the environment, yet not recycling classroom material.
- Examining fair means of conflict resolution while setting a whole-class detention and therefore punishing innocent pupils.
- Teaching about valuing diversity, yet not appreciating the diversity that exists in the classroom.
- Asking pupils to discuss differences calmly and rationally, yet not modelling this in the classroom, perhaps getting defensive when your views are challenged.
- Presenting a one-sided lesson on issues of media bias.
- Guides on beginning teaching discuss the need to establish status in the classroom (for example, Kyriacou 2001: 103). Are some ways of doing this more consistent with the aims of citizenship than others?
- Osler and Starkey (2005) suggest that citizenship, in part, involves a feeling of belonging. Do some methods of teaching, more than others, make pupils feel they belong?
- You might teach about the importance of the rights of the child, yet overlook the right to participation or freedom of expression in your own classroom.

One issue of concern to many student teachers is that of pupil behaviour. Teaching involves daily decisions about what is fair (Johnson and Reiman 2007). At the same time, citizenship education involves frequent discussion about what is and is not fair, and one of the key areas in which the two might not marry is in the establishing of appropriate learning behaviour in the classroom. Schools often have established systems of sanction and reward that you might be expected to employ.

Regardless of how effective or even fair this system is there is still a question of *why* a teacher would want to enforce any rules at all. Kohlberg (1981) argued that there are three key stages of moral thinking. Pre-conventional, where what is right and wrong is determined ultimately by what benefits the individual. On this level of thinking the teacher might hold the 'rightness' or 'wrongness' of sanctions on the basis of how they benefit them as a teacher – perhaps by making teaching easier or not. On the conventional level, right and wrong are determined by a relevant group – a peer group or society in general. On this level of thinking a teacher might believe it is right that pupils follow the rules as these are the rules that the school has decreed, or might think them wrong if enough fellow teachers show discontent. The post-conventional level involves employing ideals that transcend societal values – such as human rights or a moral theory such as utilitarianism. In these cases a teacher might hold the rightness (or wrongness) of school rules by, for example, claiming that learning behaviour from all is necessary for pupils to access their right to education, or by citing the greatest happiness of the greatest number. Many people might use justifications on all three levels. However, Johnson and Reiman (2007) suggest that teachers employing greater post-conventional moral thinking are more likely to tend towards democratic classrooms. This leads to the question of whether some systems of sanction and reward are more in keeping with the aims and ideals of citizenship education than others.

Task 4.2 **DEVELOPING A TEACHING ETHOS**

1   Now you have started teaching, what do you think is the importance of citizenship education?
2   Think of ways in which there might be disparity between the message and the method in your own classroom.
3   What would be your ideal teaching ethos? (Think of tone of voice, set up of the classroom, use of humour, emotional pitch, topicality, relevance to pupils, system of sanction and reward, level of pupil participation, expectations of yourself and pupils.)

Of course, we cannot always expect teachers to be 'paragons of virtue'. Taylor suggests that seeing teachers as sometimes fallible humans is an important learning point too (1998: 13). Further, some of your teaching ideals might be longer term goals not achievable in a short placement. In part this could be because you might not have control over certain aspects of teaching, such as choice of topics, classroom decorations, prior expectations of the class (which can lead to a sense of powerlessness (Bezzina 2006)). Also because some teaching styles might take longer to bear fruition. For example, raising your voice to very high levels in the classroom might have some immediate impact, but in the longer term might not be an effective method. Conversely a quiet, friendly resolve might take longer to become effective but eventually could bear fruit for all.

I find classroom management challenging because I don't like telling people what to do (I don't like the power dynamics involved) and it's hard at the beginning to do things the way I would ideally like; class agreements on behaviour etc.

(Student teacher D)

We should finally note that an intended ethos is not always the same as an experienced ethos and some teaching ideas, however well intentioned, might not have the desired effect (McLaughlin 2005). Precisely because of this, beginning teaching is an excellent time to experiment with different ways of teaching, to hopefully find a style that works for both you and the pupils, helping engage young people with the world around and instilling a sense that they can change it for the better.

SUMMARY AND KEY POINTS

It is normal for beginning teaching to be a very emotional time. Highs and lows can fluctuate wildly within a lesson and across a day or week. Being aware of your emotions, discussing them with colleagues and thinking about their causes can help to place them in the wider contexts of teaching and beginning to teach.

The initial stages of teaching can be difficult not least because 'powerful social processes operate within school contexts that can be foreboding and often intimidate novice teachers' (Lundeen 2004: 552). Adapting your ideals of teaching to the reality of the classroom can be a challenging process. Focusing on developing your own teaching ethos can encourage you to experiment in the classroom, keep longer term goals in mind and can also help ensure that your aims for citizenship teaching are consistent with your teaching methods.

To end on a positive note, some of the high points mentioned by the citizenship student teachers included:

- 'When pupils leave the classroom still debating the topic you were teaching that lesson.'
- 'When a Year 9 pupil came up to me the other day and said "I really enjoy politics, it's really interesting".'
- 'Being able to make a difference in the lives of the next generation.'

FURTHER READING

Ayers, W. (2006) 'The hope and practice of teaching', *Journal of Teacher Education*, 57: 269–77.
Some light hearted and inspirational guidance for the student teacher.

Hayes, D. (2003) 'Emotional preparation for teaching: a case study about trainee teachers in England', *Teacher Development*, 7(2): 153–71.
Contains a literature review and qualitative research that features some interesting quotes and insights from student teachers on their emotional experience.

CHAPTER 5

DEVELOPING SUBJECT KNOWLEDGE IN CITIZENSHIP

Liz West

INTRODUCTION

Citizenship education has been described as 'more than a statutory subject' by Sir Bernard Crick, in recognition of the transformative potential of such processes as informed and responsible action (DfEE/QCA 1999: 13). However, this does not negate citizenship's position as a subject in its own right and that such participation derives from, and is informed by, an understanding of issues, institutions, processes and concepts central to education for citizenship. Student teachers can often feel daunted by the scope of the knowledge indicated by the National Curriculum Programmes of Study for Citizenship (QCA 2007). A cohort of student teachers of citizenship might come to their training with their knowledge rooted in a wide variety of subject backgrounds, disciplinary processes, conventions and conceptual frameworks. Therefore, they might not necessarily share a common language for describing their existing subject knowledge both in substantive and procedural concepts nor in terms of what 'doing citizenship' means. This sits in contrast to most of your peers, who while having 'gaps' in substantive knowledge will have a developing appreciation of what it is to study the subject they are now training to teach.

However, you might enjoy the opportunity of finding resonances between your previous experience, such as involvement in community projects, and the procedural and substantive elements of the citizenship curriculum. It is likely that your undergraduate study will have substantive links with the citizenship curriculum. Indeed, many universities explore the links between what you have studied and your wider experience as part of the application process and pre-course preparation. This chapter seeks to prompt this on-going process of identifying the areas where your subject knowledge is secure and where it is not, to reflect upon what 'secure' subject knowledge means for citizenship teachers and to suggest activities that could be used to support subject knowledge development.

OBJECTIVES

By the end of the chapter you will be able to:

■ reflect on why subject knowledge matters and be able to identify the relationship between subject knowledge and the practical application of it in your planning, teaching and assessment of learning;

■ self-audit your subject knowledge in relation to the current National Curriculum Programmes of Study for Citizenship (QCA 2007), identify targets for development and consider strategies for extending your subject knowledge;

■ define the characteristics of subject knowledge as indicated by the Teacher Development Agency (TDA) Professional Standards for Qualified Teacher Status (QTS) (TDA 2007);

■ identify the implications for your practice of research and reports into the teaching and learning of citizenship.

WHY DOES SUBJECT KNOWLEDGE MATTER?

Subject knowledge underpins effective teaching and learning. At its most fundamental, substantive subject knowledge is required in order to frame meaningful enquiry questions that can shape lessons and to accurately and fully address questions raised by pupils in lessons. Yet the standards for QTS demonstrate that mere recitation of 'factual detail' does not meet the subject knowledge expectations of teachers in this regard (TDA 2007). Sound subject knowledge includes mastering sufficient substantive knowledge to accurately teach citizenship but this is rooted in a keen understanding of conceptual and procedural frameworks and a deep understanding of the implications of these upon pedagogical choices.

These elements are interwoven in effective citizenship education. Secure substantive knowledge allows a teacher to select the enquiries that will frame pupils' exploration of issues and themes, fully conscious of how *that* enquiry fits into the 'bigger picture'. They are able to identify the interplay between 'topics' so that the pupil experience of citizenship education is coherent and is structured to support pupils' progression. They are able to prompt or probe pupils' developing mental map of citizenship education through reference to prior learning. In this way, effective teachers support pupils' piecing together of the citizenship jigsaw. They provide clear routes for pupils to explore the dynamics of the relationships between institutions, movements and issues thereby prompting deeper understanding of the complexities of political life.

Should a teacher's own substantive knowledge only extend a 'few pages ahead of the pupils in the textbook' then they struggle to craft longer term planning that has direction, purpose and progression. They are subject to the selection and approaches determined by educational publishers and cannot critique resources vigorously – and may be unable to spot material that has been overtaken by events and is therefore inaccurate. The Ofsted *Towards Consensus* report noted that: 'Citizenship often strays into areas where a little knowledge is a dangerous thing. It is characteristic of very good teaching that the teacher's subject knowledge is secure and thus supports the treatment of controversial issues' (Ofsted 2006: 37). This highlights the crucial importance of secure subject knowledge in framing debates about sensitive issues which are rooted in knowledge.

THE IMPLICATIONS OF CONCEPTUAL AND PROCEDURAL KNOWLEDGE AND UNDERSTANDING

The National Curriculum of 2007 structured the Citizenship Programmes of Study in a pattern of Concepts, Processes, Range and Content and Curriculum Opportunities as adopted across foundation subjects. In your reflections on subject knowledge development, it can be helpful to identify how conceptual and procedural frameworks can support teaching and learning in citizenship.

A rigorous understanding of the unifying concepts and processes of citizenship enables teachers to better design opportunities for young people to interrogate topical issues, case studies and participative opportunities using the language of political discourse. Failure to engage with the concepts of citizenship could disempower pupils. Concepts such as justice, rights, representation and freedom not only provide the glue to create recurrent and resonant themes in citizenship education, they are central to critical democratic debate. Fragile understanding of these concepts and processes weakens the choices made by pupils over how to secure change. An absence of critical reflection on the contested, contingent definitions of these concepts renders our pupils more susceptible to the manipulation of such concepts by others. Rather than being critical consumers of, and participants in, political discourse they are hampered by a limited 'political vocabulary'.

Crucially, if citizenship education is to enable pupils to reflect on the world beyond the classroom then they need the space to consider, for example, why 'fairness' matters. Pupils need opportunities to interrogate and apply these concepts with increasing independence and sensitivity to the nuances of contested definitions. This knowledge then informs their strategic considerations of change-making and how they frame their advocacy of change. The rigour of the evidential base for their argument is initially shaped by the quality of evidence presented for consideration by their teacher. Therefore, the depth of substantive knowledge of the teacher creates a model for reasoned and substantiated argument.

The examination of concepts such as justice, freedom, rights and identity can support pupils' insight into what each of us cherishes, what holds an almost talismanic appeal within a society and what that reveals about that community, society and particular context. The interplay between ideological stance and the interpretation of political concepts needs to be explored by pupils in order to evaluate viewpoints.

WHAT DO WE MEAN BY SUBJECT KNOWLEDGE IN CITIZENSHIP?

In terms of your training, subject knowledge is defined not only in terms of a secure understanding of a specified substantive knowledge base but in terms of an understanding of related disciplinary process. Subject knowledge in citizenship is dynamic, blending substantive with pedagogical applications and is responsive to developments in political and societal contexts. Subject knowledge can therefore be said to include:

1   *Substantive knowledge of the institutions, political processes, ideologies and debates that a study of citizenship includes.* In terms of the National Curriculum, these are identified in the 'Range and Content' sections of the Programmes of Study (QCA 2007: 32–3 for KS3 and 46–7 for KS4). This substantive knowledge should extend to include the themes and enquiries studied at public examination and qualification levels.

2   *Conceptual and procedural knowledge and understanding.* The study of citizenship involves the critical examination and application of concepts such as power, authority and liberty, as well as those concepts such as 'Democracy and Justice' stipulated as unifying concepts within the National Curriculum. These concepts could provide the fulcrum for a series of citizenship enquiries threaded across a range of different substantive 'topics'. For example, the concept of justice could be used to frame Key Stage 3 enquiries into the debates regarding the allocation of resources within the local community, as well as exploring how young offenders are treated. In addition, citizenship teachers need an understanding of the skills and processes that shape citizenship, for example, advocacy. However, they need to be clear about what distinguishes the application of these processes and skills in citizenship from those in other subjects. For example, the process of advocacy and the skills of persuasive speaking developed elsewhere in the curriculum.

3   *Wider knowledge and understanding of topical issues and how these illuminate and illustrate concepts in action as well as the impact on substantive knowledge.* The nature of institutions, laws, processes and conventions are reshaped by events. The teacher of citizenship cannot afford to be 'out of date' in case their subject knowledge of institutions and processes becomes inaccurate.

4   *An understanding of the curricular expectations of citizenship education as well as the requirements of the qualifications available for pupils within citizenship education.* This includes an understanding of the public examination requirements for Citizenship Studies and the role of citizenship in other qualification routes, for example, its contribution to diplomas (for further exemplification of the diplomas for first teaching in schools, September 2008, see www.qca.org.uk). Citizenship is in a rapidly changing context, having seen the introduction of an eight-level 'ladder' of attainment that brings citizenship into line with other foundation subjects. In addition, the development of 14–19 pathways has seen the extension of examination and qualification pathways in citizenship.

5   *A critical engagement with models of progression within citizenship.* Put simply, this means teasing out what you mean by 'getting better at citizenship'. This will be

informed by the available research and reflections on pupils' learning in citizenship and through your reflections on your own practice. This requires you to identify and consider the difficulties that pupils experience and common misconceptions within this subject. Again, your wider research can help you secure an understanding of the skills or content areas that pupils find difficult to access. You can usefully discuss this with school colleagues based on their previous experience. These reflections should then inform your practice and enable you to plan accordingly to avoid such misconceptions.

6   *An understanding of citizenship's contribution to wider educational initiatives*. It might be argued that given the small number of specialist trained teachers of citizenship, it is vital that you identify citizenship's relevance to the wider curriculum and the school community. This will be preparation for the likelihood of taking on responsibility for your subject and collaborating with colleagues in other subject areas over how they can meaningfully explore citizenship.

7   *An understanding of the pedagogical practices of citizenship education*. For example, what are the implications of citizenship's remit to enable and empower pupils to take informed and responsible action?

8   *Knowledge of relevant research and inspection findings*. You need to be aware of this and how this impacts on your own practice as well as considering the implications for the subject community.

You will notice that many of these aspects have been described in terms of practical application to planning, teaching and learning. This is deliberate. As the 'Crick Report' noted in relation to the suggestions for a citizenship curriculum: 'It should be emphasised that the knowledge and understanding components should not be learned as a disembodied list of aspects, content and terms but embedded in issues, events and activities of significance and interest' (DfEE/QCA 1998: 42). In order to meet the standards for QTS you will demonstrate how your subject knowledge is transformed into effective teaching and learning.

AUDITING AND TRACKING THE DEVELOPMENT OF SUBJECT KNOWLEDGE

The process of identifying the 'gaps' in substantive knowledge is often part of the interview procedure for ITE courses and you may have been advised to build up particular areas of substantive knowledge ahead of your training. This process is often formalised through an audit, which identifies areas of strength and areas for development based on prior study and experience. The breadth of study in citizenship and the prominence of 'doing citizenship' provides opportunities for you to apply your involvement in relevant projects or employment, such as legal services, community projects or local government to the audit process. An effective subject knowledge audit in citizenship should highlight how your prior experience and study informs your substantive knowledge.

However, a mere recitation of modules studied at undergraduate level can become a mechanistic process, as can logging what you read, access on the web or view without any reflection on what this means for your practice. The subject audit should be a tool for reflection and action, enabling you to identify targets for research and to track your progress towards these targets. It can be helpful for you to consider your degree of subject knowledge in terms of classroom application. In other words, the criteria used capture characteristics of what 'good' subject knowledge 'looks like' in planning, in classroom practice and in assessing pupils' learning. Examples of subject audits are outlined in two chapters in the companion text *A Practical Guide to Teaching Citizenship in the Secondary School*, one by Cremin and Warwick, the other by West (Gearon 2007: 25–6 and 33–9).

Task 5.1 **HOW WILL YOU AUDIT AND DEVELOP YOUR SUBJECT KNOWLEDGE?**

Consider how your prior study and experience have equipped you for teaching citizenship. Conduct an initial audit against the National Curriculum for citizenship. Identify those areas of strength where you might be well placed to share your expertise with your peers and those where your knowledge is limited. Table 5.1 provides one example of questions that could focus your initial identification of strengths and areas for development as well as considering how you could support your peers' subject knowledge development.

Having established where there are gaps in your subject knowledge, you then need to identify specific ways in which you could develop your substantive subject knowledge.

Box 5.1 provides several examples of different training actions that could support the development of subject knowledge. Consider two 'gaps' and select an action that could be a focus for your research into these areas. You will notice that these strategies blend substantive and pedagogical knowledge. Your development of your subject knowledge should link to application in your practice. In this way, you are more likely to see a purpose and immediate outcome as well as being one way in which you can 'test' the depth and security of your developing knowledge by transforming it into a display or a lesson activity.

You might find it helpful to track your developing subject knowledge. Table 5.2 shows one example of a completed audit sheet for one theme. In this example, the student teacher has indicated their research as well as how this has translated into their practice. The grid allows for self-evaluation with 1 being a high level of subject knowledge, and 4 being inadequate subject knowledge, and is based on a training course with two school placements.

Table 5.1 How might my prior study and experience be relevant to the National Curriculum in Citizenship?

Element of National Curriculum	How does my prior study relate to these aspects?	How might my previous experience relate to these?	How could I use these in practice? Share with my peers?	Is this a 'Subject knowledge black hole'? Action?
3a: Political, legal and human rights				
3b: Law and justice system				
3c: Parliamentary democracy and government				
3d: Freedom of speech, diversity of views and role of media	Module on censorship: this could inform debates on regulation; media as a watchdog of government	Degree placement in local TV newsroom; observed and participated in editorial process and impact of regulations	Create a unit of work on media's role: create and trial with peers a newsroom simulation for higher KS3 to demonstrate editorial criteria and ways in which news is constructed	
3e: Individual/community action; the environment				
3f: Conflict resolution				
3g: Local community needs and decision making				
3h: Economic decisions and accountability				
3i: Changing nature of UK				
3j: Migrations from and within UK				
3k: EU; UN and Commonwealth and UK relations				YES. Action: read a text on this
Processes: advocacy, informed action; critical enquiry				

Box 5.1 **POSSIBLE TRAINING IDEAS TO IMPROVE YOUR SUBJECT KNOWLEDGE**

You would need to research into the relevant content area prior to completing these activities. This research could include wider reading, accessing relevant websites, watching pertinent DVDs, reading pupil texts. It can be useful to have an outcome to focus the research and to embed your learning:

• Plan a sequence of lessons on a particular topic/unit.
  OR
• Rewrite a sequence of lessons to focus on a different skill/process.
• Create a teaching resource on a topic – you could develop differentiated resources on the topic that will help you think about access and challenge.
• Make a 'guest' appearance in another teacher's lesson as an NGO/different viewpoint representative for a 'hot-seating' activity.
• Produce a display advertising the skills and purpose of citizenship (this could be very helpful to a department at 'options' time – which will probably be during your A Placement) or for an open evening.
• Produce a display on a particular theme/concept/topical issue. You can place the concept at the centre of the display and then add photographs, news stories, eye-witness accounts, statistics and other evidence to illustrate the concept with some headings and questions that help pupils to identify the relevance of the central concept to those debates.
• Create a series of role-play cards with supporting information cards that illustrate the differing viewpoints on a topical issue/central debate. This not only develops your knowledge of diverse opinions and the evidence used to support these opinions but gives you a potential lesson activity.
• Evaluate a video and create a learning activity to go with the video.
• Evaluate a website and create a learning resource for pupils to use. This includes enabling them to evaluate the website. Consider the criteria and the process of doing this.
• Compare two recent citizenship textbooks aimed at the same year group and produce a brief book review/recommendation. Be clear over your criteria.
• Create a web page on a particular topic.
• Create an IT discussion board for pupils to contribute their informed viewpoints on a particular topic. What might you use as stimulus materials/discussion board reading?
• Develop a 'citizenship in action' board that highlights stories in the news and how this links to what pupils are studying/questions of debate, and so on.
• Work with a teacher on an out-of-school project/whole-school project to support informed action/advocacy, and so on.
• Create a series of different teaching and learning resources that transform the key points of a particular debate, theme or issue into different media. For example, how could you transform the content of the UN Charter of the Rights of the Child?

Table 5.2 Subject knowledge audit: political, legal and human rights. An example of how this can be approached

Topic	Political, legal and human rights	Political, legal and human rights
Evidence of prior learning/ experience, for example, degree/work	Module on human rights and strategies to promote/protect rights. Case studies approaches: international campaigns to influence civil and political rights in Myanmar; conflicts between European courts and national judicial systems. **Self assessment (circle)** 1 2 ③ 4	**Evidence of additional reading/research and development of subject knowledge**: for example, articles on securing understanding of the main themes of this area, development of resources, subject knowledge presentations, creating displays, online research. **State where evidence can be found.**
Topics taught with overarching enquiry and key questions	**A Placement: KS3:** Developed and taught sequence of learning on enquiry: What do we mean by a 'right'? What does the UN Convention state are children's rights? Are these rights respected worldwide? How can we work to protect these rights of all children? Sequence focused on distinctions between civil, political and social rights. Developed scenario approach to promote pupils' ability to apply categorisation and debate distinctive features. Case studies on comparison of access to education across global context. Then deliberately included statistics on participation in post-compulsory education in UK to prompt thinking about how economics/social factors can affect 'rights'. Co-taught sequence on 'Why was the slave trade abolished in 1807? Why then are there campaigns now against "slavery"?' Joint citizenship/history unit: from slave trade abolition to current debates over use of child labour/trading practices. **B Placement**: Overarching enquiry: KS4: A Right to Education? School choices. This had a broad theme and focused on a series of related questions: Is the 'right to choose' a school a reality? What are the implications of choice for equality within society? Who really 'runs' the school? The latter question was linked to how we protect 'rights to an education' and how we resolve conflicts when there are competing rights. KS3: Legal rights: what does this mean for you? Series of lessons on legal rights of young people, which incorporated visit by Youth Offending Team.	**Additional Reading:** (see notes in portfolio) Chapters on concepts of rights, legal rights, EU and international definitions of human rights, consumer rights and 'social contract' definitions of rights. A-level text for Government and Politics. Anna Douglas (2003) 'They know more than they think', *Teaching Citizenship* 5, Spring 2003. Massey, I. (2006) 'Doing the rights stuff', *Teaching Citizenship* 13, Winter 2006. Starkey, H. (2007) 'Teaching and learning about human rights', *Teaching Citizenship* 18, Spring 2007. CitizED: Briefing paper: Ralph Leighton (2007): Political, Legal and Human Rights. UNICEF session notes on teaching about human rights. *Freedom: A History and Citizenship KS3 Resource to Investigate the Transatlantic Slave Trade.* National Maritime Museum. Development of archive of related teaching and learning materials for MLA. How have children's rights been defined?: a comparison of Oldham children's experiences 1840–2008. Read chapters from AQA Citizenship Studies text: Mitchell *et al.* (2002). Focus was on the right to choose schools and the responsibility of different partners in education. I linked this to the data on rise of home schooling, exclusions and conventions regarding dress, custom and school rules. I developed a carousel of case studies as a main focus for the lessons, which followed a more generic exploration of rights and responsibilities within UK society. (See teaching file for resources and IT CD of resources developed.) **Final self assessment (circle)** 1 ② 3 4

DEVELOPING CONCEPTUAL AND PROCEDURAL KNOWLEDGE AND UNDERSTANDING

Subject knowledge involves knowledge and understanding of the conceptual and procedural frameworks that unify a discipline. The 'Crick Report' highlighted the role and breadth of concepts that education for democracy includes (DfEE/QCA 1998: 41–5). Anna Douglas illustrated how explicit but contextualised examination of political concepts frames the development of political literacy (Douglas 2003).

The National Curriculum has foregrounded certain concepts and processes to be explored and practised throughout the key stages. You will need to consider how the findings of research into the pupils' understanding and application of these skills and concepts might inform your practice. For example, are there specific teaching and learning methods that support pupils' skills in advocacy or their understanding of representation? How can citizenship teachers ensure that pupils find the discussion of 'rights and responsibilities' meaningful and tangible? What kind of questioning promotes rigorous examination of these concepts?

In practice, you will shape your lessons to blend content, concepts and processes. Initially, you might wish to focus your research on single concepts or processes before pulling it all together. Task 5.2 uses this approach. At first, you are researching a concept or process and identifying how you can use this in your own practice. Task 5.3 starts to frame your growing understanding of how these different elements of Concepts, Processes and Range and Content meld together to make meaningful lessons for pupils.

One feature of the processes identified in the National Curriculum is their overlapping nature, so research in one process will inform your understanding of the other two. For example, in order to extend pupils' skills of informed and responsible action, pupils need to engage with the substance of the issue they are acting upon. This requires them to have researched the issue and to critically consider the differing perspectives held on that issue, as well as the evidence used in support of these viewpoints (critical enquiry). They then need to consider how best to express their own views or to represent the views of others (advocacy). You may wish to highlight how this could be demonstrated in the following tasks.

Table 5.3 places a concept as the unifying feature. The diagram is then divided into sections that relate to different parts of the 'breadth of study' of the National Curriculum. In these boxes identify three relevant topics from the 'Range and Content' section of the National Curriculum. Then create some key questions that might be a focus for a lesson on that topic with your named concept as a focus.

The next row allows you to locate topical issues or case studies that could be used to explore this concept and content area. In this way, you are planning how you might ground the exploration of the concept in a concrete way as well as enabling pupils to consider a topical issue. The final row focuses upon styles of learning and, in particular, how you could 'activate' the learning. This links explicitly to the processes of citizenship.

Alternatively you could place an area of 'content' at the top of the diagram and consider how you might create enquiries within that topic area that could promote examination of the three conceptual foci identified in the National Curriculum.

Task 5.2 **DEVELOPING YOUR CONCEPTUAL AND PROCEDURAL UNDERSTANDING**

Select one area of the National Curriculum's processes in citizenship, for example, critical enquiry. Research this process and consider how teaching and learning can be structured to support pupils' skill in this process. You will find useful articles and examples of school-based application on the following websites:

- CitizED. www.citized.info.
  In particular, look at the trainee briefings and commissioned research papers.
- www.teachingcitizenship.org.uk.
  The website of the Association for Citizenship Teaching (ACT) provides useful exemplification of these processes. In addition, the association's journal *Teaching Citizenship* is a resource for further exemplification and debate.
- Citizenship Foundation www.citizenshipfoundation.org.uk.
  Further case studies and forums can be found on this site. In addition, the Annual Hooper Lecture provides further points for reflection.
- Institute for Citizenship www.citizen.org.uk.
  This website provides exemplification of active citizenship approaches. This can be one way to consider how to structure informed and responsible action.

Next, identify one sequence of lessons that you will be teaching and design two learning activities that have been informed by your research. For example, creating a research guide framework for pupils focused upon researching into a Non-Governmental Organisation. Your guide should consider how you can support pupils' critical engagement with the materials and require them to identify the limitations of the websites and resources used.

Task 5.3 **PULLING IT ALL TOGETHER**

This task can be done in several ways depending upon your preference and the stage of your training. Table 5.3 provides one way in which you can track through from a concept to lesson enquiry questions and learning activities.

■ **Table 5.3** Bringing it all together

Concept			
	1	2	3
Range and content area and keywords			
Possible lesson/sequence of lesson enquiry questions			
Making it topical: case studies and topical debates that could be included			
Making it purposeful: possible teaching activities related to processes			

Finally, as your knowledge and practice develops you can amend the table so that the numbered row relates to different year groups, for example, Years 7 to 9. With the different year groups in mind, which enquiry questions would you use? How could you build up challenge through your choice of case studies and of teaching and learning activities?

Task 5.4 **UNDERSTANDING THE IMPLICATIONS OF OFSTED EVIDENCE FOR THE TEACHING OF CITIZENSHIP**

Read the 2006 Ofsted report *Towards Consensus? Citizenship in secondary schools* on the findings of inspections relating to citizenship education. This can be accessed via the website: www.ofsted.gov.uk.

You could use the following questions to structure your reading and reflection:

• What does the report suggest about the challenges and opportunities presented by the differing ways in which citizenship is delivered within schools?
• Read the summary findings and recommendations. What does the report suggest about strengths of practice in school and areas requiring improvement? What are the implications for your practice? Identify a target and training action(s) to focus on one of the areas for improvement.

It can be helpful to use reports into the teaching of citizenship as a way of seeing beyond your own practice to the experience of the wider subject community and to identify trends and common challenges.

Subject knowledge also includes an understanding of the requirements of public examination and different qualification pathways available for pupils. This is the focus of Task 5.5.

Task 5.5 **IDENTIFYING THE REQUIREMENTS OF EXAMINATIONS AND QUALIFICATIONS**

Access the following exam board websites:

- Assessment and Qualifications Alliance (AQA): www.aqa.org.uk.
- www.edexcel.com.
- Oxford Cambridge and RSA Examinations (OCR): www.ocr.org.uk.

Read the exam specifications for GCSE Citizenship Studies. Then design a leaflet, a display board or an electronic 'prospectus' page aimed at Year 9 pupils, explaining GCSE Citizenship Studies. How would you explain the following?

1   The nature of the course content. What are the distinctive features of the course? What types of issues will they explore?
2   The skills developed through the course. Which are transferable? How can this course be helpful to the pupils' development and opportunities beyond school?
3   The style of assessment and the relative weighting given to each aspect.
4   Styles of learning that will be integral to this course.

SUMMARY AND KEY POINTS

This chapter examines the role, nature and dynamics of subject knowledge in citizenship and suggests ways in which student teachers might develop their subject knowledge. As noted earlier, the standards for QTS stipulate a broad definition of subject knowledge that encompasses not only substantive, conceptual and procedural knowledge but also knowledge and understanding of related pedagogical approaches. However, this aspect of subject knowledge will be examined in more depth within other chapters. In addition, a distinctive feature of developing your subject knowledge as a student teacher of citizenship is extending your under-standing of how citizenship might be meaningfully studied through other curriculum areas. Later chapters will focus explicitly upon the relations between citizenship and specific subjects within the curriculum. Therefore, this chapter has not explored this feature of subject knowledge although you might wish to add research into these links on a knowledge audit. In fact, it could be that by clarifying what does not represent 'citizenship through . . .' in other subjects, you might well find a clearer sense of your own subject. The process of developing your subject knowledge will be continuous and will carry on throughout your teaching career. The strategies outlined in this chapter are a starting point for this process and in demonstrating how secure subject knowledge touches all aspects of teaching.

FURTHER READING

Brett, P. and West, L. (2003) *Citizenship Education and Subject Knowledge*, available via the CitizED website at www.citized.info.

This was written as a response to Ian Davies' paper and then became a commissioned research article. The authors explore the importance of subject knowledge in citizenship and some of the challenges facing student teachers in developing their sense of the subject and of a subject discipline.

Davies, I. (2003) 'What subject knowledge is needed to teach citizenship education and how can it be promoted? A discussion document for consideration by initial teacher education tutors', accessed via the CitizED website at www.citized.info.

Last accessed 5/11/08. This was a discussion paper designed to stimulate thinking about what constituted subject knowledge for student teachers of citizenship at an early stage of discrete initial teacher training in citizenship.

Gearon, L. (2007) *A Practical Guide to Teaching Citizenship in the Secondary School*, London: Routledge.

While there are two chapters dedicated to developing subject knowledge, this text can also support your understanding of examination pathways and pedagogies related to citizenship.

Rowe, D. (2008) *Concept of Justice and its Assessment at Key Stage 3*, available via the CitizED website at www.citized.info.

This briefing paper for trainee teachers of Citizenship Education builds on Don Rowe's earlier article on the development of political thinking in school pupils. The briefing paper is a useful resource in demonstrating how a concept can be used as a unifying concept around which a series of enquiries could be developed. It also examines what progression could look like and how this links to assessment.

CHAPTER 6

DEVELOPING SKILLS OF ENQUIRY

A critical dialogic approach to citizenship education and its contribution to community cohesion

Paul Warwick and
Hilary Cremin

INTRODUCTION

This chapter concerns the ways in which you and your pupils can use dialogue to critically enquire into controversial global issues within citizenship education (CE). It provides a brief overview of one such controversial issue – community cohesion. While citizenship teachers need to maintain their powers of critical analysis, and apply them to their various professional contexts, pupils also have much to gain from learning critical perspectives on their issues of concern. One way of teaching criticality, and the ability to engage in constructive dialogue, is presented here.

OBJECTIVES

At the end of this chapter you should be able to:

- understand how the current Programmes of Study for CE relate to the community cohesion agenda;
- reflect on the sometimes contested nature of being a citizenship teacher in a social and political context;
- critically engage with community cohesion, recognising it is a multifaceted agenda;
- understand a dialogue-based method for engaging your pupils in critical enquiry.

CITIZENSHIP EDUCATION AND COMMUNITY COHESION

All maintained schools in England now have a legal duty to promote community cohesion. CE can make an important contribution towards meeting this duty. The difficulty is that community cohesion is still an emerging concept and interpretations of the term are both complex and contested. The Department for Children, Schools and Families (DCSF) guidance to schools provides the following general interpretation:

> By community cohesion, we mean working towards a society in which there is a *common vision* and *sense of belonging* by all communities; a society in which the diversity of people's backgrounds and circumstances is appreciated and valued: a society in which similar *life opportunities* are available to all; and a society in which strong and positive relationships exist and continue to be developed in the workplace, in schools, and in the wider community.
>
> (DCSF 2007: 3, original emphasis)

The context within which community cohesion is emerging as an educational priority is the increasing cultural and ethnic diversity of British society. Concerns are being raised over how young people can be better equipped to navigate the complexity of the world they now live in. The fear is, as stated by Trevor Philips of the UK government's Commission for Racial Equality (CRE), that Britain is: 'Sleepwalking our way to segregation. We are becoming strangers to each other, and we are leaving communities to be marooned outside the mainstream' (CRE 2005).

This follows on from reports such as that of the Community Cohesion Review Team led by Ted Cantle, which investigated the causes of violent disturbances in towns such as Bradford and Oldham in 2001. This report expressed concern over the depth of polarisation existing within our towns and cities. It identified factors such as separate educational arrangements, places of worship, and social and cultural networks resulting in many communities operating on the basis of parallel lives with very few meaningful opportunities to touch at any point (Home Office 2001).

CE is being identified as a subject that can play a leading role in enhancing community cohesion. The *Diversity and Citizenship Curriculum Review* led by Sir Keith Ajegbo recommended the inclusion of a new 'strand' within CE entitled 'Identity and diversity: living together in the UK'. One of the components within this strand was 'critical thinking about ethnicity, religion and race' (DfES 2007: 12). This recommendation has subsequently been incorporated into the new Programme of Study for CE at secondary school level. In this programme one of the three Key Concepts underpinning the study of citizenship is stated as 'Identity and diversity: living together in the UK'. Included in an understanding of this concept are:

- Appreciating that identities are complex, can change over time and are informed by different understandings of what it means to be a citizen in the UK.
- Exploring the diverse national, regional, ethnic and religious cultures, groups and communities in the UK and the connections between them.
- Considering the interconnections between the UK and the rest of Europe and the wider world.

- Exploring community cohesion and the different forces that bring about change in communities over time (QCA 2007).

DIALOGUE AND CRITICALITY IN A POLICY CONTEXT

Before moving on to explore how you might develop dialogue for critical enquiry within your classrooms and make a positive contribution to community cohesion, it is worth pausing for a moment to consider how citizenship educators such as yourself might locate these approaches within wider educational, social and policy discourses. Can teachers and other educators increase community cohesion through pedagogic approaches alone? What else might be necessary before the messages of the 'hidden curriculum' mirror those of the taught curriculum? If it is important for all teachers to engage in critical dialogue with those who wish to regulate and influence their classroom practice, is it not doubly so for citizenship teachers to be seen as open, curious, critical and engaged intellectuals and professionals?

What then are the issues and perspectives that citizenship educators need to take into account when considering their subject's connection with community cohesion? Tomlinson suggests that, despite legislative and policy developments in the area of racial discrimination, the education system over the past 50 years has developed within a sociopolitical context in which there has been a lack of political will to ensure that all groups are fairly and equitably treated:

> The climate has been such that politicians of all parties, their advisors and civil servants have to some extent acquiesced in processes of social, political, economic and moral denigration of groups considered to be racially, ethnically or culturally different, and they have seldom provided adequate and positive leadership that work towards . . . community cohesion.
>
> (2008: 2)

It could be argued that New Labour's decision to continue a Conservative agenda of 'parental choice' has undermined the comprehensive ideal (Whitty 2002; Rutter 2003) and reinforced ethnic segregation in UK schools. Local schools have been replaced by schools offering greater specialisation, selection and diversity in the name of choice and standards. As schools are encouraged to compete for pupils, the better-funded, popular schools can use their extra resources and admissions policy to attract and select the most able and advantaged children. Some schools have used legislation to expand the number of faith schools to introduce selection by the back door (7,000 of the 22,000 maintained schools in England are faith schools). In a study by Osler *et al*. (2007) respondents in Newham and Hackney suggested that social class, and not faith, made the biggest difference to who was admitted to successful faith schools. In Blackburn the faith schools, 'which are effectively selecting their students, are also achieving the highest academic results' (Osler 2007: 11). This is resulting in further segregation along ethnic and social class lines. These government policies and their unintended (or intended) effects do not sit well with policy to inspect schools for their ability to promote community cohesion.

A fixed and Eurocentric curriculum has also been blamed for a lack of community cohesion in schools. Tomlinson (2008: 16) has argued that government has not facilitated community cohesion through its 'failure to rethink the curriculum to inform and prepare all young people for their multicultural society and a globalised world characterised by racial and religious conflicts'. Gilroy (2006: 96) cites the 'almost totemic' power of the Second World War in its centrality to British history and identity and contrasts this with 'the mysterious evacuation of Britain's postcolonial conflicts from national consciousness'.

Bhavnani (2001) highlights a pressing need to 'deconstruct whiteness' in order to situate white identities alongside those of British minority ethnic identities. It is only through brave and self-critical reflection on the part of dominant communities that racism and community segregation can be addressed. Education for citizenship should involve not the simplistic reinforcement of contentious British values, but a process of unlearning racism while exploring identity construction, including ethnicity, gender and class. How can community cohesion be achieved if these areas are ignored?

So where now for citizenship educators who would like to work towards community cohesion? The answer, we would suggest, is to find a way of embracing paradox, uncertainty and contradiction, and to work with and through them. There are no easy answers, but there are plenty of opportunities to engage, challenge and explore in classrooms, staffrooms and beyond. This is important work, and we would hope that citizenship educators would play a central role in working towards change.

DIALOGUE AND CRITICALITY WITHIN A CE CONTEXT

> Our vision defines one aspect of education for diversity as focusing on critical literacy, which allows pupils to reflect on their own cultural traditions and those of others. Pupils need to develop an understanding of how language constructs reality and the different perspectives they use to make sense of the world around them. It is crucial for education for diversity that pupils are given the skills to challenge their own assumptions and those of others.
>
> (DfES 2007: 46)

The review led by Sir Keith Ajegbo, in its identification of the need to engage pupils in critical literacy, goes on to state that there needs to be an exploration of pedagogical approaches that are effective in helping young people to develop such skills. It identifies the importance of schools having mechanisms in place to ensure that the pupil voice is heard and acted upon in order for young people to be engaged in discussions around identity, values and belonging. Ruddock (2003) provides a useful review of pupil voice within CE and offers a set of good practice principles.

Within the Ajegbo Report a number of methodologies and resources are specifically listed as being of use to educators for developing critical literacy and engaging pupils with diversity. For example, Philosophy for Children (P4C) is identified as being an effective methodology for pupils developing higher order thinking skills when exploring education for diversity. Another example of effective practice in encouraging critical literacy is highlighted as being 'Open Space for Dialogue and Enquiry' (OSDE) and it is to this innovative methodology that we will now turn our attention.

Open Space for Dialogue and Enquiry (OSDE)

OSDE is one methodology that you can use for introducing controversial issues to your pupils within CE in order to develop critical literacy. It is a method for engaging young people with issues of cultural diversity and globalisation that has been developed by Andreotti and a group of international educators and academic researchers (OSDE 2006a).

The rationale behind OSDE is that learning to live together in a diverse and unequal context involves young people developing skills and relationships that support them in dealing with increasing levels of complexity and contestability. Critical literacy is conceptualised as helping learners to 'analyse the relationships amongst language, power, social practices, identities and inequalities, to imagine "otherwise", to engage ethically with difference and to understand the potential implications of their thoughts and actions' (OSDE 2006a: 3).

The objective of OSDE is to create a learning environment where young people encounter different perspectives on pressing global issues, including the points of view of their peers. In the light of these different perspectives the participants are encouraged to critically examine their own points of view and supported in identifying and questioning the assumptions, information sources and implications of their positions. In this way OSDE aims to engage pupils in understanding where their perspectives are coming from and leading to. It represents a form of critical global CE that is not an attempt to destroy or de-legitimise a perspective on a global issue but to encourage participants to broaden their field of vision and to scrutinise their own points of view (Andreotti and Warwick 2007). OSDE does not seek to tell pupils what they should think or do about a particular global issue. Instead, through this critical engagement it aims to enable young people to be more informed and hold their own points of view with a greater sense of awareness and humility.

An OSDE workshop generally follows a sequence of steps that can be summarised as shown in Task 6.1.

Getting to grips with OSDE

A common appeal of OSDE to citizenship educators is its participatory and group-based approach to engaging pupils with controversial issues. This pedagogical approach fits the active learning mandate contained within the original CE order. However, facilitating such a dialogic learning environment for young people is not without its difficulties. Achieving a genuinely open space for critical enquiry into controversial issues can be a demanding and complex task for both yourself and your pupils.

The relative newness of this methodology highlights the importance of citizenship educators such as yourself being able to access the necessary training in order to skilfully facilitate such a dialogic approach. The OSDE network has sought to address this through providing a website of relevant training material and session resources to use, including a professional development resource pack (please see www.osde methodology.org.uk). Global Education Derby and the Centre for the Study of Social and Global Justice have also created a related web-based professional development

Task 6.1 OPEN SPACE FOR DIALOGUE AND ENQUIRY PROCEDURE

Step 1 Establishing ground rules/principles of participation

It is important that you first create the open space in which your pupils feel safe to participate, and that is conducive to a community of enquiry being formed. The key issue is that you cannot create this space on your own. You need the help of each pupil to make sure that no one is left out and that each young person feels able to share their own point of view. One mechanism for achieving this is to state a set of basic principles that the pupils are required to adopt in order to take part:

1   Every individual brings to the space valid and legitimate knowledge constructed in their own contexts.
2   All knowledge is partial and incomplete.
3   All knowledge can be questioned.

(OSDE 2006b)

Step 2 Critical engagement with different perspectives on a controversial global issue

Pupils are introduced to different and 'logical' perspectives on the chosen topic of the open space enquiry through being presented with a number of stimuli. The stimulus material presents different points of view on the issue and you can take these from a variety of sources and in different formats such as newspaper articles, cartoons, stories, photographs or video footage.

Step 3 Informed thinking and reflexive questioning

Your pupils then need to be provided with the opportunity to consider for a moment what these different stimuli have presented. They can be encouraged to consider what might be the dominant views on this particular issue and why they are dominant and how they are constructed. Participants are also invited to consider reflexive questions where they identify what they themselves think about this issue, and how their perspectives have been shaped or influenced. Encouraging participants to consider what their personal responses to the different stimuli are can involve pupils working either by themselves or in pairs, and drawing, writing down or discussing their thoughts. When conducted within pairs this begins the process of pupils sharing their points of view and encountering the considered views of their peers; potentially beginning to identify aspects of commonality and difference in perspective.

Step 4 Group dialogue

Questions that critically explore the topic further can either be provided by yourself or generated by the pupils themselves to be explored within a dialogic setting. One participatory procedure is to invite each pair to negotiate a question that they would like to discuss and then organise a voting system where the whole group identifies one or two questions that they would prefer to explore. During the resulting dialogue your role is to try to encourage the participants to engage in the challenge of exploring different angles and points of view on the issue, and to analyse assumptions, implications and contradictions.

Step 5   Responsible choices

A problem-solving task can be devised that gives your pupils opportunity to apply the skills and knowledge gained in the dialogue process to a simulated dilemma or situation of responsible decision making. The aim here is to engage the participants in considering what they might now do in a real-life situation in the light of their critical engagement with this issue.

Step 6   Debriefing

Last words – closing the open space

Pupils are invited to reflect on their participation and provide some feedback, either written or verbal, concerned with what they have learned about the topic, themselves, about others, or about the learning process.

For further guidelines on these procedures visit www.osdemethodology.org.uk.

programme 'Learning to Read the World through Other Eyes'. Written by Andreotti and de Souza this offers a free online programme of study designed to help equip educators to engage in a critical literacy-based approach to global CE. It offers a theoretical framework and a set of learning activities to help educators examine the origins of their own perceptions, values and assumptions, and to re-evaluate their own positions with regard to global issues. To access this free online course please go to www.throughothereyes.org.uk.

The dialogic approach of OSDE might represent a learning activity that is a relatively new experience for the vast majority of your pupils. If this is the case, it is strongly recommended that you implement OSDE as a series of workshops, rather than just offering a one-off bubble experience. Within the piloting phase of OSDE in the UK it was observed that by providing the opportunity for young people to take part in a series of OSDE workshops over a number of weeks they were enabled to slowly find their voices, and take on the challenge of critically engaging with their own perspectives while learning about the perspectives of others.

Another useful tactic in helping your pupils to take personal responsibility for creating the open and dialogue-based learning environment is to avoid simply stating the principles of participation at the start of the OSDE programme. Instead, getting pupils to rewrite the ground rules/principles has proved an effective mechanism for participants to carefully consider what taking part in OSDE actually entails. Adopting this practice reduces the risk of the ground rules being lost in translation, where your pupils verbally agree to the presented principles but misunderstand what is meant by them.

Finally, within an OSDE programme it is useful for you to consider how you can help equip your pupils to be able to actually take part in the desired spirit of openness, critical challenge and trust. One effective response to this is to consider incorporating into the early stages of the programme relationship and communication skills development. So, for example, pupils can be provided with the opportunity to practise listening attentively to each other or take part in team-building activities or simple trust-building exercises.

Finding safe starting points

A vast array of controversial global issues can be covered within an OSDE-based CE programme. These include transdisciplinary topics such as climate change, sustainable development, migration, poverty, globalisation and conflict. A useful approach to tailoring OSDE to your school's unique community context is to incorporate consultation activities to ascertain pupils' pre-existing issues of concern (see Warwick 2008a for an example of a consultation activity).

Consulting with your pupils first helps you to identify the current hot topics of interest for your pupils. It is these topics that often serve as good starting points within an OSDE programme; drawing out pupils' enthusiasm to take part and share their perspectives. Alternatively, consulting your pupils might highlight issues that they express little pre-existing concern about or awareness of but which you, in your professional judgement, still feel are vitally important for CE to touch upon. Such issues might be more appropriately covered towards the middle or end of an OSDE programme when pupils are familiar with the methodology and open to exploring new topic areas. Having this awareness of your pupils might also help you to realise that when this topic is to be introduced the stimuli you use would need to give extra emphasis to background information in order to help the pupils develop a basic understanding of the problem.

Adopting a consultative approach can also be useful in identifying pupils' interest in discussing controversial issues that they have personal experience of and that therefore need to be handled with particular sensitivity. For example, in one multicultural setting pupils taking part in an OSDE pilot programme expressed an interest in critically exploring the issue of racism due to a number of participants having experienced racism within their own city. Rather than avoiding this personally sensitive topic area, it was decided that this issue would be covered towards the later stages of the programme when both staff and pupils were familiar with, and competent in, the respectful and trustworthy principles for participation in OSDE. This approach proved highly successful in facilitating the opportunity for the pupils to meet with each other and, through open dialogue, appreciate not only their differences but also their commonalities.

SUMMARY AND KEY POINTS

The policy landscape of schooling continues to evolve and this has recently led to revisions being made to the CE curriculum and to a duty being placed upon schools to promote community cohesion. CE has the potential to play a leading role in helping schools navigate the community cohesion agenda due to the explicit links between the two. You as a citizenship educator are uniquely placed to cast a critical gaze on policies and inspection regimes that require you to take a particular sociopolitical stance. You are equally well placed to encourage the young people in your care to cast a similar critical gaze on the controversial issues that touch their own lives. Whether you are in the classroom, the staffroom, the lecture theatre, the town hall or the pub, your views are important! The role of the citizenship educator is a painful one if there is no coherence between ideas and action, even if those ideas are sometimes contradictory and even paradoxical.

OSDE is one methodology that seeks to contribute to the maximal potential of CE where your pupils are encouraged to critically enquire into their own perspectives on controversial global issues, the different influences upon their lives, and their identification of where changes for the common good need to take place within their own community settings. OSDE affords young people with the opportunity to develop self-understanding and learn from each other in a climate of openness and respect. Although OSDE represents a demanding and challenging educational opportunity for both yourself and your pupils, it holds the potential to build bridges of mutual understanding between young people as they grow up in an increasingly diverse and globalised context.

Note: Parts of this chapter are based upon a CitizED commissioned research report, for further details please see Warwick 2008b.

USEFUL WEBSITES

www.osdemethodology.org.uk.
www.throughothereyes.org.uk.

FURTHER READING

Claire, H. and Holden, C. (2007) *The Challenge of Teaching Controversial Issues*, Stoke on Trent: Trentham Books.
A comprehensive book that includes looking at a number of different controversial issues and, for each, considering a range of teaching approaches to support pupils' critical and creative engagement.

DfES (2007) *Diversity and Citizenship Curriculum Review* (Ajegbo Report), London: DfES.
This report provides an interesting account of the systematic change that is required within schools in order to effectively provide education for diversity, and highlights the importance of pupils developing critical literacy.

Fielding, M. (2004) 'Transformative approaches to student voice: theoretical underpinnings, recalcitrant realities', *British Education Research Journal*, 30(2): 295–311.
This article gives a compelling critique of tokenistic responses to the directive of consulting with young people about their lives in school.

Hicks, D. and Holden, C. (eds) (2007) *Teaching the Global Dimension: Key principles and effective practice*, London: Routledge.
This book explores both the theory and practice of global education and includes a range of case studies that show different teaching approaches to developing the global dimension and handling controversial issues.

OSDE (2006b) *Critical Literacy in Global Citizenship Education: Professional development resource pack*, Derby: Global Education Derby. Available online at www.osdemethodology. org.uk/keydocs/pdresourcepack.pdf.
This professional development tool helps educators to consider how they can create learning spaces where pupils critically engage with a range of global citizenship issues.

CHAPTER 7

PLANNING LESSONS AND SCHEMES OF WORK IN CITIZENSHIP

Sandie Llewellin

INTRODUCTION

This chapter provides an introduction to the process of lesson planning and the design of Schemes of Work for citizenship learning. It also includes a brief outline of the wider context and complexities of the whole planning process as it is important you have some awareness of the bigger picture.

Celebrations recognising the tenth year since the publication of the Crick Report have coincided with the introduction of the 2007 Revised Secondary Curriculum that brings welcome clarity to what distinguishes citizenship from other subjects; level descriptors to assist with progression and assessment; legislation and guidance that support citizenship aims; and research that provides relevant information to promote understanding of the role and purpose of citizenship in the curriculum. The tools for citizenship planning have never been so accessible, with key websites (QCA, Standards and the Secondary Curriculum) all available online. Making the most of this new context for citizenship and applying the available tools to school practice creates an opportunity to innovate and a challenge to demonstrate that citizenship can make a difference to teaching and learning in schools.

OBJECTIVES

At the end of this chapter you should be able to:

- explain where a lesson plan and SoW fits in the wider planning process;
- describe the purpose and component parts of a Scheme of Work;
- describe the principles underpinning lesson planning for citizenship;
- use web-based resources to design a unit of work and plan a citizenship lesson.

WHAT IS PLANNING ALL ABOUT?

The planning process

Planning forms one part of a wider process – it is not a stand alone activity:

> Good planning coordinates long, medium and short term approaches and underpins good practice; it helps to ensure teaching is focused on what pupils need to learn and make good progress and enables staff and pupils to work together to achieve jointly agreed aims.
>
> (DfES 2002)

The process of planning is cyclical and involves making decisions about how to achieve aims effectively, monitoring those decisions to identify progress, reflecting on progress and evaluating achievement to feed into future planning activities – PLAN, DO, REVIEW: 'planning is one of the three groupings that form a continuous cycle underlying the teachers decision making' (Kyriacou 1998: 113).

Planning for teaching needs to address the questions:

- What should pupils learn?
- Why should they learn?
- When should they learn?
- Where should learning happen?
- Who should teach pupils?
- How should pupils learn?

Planning in citizenship education

Since the introduction of citizenship as a statutory subject in the 2002 National Curriculum at KS 3 and 4, planning for citizenship within the curriculum has presented difficulties for schools. The 'problem with the term "citizenship" itself and the many ways in which the term has been interpreted' (Ofsted 2006) has resulted in a wide variety of ways in which citizenship is taught, learned, assessed and practised in schools.

The 2007 Revised Secondary curriculum creates new and enhanced opportunities for citizenship learning by placing becoming 'responsible citizens who make a positive contribution to society' as one of its three underpinning aims. It also provides for, and supports, the wide variety of approaches to citizenship learning by stating that:

> The curriculum should be seen in its widest sense as the entire planned learning experience. This includes formal lessons as well as the events, routines, visits and learning that take place outside of the classroom and beyond the school.
>
> (QCA 2006)

The requirements to meet the outcomes of 'Every Child Matters', increased encouragement from the DCSF to involve young people in decision-making processes in schools, and the curriculum 'big picture', developed by QCA to reinforce the concept of curriculum as the entire planned learning experience of a young person, have all contributed to the importance of citizenship education in schools. Furthermore, there is recognition that 'real and relevant' citizenship learning has a contribution to make: 'The new curriculum offers real opportunities for schools to raise the aspiration and achievement of their students by making learning relevant, engaging and irresistible for our youngsters' (Mick Waters, Director of Curriculum, QCA).

Planning for effective citizenship learning across a range of models of delivery, teaching led by non-specialist staff, involving community partners and providing learning beyond the classroom and ensuring progression and continuity across key stages demands clear coordinated thinking about what needs to be achieved, confident decision making about how to achieve aims effectively, continual monitoring to identify progress, reflection on progress, evaluation of achievement and review to feed into future planning activities. These are the elements of the planning process. The complexities of citizenship education require careful planning if it is to bring real benefits to young people, organisations and to society.

Levels in planning

Planning for teaching citizenship is an essential and structured activity that operates continually at a range of different levels to meet a complex set of requirements. Lesson planning is, in a sense, at the 'sharp end' of the planning process and is a vital part of becoming a good teacher but it is important to recognise it has a distinct context. Many (although not all) of the difficulties encountered in teaching can be overcome by good lesson planning, but avoid the temptation to start lesson design before you are confident about the long-term aims for citizenship in terms of the fundamental purposes of education, societal responsibility and the specific aims of the subject.

Many schools work with three levels of planning: long-, medium- and short-term plans.

WHAT IS A SCHEME OF WORK?

A Scheme of Work shows how the citizenship Programmes of Study can be translated into manageable units of work and how units of work fit into the whole picture by sequencing the units. The purpose of the Scheme of Work is to ensure progression by building on prior knowledge and providing continual challenge and increasing demand.

QCA and the DfES have produced Schemes of Work for citizenship. The materials in the Schemes of Work are designed to help schools plan and develop citizenship. At Key Stage 3 and Key Stage 4 the materials support schools as they plan and develop provision to meet the requirement of the National Curriculum Programmes of Study. Each scheme contains:

• A *Teacher's Guide*, with practical ideas about whole-school planning, approaches to and delivery of citizenship.

■ **Table 7.1** Levels of planning

Long-term plans	Medium-term plans	Short-term plans
'A long-term plan is the planned programme of work for a subject across the school, covering one or more key stages. Long-term planning for a subject happens in the context of a school's overall **Curriculum Plan** (the long-term planned programme of work in all subjects covering every year group in a school). Schools develop their own individual curriculum plans to reflect their context and characteristics, as well as their values, aims and priorities. A long-term plan shows how units of work in a subject are sequenced and distributed across years and key stages. Schools make decisions about the order and timing of units in a subject, focusing on curriculum continuity and progression in pupils' learning. These decisions might change from year to year to take into account new initiatives or other changes. Many schools also identify opportunities to highlight important links with work in other subjects in their long-term plans.'	'A medium-term plan is a planned sequence of work for a subject (or for more than one subject) for a period of weeks, such as a half term or term, or for a number of lessons. Medium-term planning focuses on organising coherent units of work. Medium-term plans identify learning objectives and outcomes and indicate the activities that will enable these to be achieved. They usually show a sequence of activities that will promote progression and some information about the amount of time needed to cover the objectives (whether in blocked periods or regular lessons over a period of weeks).' A **Scheme of Work** is used to assist with medium- and short-term planning.	'A short-term plan is a set of activities for a week, a day, or a lesson. Short-term planning is based on the needs of individual schools and teachers. Teachers often use short-term plans to think through the structure and content of a lesson and to note information such as key questions, resources, differentiation and assessment opportunities, especially where this is not already included in the medium-term plan.' A **Lesson Plan** is a short-term plan.

Source: taken from www.standards.dcsf.gov.uk/schemes3/planning/?view=get

- *Exemplar units* that reflect the flexible nature of the citizenship Programme of Study requirements. The units can be adapted by schools to meet the needs of their pupils and to fit in with their provision.
- *Subject leaflets* (Key Stage 3 only) which map where citizenship and other subject Programmes of Study are compatible and suggest opportunities for teaching citizenship through other subjects.
- A *booklet of ideas* about involving pupils in different aspects of school and community-based activities: *Getting Involved: Extending opportunities for pupil participation.*

The schemes can be found at www.qca.org.uk/qca_4840.aspx. You should use this website in conjunction with this chapter. Appropriate parts of this website are sign-posted throughout this section of the chapter on Schemes of Work.

WHAT SHOULD A SCHEME OF WORK FOR CITIZENSHIP INCLUDE?

The key components of a Scheme of Work are:

- description of the unit;
- a distinctive citizenship focus;
- reference to the Programme of Study – Key stage, Key Concepts, Key Processes, Curriculum Opportunities;
- cross-curricular links;
- resources;
- key words;
- learning objectives;
- activities;
- learning outcomes;
- assessment opportunity.

Description of the unit

The Scheme of Work should be broken down into key stages, years, terms and units of work. Four to six lessons is a useful 'rule of thumb' for unit size. 'Units of work are best drawn up in terms of themes based around the sorts of real life issues that are relevant to young people, for example, youth crime, animal rights, discrimination, environmental change' (Huddleston and Kerr 2006: 131).

A distinctive citizenship focus

Citizenship units of work need to reflect what is distinctive and different about the subject and should be R – E – A – L: Relevant, Engaging and Active Learning.

R – RELEVANT

Pupils react and respond to topical, real issues that are current and actually affect people's lives; moral issues that relate to what people think is right or wrong, good or bad, important or unimportant in society, and sensitive and controversial issues that can affect people at a personal level, especially when family or friends are involved. Young people are aware of, and affected by, controversy. They want to talk about and understand it. Learning should be relevant to young people's experience and interests. For example, consider the responsibilities of the press by discussing the images presented in teenage magazines.

E – ENGAGING

Learning from real-life experience is central to citizenship education. Engaging directly with real issues and events in the life of their school or college or in the wider community gives pupils first-hand experience of citizenship in action – for example, through involvement in:

- school democracy, e.g. class and pupil councils;
- local democracy, e.g. youth councils, area forums;
- problem solving, e.g. how can we make this fairer?;
- community events, e.g. Refugee Week;
- campaigns, e.g. public transport, personal safety;
- regeneration projects, e.g. recycling, conservation;
- public consultations, e.g. lowering the voting age;
- researching, planning and running charity support, e.g. Disaster Relief.

(Adapted from DfES 2006: 108)

A – ACTIVE

Active learning is important in citizenship education because being a citizen is essentially a practical activity – it is something we 'do'. Active learning can be achieved indirectly through the use of activities based on imagined or hypothetical situations. We learn about democracy by engaging in the democratic process, how to debate by taking part in debates, and what it is to be responsible through the exercise of responsibility. Learning through discussion is important in citizenship education because it is an important vehicle for learning and a citizenship skill in its own right and gives young people a voice. It is important to recognise, however, that not all discussions are citizenship discussions. Citizenship discussions:

- are about real-life issues;
- deal with the public dimension of life;
- relate to young people as citizens.

(Adapted from DfES 2006: 111)

Project work is important in citizenship because it is an opportunity for young people to take responsibility for their learning and is a form of active learning. Project work can be a powerful motivator for citizenship learning. The opportunity to use initiative on an issue that concerns them can stimulate in young people a desire to find out more about how their community is run, what the barriers to change are and how these might be overcome. It also helps them to learn where they can find out these things. It also has a valuable role to play in the consultation process. Young people as researchers are able to provide information useful for decision making in schools, other organisations and in the community at large.

L – LEARNING

Citizenship learning is most effective when it takes place in a climate that is non-threatening, in which young people can express their opinions freely and without embarrassment and use their initiative without undue fear of failure. Such an atmosphere takes time to develop and is built up gradually. There are a number of strategies that can help you with this. They include:

- Ground rules – these work best when young people are involved in developing and testing their own, for example, for activities such as discussion, or group work.
- Paired and small-group work – less threatening than facing the whole group all the time.
- Seating arrangements – to create a more open and inclusive atmosphere, for example, sitting in a circle for discussion.
- Warm-ups and debriefs – these help young people to get to know and trust each other and feel a valued part of the process.
- Giving everyone something to do – full participation prevents individuals feeling left out and builds up a sense of group solidarity, for example, having a vote, 'round robins', assigning different responsibilities to group members.
- Achievable goals – to create a feeling of success for all and avoid any unnecessary sense of failure.
- Catering for different learning styles – a range of activities employing different kinds of learning, for example, visual, physical, written, oral.

Reference to the Programme of Study – Key stage, Key Concepts, Key Processes, Curriculum Opportunities and Cross-curricular links

The 'themes' should ensure all pupils have opportunities to understand the Key Concepts of 'Democracy and justice', 'Rights and responsibilities', 'Identities and communities: Living together in the UK' that underpin the study of citizenship:

It is important to ensure that understanding is developed in each concept and that pupils make sense of the concepts through concrete examples. Applying the concepts to different topical issues and in a range of contexts (local, national, global) will reinforce conceptual understanding.

(http://curriculum.qca.org.uk 'Citizenship at KS3
Planning across the Key Stage')

Planning should also provide for the continuous development of the three Key Processes of critical thinking and enquiry, advocacy and representation, and taking informed action 'to ensure that pupils continue to be challenged and are able to progress'. QCA guidance states that:

Planning should ensure that pupils have opportunities to:

- develop questions to investigate;

- use different approaches for their enquiries and research;
- use and analyse real data including statistics and primary sources of research, such as surveys of or interviews with their peers;
- work with others, including different people from their peer group, people of different ages and backgrounds and those from the wider community;
- try out new roles or ideas as they plan and undertake different courses of action in project teams and groups;
- practise different ways of presenting a case in informal discussions and in parliamentary style debates, with familiar and unfamiliar audiences;
- use a wide range of increasingly complex and challenging materials and sources, including those that are ICT-based or that are derived from the media.

(http://curriculum.qca.org.uk 'Cit KS3 Planning across the key stage')

Pupils should cover all relevant Key Concepts and Key Processes at least once in each key stage but this can be done in combination within the same unit of work, for example, gun crime, the law and community cohesion. Some Key Processes may be developed within 'host' subjects such as Persuasive speech in English set out in QCA Citizenship for KS3 subject leaflets, or within Cross Curriculum Dimensions such as Sustainable development, or through 'special' specific activities such as voting for a representative for the UK Youth Parliament that would contribute to a unit on democracy.

Resources

The problem with citizenship is that there are almost too many resources and selecting the most appropriate becomes an issue. It is essential to audit resources regularly and to develop criteria for selection to ensure resources for citizenship support the learning objectives and outcomes for all aspects of citizenship Programmes of Study as a whole not just for knowledge-based Key Concepts. This means that in addition to websites and ICT-related resources including video and CD-Rom, texts for teachers, photocopiable resources for pupils, fiction and non-fiction, there should be recognition of the contribution of visits and visitors together with current materials in the form of newspapers, photographs and magazines.

Pupils should be given opportunities to engage with the wider community, communicate with, represent, and take action alongside others both in school and beyond. Activities or sequences of work involving contact with groups, organisations and individuals in the local community are important ways to achieve this. QCA have produced a *booklet of ideas* about involving pupils in different aspects of school and community-based activities: *Getting involved: extending opportunities for pupil participation* (www.qca.org.uk/qca_4840.aspx). Elements of ICT such as using the internet, PDAs (hand-held computers) and webcams offer direct opportunities to engage with audiences in different communities, both within the UK and internationally. The DfES 'Self evaluation tool for citizenship education' includes a useful section on 'Resources and their management' that enables schools to audit resources and 'ensure that selected resources promote equality, inclusion and diversity and where possible involve pupils in their selection' (www.citizenshipfoundation.org.uk/lib_res_ pdf/0732.pdf). Teachers of citizenship should appraise resources critically to be sure of relevance and real citizenship focus. The ACT booklet 'Identity, diversity and citizenship: a critical review of resources' followed findings in the Ajegbo Report that: 'teaching about issues of identity and diversity in Citizenship is often unsatisfactory in terms of coverage, conceptual depth, contextualization in real-life issues and links to political understanding and active participation'.

Applying the approach used by ACT to resources that support the development of other Key Concepts and Processes in citizenship should improve the selection of more appropriate teaching resources. QCA have produced an extensive list of useful resources that include citizenship documents and websites (www.qca.org.uk/qca_ 4850.aspx).

Key words

QCA have produced a citizenship glossary that provides teachers with definitions of key words and terms used in teaching citizenship. The A–Z glossary is easy to search and may be printed out for reference (www.qca.org.uk/qca_4826.aspx).

Planning to achieve learning outcomes

Learning objectives and learning outcomes are the small steps that enable the broad aims of citizenship to be achieved. In citizenship lessons pupils should be encouraged to participate in the process of setting learning objectives by generating and discussing options, and developing, and using, decision-making skills to select appropriate approaches to achieving learning. The specialist citizenship teacher should take the role of facilitator in the process of empowering pupils to take responsibility for their own actions. Decisions on learning outcomes can be decided in advance by the teacher but should increasingly be negotiated with pupils depending on their preferred learning style, strengths and weaknesses. Outcomes need to be written, clearly explained and confirmed by teachers and pupils to avoid any misunderstanding.

Assessment

In all National Curriculum Subjects, including citizenship from 2008, the criteria for assessing progress are set out in descriptions of performance at eight levels. These national standards allow teachers, learners and their parents or carers to see how well they are doing in relation to their prior attainment and to expectations for learners of their age. The descriptions have been written so that:

- Level 2 represents expectations for the average 7-year-old.
- Level 4 represents expectations for the average 11-year-old.
- Level 5–6 represents expectations for the average 14-year-old.

■ **Table 7.2** Learning objectives and learning outcomes – what's the difference?

Learning objectives	Learning outcomes
Learning objectives focus on what pupils will learn in the lesson and need to be developed with pupils and made explicit in a language that they can understand. The purpose of the objective is to support pupils as they move from what they know towards new knowledge, skills and understanding. For example, KS3 pupils should learn about the age of criminal responsibility.	Learning outcomes are what pupils have 'learnt' and can demonstrate as a result of a lesson, an experience, programme or event. They are the precise stepping stones that achieve the learning objective and can be very specific (list ten key facts about Parliament) and very broad (show a more positive attitude to participating in discussion). Outcomes can be set by teachers, organisations or by the learners themselves. They can be used to assess, describe and evidence the learning that has taken place. For example, KS3 pupils are able to understand the concept of the 'age of criminal responsibility' and discuss this critically.

Sources: www.standards.dfes.gov.uk/schemes2/citizenship/cit13/?view=list&column=objective; www.standards.dfes.gov.uk/schemes2/citizenship/cit13/?view=list&column=outcome

Assessments should be planned as part of citizenship teaching and learning. This requires teachers to clearly establish what pupils should:

- know – the essential knowledge drawn from Range and Content;
- understand – conceptual understanding;
- be able to do – citizenship skills and processes.

Teaching of the Key Processes at KS3 should take account of pupils' previous experiences to link with and build on their previous learning in KS2.

Pupils should be given regular feedback on how to improve in order to help them meet the expected standard by the end of the key stage. New level descriptions for citizenship will help teachers and learners to understand the standards to aim for, and will provide a framework for progression in the subject. The challenge for schools will be to embrace the breadth of activities that constitute citizenship education and provide opportunities for pupils to collect evidence of achievements, actively involve pupils in planning and assessing learning objectives and outcomes, give pupils opportunities to give and receive feedback assessment and develop a whole-school approach to assessing and recording progress in citizenship.

Although written before the level descriptors, the QCA booklet 'Assessing citizenship: example assessment activities for KS3' (2006) provides some useful guidance for appropriate approaches to assessment.

At KS4 all three awarding bodies offer Level 1 and Level 2 GCSE short course in Citizenship Studies and from September 2009 will offer Levels 1 and 2 full GCSE course in Citizenship Studies. For full details visit www.accreditedqualifications.org.uk

---

Task 7.1 **PLANNING A SCHEME OF WORK FOR FIVE LESSONS**

Taking into consideration what you have learnt from this chapter and related websites use the suggested template to write a KS3 Scheme of Work for five lessons for Year 7 pupils on one of the following themes – the role of the media, crime and punishment, the environment. It is important that you include opportunity for pupils to 'take informed and responsible action'.

WHAT IS A LESSON PLAN?

A lesson plan is a guide to aid planning, delivery and reflection on classroom practice. It is a tool for sharing and following practice, a time sheet for a single event and a vital part of becoming a good citizenship teacher. The lesson plan gives the teacher clarity of purpose, improves pace and challenge in delivery, provides structure, is a reminder of resources, Key Concepts and Processes, sequence and tasks, and provides a tool for reflection and improvement. Most importantly, lessons are about learning. In successful lessons pupils are put first, they will have contributed to lesson planning, they are clear about expectations and what is to be learned, they are actively engaged in learning, able to work independently and in groups, able to use assessment to improve and confident of success because the right conditions prevail. Coordinating the timing, handling resources, catering for a variety of needs and abilities and ensuring learning expectations are communicated and outcomes achieved, are complex and demanding tasks. Much more goes into behind-the-scenes preparation and follow-up than is seen in the short performance!

HOW IS A CITIZENSHIP LESSON PLAN DESIGNED?

Lesson planning is a continual process of plan, do, review and in citizenship it is an opportunity to contribute to changing the culture of classrooms by modelling the behaviours that will encourage pupils to grow into effective citizens. The research findings from the EPPI Review make essential reading for teachers of citizenship who are ambassadors of the approaches that are likely to foster pupil empowerment (Deakin Crick *et al.* 2004a).

WHY IS PLANNING A CITIZENSHIP LESSON DIFFERENT FROM OTHER SUBJECTS?

Citizenship has integrity and can be distinguished from other subjects in the curriculum by its content, focus and approach. It is the responsibility of specialist teachers of citizenship to make this distinction explicit whether teaching a discrete citizenship lesson or within other subject lessons, tutorial programmes or special events.

Table 7.3 A suggested template for a Scheme of Work for five lessons

Subject: CITIZENSHIP Focus/introduction	Member of staff	Topic	Term 1/2/3/4/5/6 Lesson dates:		Year

Overall aims

Links to programmes of study | **Cross-curricular links**

Resource | **Key words**

Assessment

Lesson and focus	Learning objectives Students will learn …	Activities/content – Starter/main/plenary	Learning outcomes Students will …
1			
2			
3			
4			
5			

Box 7.1 **THE LESSON-PLANNING PROCESS**

Plan

- Have a clear purpose for the lesson and locate it in the context of the Scheme of Work.
- Consider the content in relation to the appropriate Programme of Study, pupils' prior knowledge, current issues and their relevance to pupils' real-life experience.
- Involve pupils in the process of setting objectives and outcomes for learning.
- Include a 'hook' starter, engaging main learning activities and a plenary for reflection.

↓

Do

- Involve pupils in explaining purpose, lesson objectives and learning outcomes.
- Involve pupils in agreeing rules for ways of working.
- Facilitate variety in pace, methods and use of media.
- Use appropriate methods for learning that include opportunities for active participation and ensure all pupils are able to engage.
- Make links with National Strategies.
- Ensure a logical sequence of stages through starter, main activity(ies) to plenary.

↓

Review

- Use a range of approaches to assess that learning outcomes have been achieved.
- Make sure feedback to, from and between pupils enables improvement.
- Share evaluation of the lesson with pupils (not necessarily all) to identify successes, strengths and areas to develop.

Lesson content

There is a core of subject knowledge that is not covered in other parts of the curriculum – criminal and civil law, government and politics, electoral systems, taxation and the economy, the role of the EU, UN and Commonwealth and concepts of democracy and justice and the rule of law. There is also a set of skills that is distinctive to citizenship and not covered in other parts of the curriculum – critical thinking, advocacy and representation, taking informed and responsible action.

Lesson focus

A focus on real, topical, controversial issues is 'core business' for citizenship and when planning lessons you need to be aware of issues that interest and engage young people (at local, national and global levels), research and use current information and real case studies and be aware of changes and updates. Controversial issues must address matters of public concern to be real citizenship – personal issues are the responsibility of PSHE. Making the purpose of learning about an issue is essential.

Lesson approach

Citizenship education is not just about what pupils learn but the way they learn. Learning for citizenship is best when pupils are involved as partners in the process of 'doing it' – choosing the focus for the lesson, planning a lesson, participating on the school council, discussing an issue. Effective citizenship learning is enquiry based, posing a question about a current political or social matter of controversy to 'hook' a response that can be explored in greater depth, for example, should the voting age be lowered to 16?; could car crime be reduced if the driving age was lifted to 21? Effective citizenship uses active learning approaches that are stimulating and fun and involve and engage pupils and can take place beyond the classroom, for example, discussion carousel, opinion finders, debates, working in partnership with a community organisation to run special events, VLE discussion forum. This approach provides a rehearsal for forming opinions, making decisions, having a voice and making decisions in real life.

The following checklist (Table 7.5) has been designed to focus lesson planning for citizenship lessons on those features that make citizenship distinctive and different from other subjects in the curriculum. It can be used as part of your own personal evaluation and improvement process.

Starting to plan a lesson

As a citizenship student teacher on a teaching placement it is likely you will be allocated topics or units from the Scheme of Work. You may start by planning and delivering a starter activity or a plenary session. The scenarios below are typical of what to expect.

Task 7.2 **PLANNING AN ENGAGING STARTER ACTIVITY**

Scenario 1
You have been asked to plan a Y8 introductory lesson on a unit of work on electoral systems. Think of an appropriate *starter activity* to engage pupils in learning about the key concept of democracy with particular reference to PoS1.1a 'participating actively in different kinds of decision-making and voting in order to influence public life'.

Task 7.3 **PLANNING AN EFFECTIVE PLENARY**

Scenario 2

Y9 have shown little interest in two lessons on human rights led by their subject teacher. She asks you to take responsibility for planning a plenary in the third and final lesson in the unit focusing on the role of pressure groups. Plan an activity that will encourage and motivate pupils to investigate how they could get involved and take responsible action on an issue(s) that interest them.

You may then move onto planning one lesson from a unit of work. The scenario below is a typical example of what to expect.

Task 7.4 **PLANNING A THREE-PART CITIZENSHIP LESSON**

Scenario 3

You are asked to take responsibility for a sequence of three lessons on local democracy for Key Stage 3, Year 8. Plan a 50-minute introductory citizenship lesson referring to the Secondary Curriculum for Citizenship, the Standards and Electoral Commission websites.

Complete all parts of the lesson plan template (Table 7.4) and evaluate it against the checklist for a good citizenship lesson (Table 7.5).

The lesson plan template guides you through the component parts of a lesson and if used in conjunction with key resources that include QCA Schemes of Work (www.standards.dfes.gov.uk/schemes2/citizenship/ and www.citized.info/?r_menu= sow&strand=2) to provide a format; lesson plan ideas from previous student teachers (www.citized.info/search/?q=lesson+plans&x=0&y=0); the BBC website to give information on current issues (http://news.bbc.co.uk/cbbcnews/hi/newsid_1790000/ newsid_1793900/1793997.stm); and the Electoral Commission's *Democracy Cookbook* (www.dopolitics.org.uk) to give ideas for learning activities, you should be equipped to start planning. Remember an active and engaging starter activity (www.tidec.org/) and plenary.

Lesson evaluation

An important part of your development is self-improvement – the checklist for an effective citizenship lesson (Table 7.5) prompts you to plan and evaluate lessons to ensure they are distinctively citizenship.

Table 7.4 Citizenship lesson plan template

Class/group		Date		Lesson time
Key citizenship question/issue		Secondary curriculum: Scheme of Work		
Key words		Links to National Strategy: literacy/ numeracy/ICT		
Differentiation (SEN and G&T)		Group Profile		
Lesson/learning objectives and purpose		Learning outcomes: by the end of the lesson		

Time/stage	Teacher activity	Student activity	Resources	Assessment
Actual time starter				
Actual time main activity(ies)				
Actual time plenary				

Homework/action/follow-up
Teacher evaluation

■ **Table 7.5** Checklist for an effective citizenship lesson

	Have you considered the following when you are planning your Citizenship lessons?	✓ ✗
1.	Is the lesson framed around a 'hook' Enquiry Question or citizenship issue?	
2.	Have you made links to the Secondary Curriculum for Citizenship?	
3.	Does the lesson develop learning of Key Concepts? Democracy and Justice ☐ Rights and responsibilities ☐ Identities and communities: living together in the UK ☐	
4.	Does the lesson provide opportunities to develop key process? Critical thinking and enquiry? ☐ Advocacy and representation ☐ Taking informed and responsible action ☐	
5.	Is the purpose of the lesson clear?	
6.	Are your Learning Objectives related to the Secondary Curriculum for citizenship?	
7.	Is the topic relevant to young people's lives? Were pupils involved in the selection and planning?	
8.	Are your examples/case studies real, current and topical?	
9.	Have you considered the use of a controversial issue?	
10.	Have you considered active learning styles to encourage participation? Debate ☐ Forming an opinion ☐ Discussion ☐ Taking a point of view ☐ Group work ☐ Presentation ☐ Decision making ☐ Representing others ☐ Research ☐ Analysing ☐ Simulations ☐ Games ☐ Role play ☐ Critical thinking ☐ Problem solving ☐	
11.	Have you considered the use of outside organisations/community? School ☐ Local ☐ National ☐ Global ☐	
12.	Can your students take individual/group action based on the information given? Campaign ☐ Raise awareness ☐ Petition ☐ Display ☐ Vote in an election ☐ Letter writing ☐ Consultation ☐ Emails ☐ Assembly ☐ Have a voice in an organised committee/group ☐ Pressure groups ☐	
13.	Do your pupils know how they can get more involved in the issue?	
14.	Have you given a choice of appropriate types of evidence of achievement?	
15.	Have you planned for assessment for/of learning and feedback? Peer assessment ☐ Self assessment ☐ Teacher assessment ☐	
16.	Have you involved pupils in the evaluation of the lesson?	
*	Have you evaluated the lesson in terms of strengths and areas that need improvement?	

SUMMARY AND KEY POINTS

Planning for any subject is a challenging and complex process but as citizenship evolves as a recognised curriculum subject it continues to present additional difficulties particularly with the lack of specialist teaching staff and range of delivery models. The wider government context that supports citizenship intentions together with an increasing number of online tools for planning, and forthcoming national qualifications should contribute to further improvement – however, recently announced statutory PSHE could add complications in the foreseeable future.

Planning for citizenship will continue to be demanding. It will require confidence to locate the subject in the curriculum of real life; understanding that citizenship is distinctive with its own content, focus and approach; coordination to enable all pupils to access the statutory requirements; interest in current events and affairs; creativity to keep citizenship alive, topical and real; a commitment to involve pupils as partners in the learning process; enthusiasm to engage pupils and change the way young people experience learning; competent ICT skills; and a positive attitude to working with the wider community.

FURTHER READING

DCSF: Standards Site www.standards.dfes.gov.uk/schemes2/citizenship/cit13/?view=list& column=objective.

DCSF: Standards Site www.standards.dfes.gov.uk/schemes2/citizenship/cit13/?view=list& column=outcome.
The Standards site lists Learning Objectives with Learning Outcomes for each theme.

Department for Children, Schools and Families: Standards Site www.standards.dcsf.gov.uk/ schemes2/citizenship/teachersguide?view=get.
Although in need of update in the light of the revised curriculum the DCSF Standards website remains a useful starting point when planning Schemes of Work and lessons and is particularly useful at Key Stage 3. The KS3 Teachers Guide provides a structured 12 unit-based approach to the curriculum with learning objectives, learning outcomes, pupil expectations, suggested resources, links with other curriculum areas and teaching and learning ideas. It is based on the 2002 National Curriculum Programme of Study so users will need to cross-reference to the 2007 Revised Secondary Curriculum Programme of Study at Key Stage 3.

DfES (2004) 'Working together: giving young people a say'.
Document that provides guidance on what the Government believes participation in schools should mean, DfES/0134/2004. Available at www.wiredforhealth.gov.uk/PDF/ Final%20PDF%20April%2004.pdf.

The Electoral Commission (2005) *Democracy Cookbook: Doing politics with young people.* Also available at www.dopolitics.org.uk.
This resource provides everything you need when you take those first steps to planning lessons to introduce pupils to politics and democracy. It is well presented, practical, accessible, highly usable and free. The folder is divided into sections that cover many aspects of the key concept of democracy and justice (representation, democratic

institutions, law making and electoral processes). High-quality materials include information, activities, posters and photocopiable sheets. Whether you have a sound subject knowledge in politics or have limited understanding, this resource will make lesson planning possible.

Hicks, D. and Holden, C. (eds) (2007) *Teaching the Global Dimension: Key principles and effective practice*, London and New York: Routledge.

The blend of conceptual clarity, theoretical underpinning and examples of effective classroom practice make this an essential read for those interested in global issues and wanting to have impact in their teaching of citizenship. The emphasis is on practical approaches to teaching about challenging and controversial global issues and includes strategies, case studies, excellent examples of lesson plans, learning activities and a focus on action and change.

ASSESSING CITIZENSHIP

Marcus Bhargava

INTRODUCTION

Assessment is a fundamental element of the teaching and learning process and an area of regular debate within education and society alike. Assessment plays an extremely important role in education and, when used effectively, helps to support learning and raise attainment. As new citizenship teachers, it will be important for you to grasp the different approaches to citizenship assessment early in your teaching practice and to experiment with a variety of different assessment techniques.

The 2007 revised National Curriculum for England is the first major overhaul of the curriculum since its inception in 1988. The former emphasis on knowledge and understanding has been replaced with a focus on Key Concepts and Processes across every subject. Teachers are being encouraged to think creatively about the way in which they frame learning in order to develop conceptual understanding and subject-specific skills and processes, providing opportunities for pupils to learn in different contexts. In citizenship, a major change is the introduction of attainment levels (QCA/DCSF 2007).

This chapter will initially explore some of the challenges involved in assessing citizenship, as well as some key principles of assessment for learning in the subject. A number of case studies will be used to illustrate these principles in relation to assessment in everyday teaching, across sequences of learning, when making periodic judgements, and at the end of Key Stage 3.

OBJECTIVES

At the end of this chapter you should be able to:

- recognise some of the challenges involved in assessing citizenship;
- apply key principles of assessment for learning when planning assessment in citizenship;
- devise appropriate assessment methods applicable to everyday teaching, across sequences of learning, when making periodic judgements and at the end of Key Stage 3.

THE CHALLENGE OF ASSESSING CITIZENSHIP

Citizenship education should prepare pupils for their future lives as informed, participating citizens within a democracy. Much of what we hope a citizenship education will do for pupils, such as developing a propensity to vote, encouraging active participation in public life and so on, might not be realised until many years after their education; it would be impossible to assess whether citizenship provision in a certain school context had been successful in its ultimate aim. Nevertheless, pupils' positive engagement in public life in adulthood might well be linked to the effective citizenship lessons they experienced in school. We should certainly look forward to the days when politicians in the future cite their citizenship lessons as an important element in their desire to enter political life!

At the heart of citizenship education are sets of values, dispositions and ethical dimensions related to the key concepts underpinning the subject and vital for pupils to understand, explore, question and, perhaps, inculcate. The National Curriculum adds statutory weight to these intentions. The Crick Report made it clear that values and dispositions form an important element of citizenship education:

> Pupils should be encouraged, as they progress through the key stages, to recognise, reflect and act upon . . . values and dispositions. They should be helped, in particular, to reflect on and recognise values and dispositions underlying their attitudes and actions as individuals and as members or groups or communities.
>
> (Crick 1998: 41)

Effective assessment strategies should ensure appropriate opportunities are provided for pupils to demonstrate their recognition of, and reflections on, such values and dispositions. This would impact on the criteria used to assess citizenship and the attainment level they may ultimately receive at the end of the key stage. With this come other potential challenges, including the fact that some pupils might offer responses that they do not personally believe, but which might receive a more favourable response from the teacher or examiner, especially if their response is more consensual or socially acceptable.

Halstead and Pike raise a crucially important question, asking if assessment in citizenship is 'assessment by the people *of* the people or assessment by the people *for* the people'. They suggest citizenship assessment must encourage 'citizens to critically evaluate democratic values and to reflect upon the extent to which these are congruent with their own'. Such approaches might well be best served by assessment for learning strategies, since this 'represents open communication between teachers and pupils which in itself can be a lesson in citizenship' (Halstead and Pike 2006: 151–2).

Ofsted have highlighted some key problems with citizenship assessment. Their criticisms, which acknowledge the embryonic nature of the subject, have highlighted the 'tentative view of standards and progression in citizenship' among teachers, and the limited forms of assessment used, often taking a written format and focusing on knowledge rather than the ways such knowledge is developed, communicated and practised (Ofsted 2006). This is partly due to the comparative lack of citizenship teachers in schools and the absence, until recently, of attainment levels to give a greater sense of progression in the subject. Citizenship tends to have less curriculum time than other subjects, making it harder to provide timely feedback to pupils, and reducing the evidence base for assessment judgements.

Such issues are not insurmountable and most of the approaches suggested in this chapter are designed with these considerations in mind; they are issues worth reflecting upon when considering the different models and stages of development in citizenship provision you are likely to encounter in your student teaching experience and beyond.

ASSESSMENT FOR LEARNING IN CITIZENSHIP

There is a statutory requirement for pupils to be assessed in citizenship during Key Stage 3, with teachers expected to make an end of key stage judgement to be shared with pupils and parents. Until now, this has been measured against a single attainment target. From summer 2011, this judgement will need to be based upon the new citizenship attainment levels, though schools might choose to use these earlier. At Key Stage 4, there are no statutory assessment requirements in the same way, though it is expected that schools will continue to use effective assessment strategies to support learners in making progress. Schools may instead offer GCSE Citizenship Studies as a way of formalising assessment and accrediting their pupils.

Formative assessment strategies, known as 'assessment *for* learning', can play a major role in helping to make assessment a positive experience for pupils, ensuring assessment is part of learning rather than something separate. Assessment for learning requires teachers to constantly use information from the learning process to feed into planning the next steps in learning and to provide pupils with constructive feedback, so they may take personal responsibility for their learning (Black *et al.* 2003). It is becoming a key element of the culture of assessment in schools and has been heavily promoted on a national basis, most recently by the DCSF's *Assessment for Learning Strategy* (DCSF 2008).

The Assessment Reform Group (2002) has suggested ten principles of assessment for learning. In this chapter, these have been used to suggest five key elements for effective assessment practices in your lessons:

- the importance of aligning citizenship learning with assessment;
- the importance of a wide evidence base for assessment judgements;
- the importance of personalising assessment;
- the importance of pupil participation in assessment;
- the importance of feeding back and feeding forward.

The importance of aligning citizenship learning with assessment

Learning is most effectively planned when there are clear links between the objectives of a lesson or sequence of lessons, the intended learning outcomes, the learning activities and the assessment strategies used. This has sometimes been referred to as 'constructive alignment' (Biggs 1996).

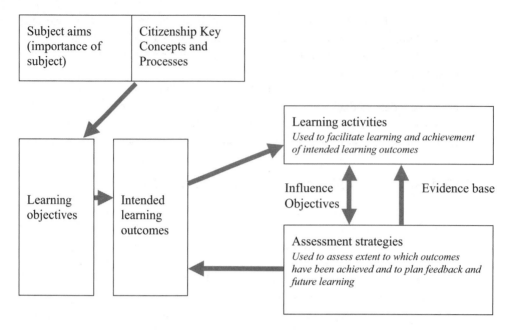

■ **Figure 8.1** Constructive alignment of learning in citizenship

Figure 8.1 indicates a clear link between elements both in lesson and medium-term plans. This is important because:

- It enables your objectives and learning outcomes to weave through the key elements of the lesson, including the learning activities.
- As learning activities are influenced by and designed to meet learning outcomes, it makes it easier to assess their achievement.
- Assessment becomes an integral part of the learning process, based upon what's happening during learning. You can use this information to provide immediate feedback to pupils and adjust activities if necessary. This will also feed into future planning.

This last point is particularly important. Teaching cannot be seen as an element coming between curriculum intentions and assessment of these intentions, nor can the creation of intended learning outcomes and assessment emerge from distinct processes (Earl 2003: 83).

Assessment should take into consideration longer-term goals as well as those specific to the learning episode (Orsmond 2004: 231). Day-to-day planning should be based upon objectives and intended learning outcomes as realised and indicated in medium-term plans. These plans should be clearly linked to the subject aims and Key Concepts and Processes indicated within the National Curriculum; they must also enable pupils to make progress through the attainment levels for citizenship.

The Key Concepts outlined in the Programmes of Study for citizenship are an important starting point for planning intended objectives and outcomes, though these

■ **Table 8.1** Citizenship concepts

National Curriculum Programmes of Study Key Concepts (QCA/DCSF 2007)	The Crick Report concepts (Crick 1998)
Democracy and justice	Democracy and autocracy
Rights and responsibilities	Cooperation and conflict
Identity and diversity	Equality and diversity
	Fairness, justice, the rule of law; rules, law and human rights
	Freedom and order
	Individual and community
	Power and authority
	Rights and responsibilities

are broad concepts within which other concepts are located. For instance, within the concept of democracy exist other concepts such as representation, legitimacy and mandate. The concepts identified in the Crick Report may help you to break down these broader concepts.

The Key Processes included in the Programmes of Study are useful in framing the types of learning activities. For instance, a teacher might decide to develop her pupils' understanding of justice through exploring views surrounding Anti Social Behaviour Orders. She might ask pupils to analyse pieces of evidence showing different viewpoints. Such an activity would clearly link to the process of 'critical thinking and enquiry'. Her assessment focus would then be based upon the extent to which the pupils were able to identify the issues surrounding a justice issue (concept) *through* analysing a number of sources of evidence (process).

For the purposes of assessment within a lesson, or even across a sequence of lessons, it might be easier to assess one concept and one or two processes. This will help you to create more focused assessment criteria, which can be shared with pupils.

Using a range of learning activities to generate assessment evidence

Assessment for learning requires teachers to use a range of evidence drawn from everyday teaching activities. Assessment will occur at many different stages of the entire learning experience: much will be informal, based upon teacher perceptions and engagement tasks and activities, though there is also a major role for extended activities and holistic assessment of pupil progress.

Relating learning activities to your citizenship intended learning outcomes makes it possible to use any number of activities in your lessons as assessment evidence, for example:

- *Mind mapping activities.* Often useful to capture initial ideas and conceptions of issues within lessons. You can encourage pupils to revisit these at the end of a sequence of learning to reconsider their ideas or add further detail, giving you and the pupils a sense of their learning journey.

- *Discussion work*. This could be a formal process (e.g. staging a class discussion on an issue) or more informal, through listening to individuals or groups of pupils discussing issues or solving problems. Some teachers find it useful to utilise a recording mechanism such as a tick chart, linked to intended learning outcomes, to ascertain the quality of contributions.
- *Role-play*. Different stages of a role-play can be assessed including the planning stages, the development of certain characters or the final product. In citizenship, the focus might be on the way the play demonstrates pupils' understanding of a particular concept alongside the way in which it might influence others to change their views (advocacy and representation).
- *Researching*. The focus here could be on the way pupils organise the process of investigating citizenship issues (critical thinking and enquiry) or how they use the information they researched to inform their opinion or advocate a view (advocacy and representation).
- *Informed action group work*. Often seen as difficult to assess, it is often easier to focus on the individual contributions made to the organisation and success of the action undertaken. It is important to assess different stages of the action, rather than the end-stage. Peer and self-assessment strategies can help with this process too.
- *Information and Communications Technology*. Many teachers now base a number of their activities on the use of ICT, including digital photography, film making, website creation and 'blogging'. Pupils could develop posters or make campaigning films about citizenship issues. It is important, however, that the focus of the assessment is on the citizenship concepts and processes identified and developed, rather than the technical expertise demonstrated.
- *Written activities*. These still play an important assessment role, as well as developing broader literacy skills. Pupils could write newspaper articles, drawn upon what they have learned about particular citizenship issues, for instance. However, written tasks are sometimes over-used as they are seen as easier to organise and assess.

Evidence collected can be assessed in terms of immediate considerations relating to the realisation of lesson and medium-term intended learning outcomes, but can also be used when making 'periodic' judgements about pupil attainment. Therefore, the same pieces of evidence may be interpreted in different ways depending on the particular assessment context.

Personalising assessment

Using a variety of learning activities to assess learners should help pupils to show what they know and can do in different ways, supporting differentiation. It is important to use this range of evidence available when making assessment judgements. You could also ask pupils to explain their understanding where their work might not explicitly show this, and allow them to review and revise their work in light of your feedback. Remember, it is vitally important that assessment supports learning: your assessment should not be the end of the process.

Differentiating learning outcomes will help you structure activities to enable all pupils to make progress. Likewise, allowing pupils choice over the format they use to communicate their knowledge, understanding and skills can be extremely enjoyable, motivating and challenging for all pupils. Instead of an essay, pupils might choose to design a poster, write a newspaper article, prepare a role-play or write a song. These approaches require pupils to clearly understand the assessment criteria, but hand considerable ownership and responsibility to them.

Personalisation must provide an appropriate level of challenge in the learning activities undertaken for all pupils (Kotze 2004: 48). More able pupils should be encouraged to apply their understanding and skills of citizenship to new and unfamiliar contexts. As pupils make progress in their citizenship attainment, they should use appropriate citizenship terminology; increasingly using conceptual terms such as 'legitimacy' accurately and in appropriate contexts. Effective assessment for learning strategies should encourage pupils to use these regularly.

Maximising pupils' participation in assessment

Self-assessment is a crucial element in learning: in identifying the problems in your understanding and skills, you are on the road to identifying what you need to do next. Self-assessment promotes the skills of independent learning, while peer assessment provides collaborative input into this process (QCA, undated). The skills of peer and self-assessment need to be developed over time but, conducted effectively, they will shed light on pupils' understanding and learning needs. Earl suggests pupil participation in assessment develops vital life skills as it encourages them to take responsibility for issues they have control over (Earl 2003: 25).

Pupils should understand how they are being assessed. This might be through sharing your intended learning outcomes, explaining the relevance of activities in relation to intentions. You could also offer and model some criteria you will use to assess their work. As pupils become aware of expectations in citizenship, you can involve them in the development of the criteria used for assessment, enabling pupils to take greater ownership of their learning and facilitating the development of a democratic culture.

The importance of feeding back and feeding forward

To make progress pupils need teachers to provide effective feedback, highlighting their strengths and areas for development. Crucially, this impacts future planning since teachers must provide pupils with opportunities to demonstrate improvement in weak areas identified. Harlen uses a thermostat analogy to emphasise the importance of this feedback for teachers:

> Just as feedback from the thermostat of a heating or cooling system allows the temperature of a room to be maintained within a particular range, so feedback of information about learning helps ensure that new experiences are not too difficult nor too easy for students.
>
> (Harlen 2006: 104)

Your feedback must help pupils to make progress in citizenship, so strengths and development areas should relate to understanding and skills in the subject. Feedback can be provided in different ways; some teachers use 'discussion assessment', in which they verbally identify strengths and weaknesses in the work and ask the pupil to suggest possible 'next-steps' targets.

Using assessment evidence from single lessons or lesson sequences, you should adjust your planning to take account of what you now know about pupils' conceptual understanding and skills. This might mean adjusting future lessons in the sequence to remedy some of the problems in learning. At the end of a sequence you might adjust future medium-term plans to revisit difficult areas or capitalise on additional progress made.

Practical assessment approaches are available on the CitizED website, including a pack written by Lee Jerome:
www.citized.info/pdf/commarticles/Lee_Jerome_Assessment_workshop.pdf.

CITIZENSHIP ASSESSMENT CASE STUDIES

Assessment within a lesson

Case study: Russell

Russell uses a departmentally produced medium-term plan to structure his lessons for his Year 8, mixed-ability class:

Box 8.1 **MEDIUM-TERM PLAN**

Medium-term plan objectives
Through enquiry, pupils identify situations where rights might need to be balanced and suggest how citizens, government and organisations have a role in balancing rights.

Concept: 1.2b, Process: 2.1b.

Intended learning outcomes
- All should explain why rights sometimes have to be balanced, using three examples from their enquiries.
- Most should recognise difficulties with balancing rights in particular situations.
- Some should suggest appropriate action that individuals, government and other organisations can take in order to ensure rights can be balanced in different contexts.

The class complete their enquiry and have identified a number of examples of people campaigning for their rights. Russell plans to use these to explore the potential conflict involved in upholding such rights. Russell plans the following lesson (Box 8.2), aligning his key elements:

Box 8.2 **LESSON PLAN**

Learning objectives
To appreciate how upholding one group of people's rights might affect the rights of others.

Intended learning outcomes	All	Should accurately identify and explain three rights affected in your enquiries
	Most	Should explain how upholding a set of rights might affect other people's rights
	Some	Should suggest the types of rights that might conflict

Learning activities

Starter: Match rights being denied to pictures, followed by class discussion about the impact of upholding these rights on others.

Individual: Using the UNDHR, identify the rights being denied in your case studies with explanation.

Group: After discussing how upholding these rights might affect other people in one case study, plan a play showing this, including the difficulties involved in balancing these rights.

Class: Watch plays. Identify the rights in conflict.

Plenary: Following discussion, suggest types of conflicting rights.

Homework: Image collage about one enquiry case study, showing conflicting rights.

Task 8.1 **USING ACTIVITIES TO ASSESS THE LEARNING OUTCOMES**

With reference to the learning activities above, suggest:

- the role of each activity in assessment of learning;
- who might be involved in assessing parts of the lesson and the role of pupils in this process;
- how assessment might be personalised for different learners;
- methods Russell could use to feedback to pupils;
- aspects that might impact on his future planning.

Assessment across a sequence of lessons

Case study: Stefan

Stefan has been asked to produce a medium-term plan for a sequence of six lessons based upon the Key Concept of 'Identity and diversity: living together in the UK', focusing on the impact of migration on the local area (1.3d) with his Year 9 mixed-ability group. He hopes to develop pupils' advocacy and representation skills, in communicating an argument, taking account of different viewpoints (2.2d).

He decides to base his assessment of learning across the sequence on four key tasks (Box 8.3). Stefan will give a National Curriculum level for each task. At the end of the sequence, he will aggregate the levels to give an overall level.

Box 8.3 USEFUL ASSESSMENT EVIDENCE?

1 Test, to assess understanding of migration (peer marked).
2 Article for the local newspaper, showing reasons for migration to the area over the last 50 years.
3 Speech about migration to the local area, focused on different arguments for and against.
4 Self-assessment written activity (peer assessed).

There are some potentially good ideas here, alongside some key problems. Stefan has attempted to use different activities to assess learners, linked to the concept and process he wishes to focus on. However, there are problems in using just four key assessment tasks, which are summatively assessed and aggregated; the focus becomes based on assessment 'of' rather than 'for' learning. He might also miss out on other assessment emerging from the everyday learning process.

Level descriptions should not be used to assess individual pieces of work in this way as they are designed to encapsulate levels of attainment across a key stage. Aggregating levelled assessment tasks completed across a sequence of lessons to provide a summative levelled judgement might do very little to help pupils make progress (Gardner 2006: 2). When suggesting pupils are demonstrating characteristics of particular levels, it should always be based upon a sufficient range of evidence.

Stefan could share his differentiated intended learning outcomes for the sequence of lessons when introducing the topic for the first time, regularly returning to this in his teaching. Used as 'success criteria', these would enable pupils to check their own progress, having a sense of where they should be heading. While these outcomes may, in some way, be related to the levels to help plan for progression, this need not be shared with pupils.

The pack 'Right here, right now: teaching citizenship through human rights' (Ministry of Justice/British Institute of Human Rights 2008) includes useful examples of differentiated success criteria for sequences of lessons. (www.teachernet.gov.uk/teachingandlearning/subjects/citizenship/rhrn/).

Task 8.2 IMPROVING ASSESSMENT ACROSS A SEQUENCE OF LESSONS

Using the five principles for effective assessment for learning given earlier in the chapter, suggest ways Stefan could improve his assessment across the sequence. You might wish to focus on the following areas:

- What might Stefan's intended learning outcomes for the sequence of lessons look like for different groups of learners in the class?
- What broader range of evidence might Stefan use to make assessment judgements at the end of the sequence?
- How could Stefan effectively involve pupils in the assessment process?

Periodic assessment: making judgements across sequences of learning

QCA have launched a new approach to assessment called 'Assessing pupils' progress' (APP). An aim of APP is to enable teachers to make more effective periodic judgements about their learners using a broad range of different types of evidence, using a number of level-related 'assessment focuses' and drawing upon effective practices in assessment for learning (QCA 2008). Teachers are often required to make periodic assessment judgements about their pupils' current attainment for reporting to parents or target setting. The APP process is designed to make such judgement both simpler and accurate.

At the time of writing, these 'assessment focuses' for citizenship and supporting materials are currently being developed, but the intention is for APP to become a key element of assessment across the curriculum (DCSF 2008). In the case study provided the attainment levels have been used instead of the new 'assessment focuses' to make a periodic judgement, though teachers could use the same process. Care must be taken, however, when evidence used for formative purposes is reinterpreted for summative judgements. Whereas assessment for learning is designed to support the learning process, including the motivation of pupils, summative assessment of learning must be applied in a consistent manner, based upon the external criteria indicated in level descriptors, in order to ensure fairness and support further moderation of judgements by other colleagues (Harlen 2006: 111).

> For further information on the relationship between day-to-day and periodic assessment, see: http://curriculum.qca.org.uk/key-stages-3-and-4/assessment/index.aspx.
>
> For further information on Assessing pupils' progress (APP), see: www.qca.org.uk/qca_19890.aspx.
>
> For further information on The Assessment for Learning strategy, see: http://publications.teachernet.gov.uk/eOrderingDownload/DCSF-00341–2008.pdf.

Case study: Asha

Asha is asked in January to indicate her Year 7 pupils' individual levels of attainment for subject reports and a forthcoming parents' evening. While she has not been teaching them for very long, she has covered elements of all of the Key Concepts and Processes in the KS3 Programme of Study. She has also used assessment for learning strategies to support pupils in making progress.

She decides to use the following sources of evidence to make a level judgement:

Box 8.4 **PERIODIC ASSESSMENT**

Informal sources of evidence	This includes observations of pupils in discussion and group work and focused conversations with pupils to ascertain understanding.
Evidence from key learning activities showing engagement across the Key Concepts and Key Processes	These would be an important basis for making judgements, but these are considered only when pupils had been given a chance to improve following feedback provided.
Self-assessment activities at end of each sequence of learning	Asha asked pupils to assess themselves against intended learning outcomes for the two sequences of lessons she has taught. She moderates these with her own assessment of pupils' achievement and progress.
Periodic activities to engage pupils with levels	Asha has shown pupils the citizenship levels and asks them to identify examples from their work when they feel they have shown certain characteristics of these. She also encourages them to set targets based on these.

Task 8.3 **ASSESSING PERIODICALLY**

Taking into consideration the evidence base Asha will use to make a periodic judgement:

*   Where can you see benefits in the process and evidence base she uses?
*   Where can you see potential problems?
*   Are there other forms of evidence Asha could use to make her judgements?
*   How can she make the process motivating and supportive of pupils' progress, bearing in mind the risk of 'labelling' them?

End of key stage judgements at Key Stage 3

Earlier, we discussed the requirements for making level-based judgements at the end of Key Stage 3. This judgement should be based upon the widest possible evidence, drawing upon good practice in assessment across the key stage. If effective day-to-day and periodic assessment have been utilised, it should be fairly straightforward to make a meaningful judgement. However, this can be difficult when certain evidence might be lacking, especially when the same teacher has not taught the pupil across the key stage.

In such circumstances, there might be a temptation to use written activities or tests to fill in gaps in evidence. However, this would be to the detriment of many learners in the group and could not, in its own right, be a useful measure of what a pupil might understand or be able to do. Instead, you might wish to use an issues-based enquiry as the basis of a sequence of lessons in Year 9. For instance, pupils might explore a citizenship issue of their own choosing. Such an enquiry could be carefully constructed to enable pupils to develop and demonstrate their conceptual understanding of some or all of the Key Concepts and Processes and skills during the course of the enquiry.

SUMMARY AND KEY POINTS

Assessment can take many forms but is best when rooted in your everyday classroom practice, providing you are clear about what you are trying to achieve, you share this with your pupils and you ensure your activities clearly relate to your learning intentions. Second, it is vitally important that you use your assessment of these everyday learning activities to inform the pupils of what they need to do next as well as feeding into your future planning. Third, involving pupils in this process will enable them to take increasing responsibility for their own progress and will further improve your understanding of their needs. This, in itself, is a vital citizenship skill. You should try different approaches out during your student teaching year so you can build up a repertoire of methods that work with different groups of learners and, importantly, help you to shed light on what pupils know, understand and can do.

FURTHER READING

Black, P. and Wiliam, D. (1998) *Inside the Black Box: Raising standards through classroom assessment*, London: King's College School of Education.
This seminal piece clearly states the importance of assessment for learning in raising achievement, with a sharp criticism of the predominance of summative assessment in classroom practice.

QCA (2006) *Assessing Citizenship: Example assessment activities for Key Stage 3*, London: QCA.
Although written before the introduction of the revised Programmes of Study, this useful guide provides detailed examples of assessment activities alongside examples of pupil work.

Urban-Smith, J. and Crawford, N. (2005) *Assessing Citizenship. Making it manageable and meaningful*, Gloucestershire: Gloucestershire County Council.
A resource designed to support assessment in citizenship and PSHE, with a number of examples at Key Stages 3 and 4, it makes use of an interesting 'focused assessment dilemma' approach.

PART III

CITIZENSHIP BEYOND THE CLASSROOM

POLITICS AND PEDAGOGY

Citizenship beyond the classroom

Liam Gearon

INTRODUCTION

A major empirical study of initial teacher training institutions in England defines education outside the classroom 'in its broadest sense, as any structured learning experience that takes place beyond the classroom environment, during the school day, after school or during the holidays'. It can include, 'amongst other activities, cultural trips, science and geography fieldwork, environmental and countryside education, outdoor and adventurous group activities, learning through outdoor play, and visits to museums and heritage sites' (Kendal *et al.* 2006: i). Focusing on such activity relevant to your training in citizenship, this chapter provides some theoretical reflections underpinning learning outside the classroom, in particular on the relationship between democracy and education, and, more broadly, on the historical and contemporary links between politics and pedagogy. These insights are used then as a theoretical framework upon which to develop practical strategies for citizenship education beyond the classroom, including the use of external organisations and visits. It draws upon some classic sources in the political philosophy of education to provide insight into why citizenship education encourages learning beyond the classroom, dissolving any perceived barriers between classroom learning and learning beyond it, or between school and community. The chapter also argues for critical citizenship and a critical pedagogy in which the reasons for extending learning beyond the classroom are fully justified, bearing in mind the health and safety of pupils but also their more general well-being, including special educational needs.

OBJECTIVES

By the end of this chapter you should:

■ be aware of some of the complex historical and contemporary relationships between democracy and education;

■ be able to conceptualise your teaching of citizenship within a wider context of politics and pedagogy;

■ be able to plan individual lessons and Schemes of Work using external organisations and visits.

Task 9.1 CITIZENSHIP AND ACTIVE SOCIAL/POLITICAL PARTICIPATION

Individually or in small groups, think about the broad relationship between education and society, considering, for example:

• Why do we have schools?
• Why are politicians concerned with education?
• Is education political?
• In what ways are schools integral to the (local/national/international) communities in which they are set?

Now read through the *National Curriculum Citizenship* (http://curriculum.qca.org.uk, and follow links). In the most fundamental way, what is this subject trying to achieve educationally as well as in terms of wider social and political goals?

In what ways does citizenship try to encourage the active participation of pupils with the wider community, locally, nationally and internationally?

Why does citizenship education try to encourage this?

Make notes on your reflections, using these as a basis for discussion, reflection and planning.

Task 9.2 LEARNING OUTSIDE THE CLASSROOM

Visit the website for Learning Outside the Classroom (www.lotc.org.uk). Read the *Manifesto for Learning Outside the Classroom* (2006).

In relation to this document consider the following questions:

• In what ways does the Manifesto provide a good framework for learning beyond the classroom?
• In what ways is the Manifesto useful for citizenship education?
• Are there any risks in applying the Manifesto in citizenship education?

POLITICS AND PEDAGOGY

In contemporary context, the domains of citizenship were classically outlined by Marshall (1950) as consisting of the civic, the political and the social. Marshall's framework provided a clear foundation for the educational application of the principles evident in the Crick Report (1998), set up by the New Labour Government to assess whether a new National Curriculum subject of citizenship would be desirable and, specifically, whether it would address the perceived apathy of young people to mainstream political engagement, particularly voting in elections (Crick 1998). An often cited sentence from the Crick Report indicates the wider political intentions behind the introduction of citizenship education: 'We aim at no less than a change in the political culture of this country both nationally and locally: for people to think of themselves as active citizens, willing, able and equipped to have an influence in public life' (Crick 1998: 7). Citizenship education was, and remains, an attempt to provide pupils with the knowledge, skills and understanding to undertake active political engagement within public and, especially, political life. Marshall's influence is most clearly evident in the three core strands proposed for citizenship:

- *Social and moral responsibility*: children learning from the beginning self-confidence and socially and morally responsible behaviour both in and beyond the classroom, both towards those in authority and towards each other.
- *Community involvement*: pupils learning about and becoming helpfully involved in the life and concerns of their communities, including learning through community involvement and service to the community.
- *Political literacy*: pupils learning about how to make themselves effective in public life through knowledge, skills and values.

(Crick 1998)

The principle of an active citizenship education that extends teaching and learning beyond the classroom pervades these strands.

The Crick Report, in turn, provided the framework for the subsequent National Curriculum Citizenship (1999), underpinned by expectations of raised participation by young people in social, political and related contexts beyond the classroom, determining that pupils should have:

- knowledge and understanding about becoming informed citizens;
- developing skills of enquiry and communication;
- developing skills of participation and responsible action.

(DfEE 1999)

The National Curriculum Statutory Requirements (DCSF/QCA 2007) significantly altered the format for citizenship in line with other National Curriculum subjects under four headings with an equal emphasis upon citizenship beyond the classroom (for instance, as highlighted in, but not restricted to, those explicit areas in bold on p. 126):

1   Key Concepts

    1.1   Democracy and justice
    1.2   Rights and responsibilities
    1.3   Identities and diversity: living together in the UK

2   Key Processes

    2.1   Critical thinking and enquiry
    2.2   Advocacy and representation
    2.3   Taking informed and responsible action

3   Range and Content [*abbreviated, and Key Stage 3 cited here*]

    a   political, legal and human rights, and responsibilities of citizens
    b   the roles of the law and the justice system . . .
    c   key features of parliamentary democracy and government . . .
    d   freedom of speech and diversity of views . . .
    e   actions that individuals, groups and organisations can take to influence decisions . . .
    f   strategies for handling local and national disagreements and conflicts . . .
    g   the needs of the local community . . .
    h   how economic decisions are made . . .

4   Curriculum Opportunities [*abbreviated and Key Stage 3 cited here*]

    a   debates, in groups and whole-class discussions
    b   develop citizenship knowledge and understanding . . .
    c   work individually and in groups . . .
    d   participate in both school-based and community-based citizenship activities
    e   participate in different forms of individual and collective action
    f   work with a range of community partners and organisations to address issues and problems in communities
    g   take into account legal, moral, economic, environmental, historical and social dimensions of different political problems and issues
    h   take into account a range of contexts, such as school, neighbourhood, local, regional, national international and global . . .
    i   use and interpret different media and ICT both as sources of information and as a means of communicating ideas
    j   make links between citizenship and work in other subjects and areas of the curriculum.

(DCSF/QCA 2007: 27–34)

For a review of its success or otherwise a decade after its introduction, see the House of Commons report 'Citizenship Education' (House of Commons 2007), and for a wide-ranging critical evaluation of citizenship in national and international contexts, see Arthur *et al.* (2008).

Task 9.3 **SELECTING CITIZENSHIP EDUCATION OUTSIDE THE CLASSROOM**

Visit the Learning Outside the Classroom website (www.lotc.org.uk) and look at their list of 20 key hubs for active participation, notably:

- Nature Detectives website
- Growing Schools website
- Creative Partnerships resources
- High Quality Outdoor Education
- Field Studies Council fold-out charts
- FACE website
- Outdoor learning cards
- Heritage Explorer website
- A week of storytime outdoors
- Royal Horticultural Society website
- Heritage Learning magazine
- NATRE resources website
- Shaping Places: built environment design education
- CABE website
- Learning maths outside the classroom
- Bringing the classroom to the countryside: research notes
- Holocaust Education Trust
- Culture and Learning: Creating arts and heritage education projects
- Demystifying Risk Assessment
- Visiting places of worship.

Grading in a list of 1 to 20, discuss which of these have the potential to be of most use in relating to citizenship education and why.

DEMOCRACY AND EDUCATION

As Derek Heater highlights in the opening chapter of this volume, it is important to be aware that these educational principles have a longer antecedence than Marshall or Crick or House of Commons reports (see also Heater 2004). The late eighteenth century is of particular relevance to citizenship. This period is marked by the forceful, literally revolutionary emergence of the political concepts, ideals and values that underpin modern polity and governance as well as much of our current citizenship education – democracy, citizenship and human rights (Himmelfarb 2004). Of critical significance here are the late-eighteenth-century revolutions in America and France. In America, the 1776 Declaration of Independence, the 1787 United States Constitution, and the 1789 Bill of Rights, and in France the 1789 Declaration of the Rights of Man and of the Citizen all encapsulate models of citizenship, democracy and rights upon which the very language of contemporary polity and governance depend. These revolutions left an indelible mark upon social and political life, creating the foundations for contemporary models of democracy, and thus impinge directly upon our notions of citizenship today – politically and educationally.

In the eighteenth century, however, only marginal amounts of attention was paid to the relationship between democratic politics and education. Rousseau was a notable exception. He presents an excellent example of an influential Enlightenment philosopher who realised that a new politics would require a new form of education. Rousseau's *political* philosophy was encapsulated in *On the Social Contract* (1762), emphasising in a society of citizens with equal right, the key principle of democracy, that valid governance is an agreement (a 'social contract') between government and people. Rousseau's philosophy of *education* is found in *Emile* (1762), and it is a curiosity when we are talking about the relationship between politics and education that *Emile* and *On the Social Contract* were published in the same year. In *Emile* Rousseau takes the case of an imaginary child and develops an ideal education. Rousseau's philosophy portrays this ideal educational process as one that allows the unfolding of the child's exploration of the world, placing a strong emphasis upon developing in the young their independent personal *experience* as autonomous and free individuals. Teaching here is less simply about imparting knowledge but more closely related to guiding, facilitating the child's enquiry. With its emphasis upon the importance of Emile the child as a free, autonomous individual, Rousseau brings his democratic philosophy to education. Rousseau's philosophy of education is thus integrally related to his political philosophy.

The nineteenth century saw many attempts to conceptualise democracy – what it meant, what its limitations were, how it could be progressively implemented – and two classic texts here are de Tocqueville's (1836) *Democracy in America* and John Stuart Mill's (1859) *On Liberty*. In texts such as these, the nineteenth century saw increasingly sophisticated reflections on democracy. The century is also notable for increased awareness that a wider (though still far from inclusive) political enfranchise-ment necessitated mass, compulsory education. The origins of this might be said, in England at least, to be evident in the 1870 Education Act, making compulsory elementary schooling. Growing mass, democratic politics is thus also the era of mass *education*, a significant correlation between politics and pedagogy, between aspiration for governance and education as a means of obtaining political goals. It was thus one of the unexpected (if belated) outcomes of democratic revolution that a mass education would become necessary in order to sustain the polity of the people by the people.

Yet it was after de Tocqueville and Mill before the relationship between politics and pedagogy was significantly theorised, and specifically the question of why the new democracy would require a new form of education. John Dewey's (1916) *Democracy and Education* is thus equally well known for its pedagogical theory as for its political philosophy. Dewey saw the relationship between politics and pedagogy as critical if democratic society was to be maintained, just as the title of his famous book indicates. Thus, and somewhat in the mould of Rousseau, Dewey argued that pupils need to be taught not simply through the imposition of knowledge but by allowing them to develop experience of the world, hence the common association between Dewey and 'experiential learning'. For Dewey, democratic societies needed a democratic education, and a democratic pedagogy. In citizenship education terms, this fits well with teaching and learning beyond the classroom.

Yet some theorists have suggested the democratic forms of the eighteenth and nineteenth centuries have left still a remnant of vastly unequal societies, which may be as directly the responsibility of educationalists as politicians. Paulo Freire's (1972) *Pedagogy of the Oppressed* stands as a late–twentieth-century example of an educational philosophy that extends and radicalises this relationship between politics and education. Freire attracted an emergent group of similarly radical educators, and a form of education often referred to as a 'critical pedagogy' (Kincheloe 2004; Darder *et al.* 2008). Critical pedagogy argues that even supposedly egalitarian democratic education does little to challenge social injustices and the imbalances of power in wider political and social life. This perspective also argues that current educational systems in Western societies actually *perpetuate* such imbalances, maintaining oppressive structures that disadvantage the poor and the powerless, arguing for a pedagogy that challenges and overturns the injustices of the status quo. The pedagogy argued for highlights the role of teacher as facilitator, and stresses the experiential learning of the pupil – so even in a simplistic analysis we can see some commonalities between these historically diverse educational and political philosophies.

Task 9.4 **EVERY CHILD MATTERS**

Read the Government agenda in *Every Child Matters* (www.dcsf.gov.uk or www. qca.org and follow links). Now visit the DCSF website at www.dcsf.gov.uk and find links for Special Educational Needs and/or Appendix 2 'Citizenship and special educational needs: key resources and guidance'.

How might you conceptualise these educational policies as philosophies of education? What kind of political philosophy do they espouse – for example, through ideas of rights, equality and well-being for children and young people?

CRITICAL CITIZENSHIP AND CRITICAL PEDAGOGY

For each of the historical contexts dealt within this chapter, there are without doubt deep chasms between stated political or educational ideals and their social actuality. Thus by no means might we imply that the ideals of citizenship, democracy and rights are beyond criticism when placed in historical context. In France, the 1789 Declaration of the Rights of Man and of the Citizen was followed by unsettling violence, not only against aristocracy and monarchy but against any offering dissent against the Revolution – the guillotine remains an abiding image of the time. Thus the

English political philosopher Edmund Burke's reflections on revolutionary France display shock at the violence of the Revolution. Burke used this violence to condemn the ideals that lay behind the Revolution. (In this volume, Moss discusses the use of teaching citizenship through English, and arguably there is no better fictional account of the time than Charles Dickens' *A Tale of Two Cities*.) Thomas Paine's (1791/2) *Rights of Man* was a direct response to Edmund Burke, and a defence of the ideals of citizenship, democracy and rights that underpinned the French and American Revolutions. The eighteenth- and nineteenth-century political contexts were fraught with other contradictions – in America the prevalence of slavery; in France the deep intolerance towards and violence against religion; and in England, the nineteenth-century liberalism of Mill must be set against a backdrop of British Empire abroad and little evidence of universal enfranchisement at home, where many working people and women remained without the vote. Today, ideas of citizenship, democracy and rights might be similarly interrogated for the distance between ideals and political realities – take Wolin's challenging view of 'managed democracy and the spectre of inverted totalitarianism' (Wolin 2008).

Thus when we are encouraging learning beyond the classroom in citizenship, through active participation or community involvement, it is worthwhile also to interrogate closely the ideals that underpin such involvement. This is clearly because citizenship presumes (perhaps sometimes too easily) a relationship between education and a particular set of political values. As Ralph Leighton and Tony Rea make clear (respectively, Chapters 10 and 11 in this volume), if we are encouraging pupils and students to engage, the engagement, if it is to be useful educationally, has to be critical engagement. If it is to be open rather than indoctrinatory, citizenship education needs to encourage critical engagement with political concepts, ideals and values rather than an unthinking and unquestioning adherence to certain values, however apparently benign or seemingly beneficial, even the fundamental concepts of citizenship, democracy and human rights themselves. This is, arguably, even more important when using external organisations and visits as these activities beyond the classroom considerably extend the scope for experientially enriching young people's experience, but also (because of the heightened impact of some experiential learning) for unfairly influencing them.

Thus the values of citizenship, democracy and rights – and understanding of the ways in which participation, with the social and political change these imply – are *contested*. Beyond this, little is known of the actual *impact* of these values within education, though an emergent body of research is telling us more:

- Ajegbo (2007) http://publications.teachernet.gov.uk (and follow links).
- EPPI (2004, 2005) www.eppi.ioe.ac.uk (and follow links).
- Gearon (2003) www.bera (and follow links).
- House of Commons Report (2007) www.gov.uk (and follow links).
- NFER (2007) www.nfer.ac.uk (and follow links).
- Osler and Starkey (2006) www.bera (and follow links).

Task 9.5 **CITIZENSHIP AND CONTROVERSIAL ISSUES**

1   Consult the DCSF Standard site, and look at the DCSF/QCA guidance on teaching controversial issues (www.standards.dfes.gov.uk/schemes2/ citizenship/teachersguide, or via www.qca.org.uk, and follow links). Now revisit the Learning Outside the Classroom website and look at their list (as above) of 20 key hubs for active participation. Select *one* of these 20 hubs and note any points in which the QCA guidance on teaching controversial issues might apply.

2   Role-play a scenario where a parent or guardian is enquiring about the educational value of a child being taken out of school for a visit.

Of critical importance when using external organisations and external visits is the health and safety of those in your care. Your school will have strict guidance on procedures and these will be monitored and implemented by senior school staff but all staff need to be aware of their responsibilities. As the DCSF summarise in general terms and in particular regard to visits:

The statutory responsibility for the health and safety of school staff and pupils rests with the employer of staff at the school. Health and safety responsibilities in schools is governed by 'The Health and Safety at Work Act 1974.' This is enforced by the Health and Safety Executive. Local authorities as employers have responsibilities for protecting the health and safety of staff, pupils and visitors on the school premises, and on organised activities. The Government has produced a range of guidance including that on management of the health and safety of pupils on educational visits.

Specific and detailed guidance, including risk assessments, responsibilities and practical procedures are found in the booklet *The Health and Safety of Pupils on Educational Visits* (DfES 1998). This was later supplemented by:

*   *Standards for LEAs in Overseeing Educational Visits*: sets out the functions of the educational visits coordinator in schools and the levels of risk management that Local Authorities and schools could use.
*   *Standards for Adventure*: is aimed at the teacher or youth worker who leads young people on adventure activities.
*   *A Handbook for Group Leaders*: is aimed at anyone who leads groups of young people on any kind of educational visit. It sets out good practice in supervision, ongoing risk assessment and emergency procedures.

Box 9.1 **HEALTH AND SAFETY RESOURCES**

HSE website – www.hse.gov.uk

HSE 'Five steps to risk assessment' – www.hse.gov.uk/pubns/indg163.pdf

HSE 'A guide to risk assessment requirements' – www.hse.gov.uk/pubns/indg218.pdf

Health and Safety Commission (HSC) 'Managing health and safety in schools'

HSC 'Health and safety guidance for school governors and members of school boards'

DfES (2001) 'A Guide to the Law for School Governors' – Community Version – Voluntary Aided Version – Voluntary Controlled Version – Foundation Version. Website www.dcsf.gov.uk/governor/info.cfm

DCSF School Security website, www.dcsf.gov.uk/schoolsecurity

DCSF 'Health and Safety of Pupils on Educational Visits: a good practice guide', www.dcsf.gov.uk/h_s_ev/index.shtml

DCSF/DH 'Supporting pupils with medical needs: a good practice guide' – www.dcsf.gov.uk/medical

DCSF 'Guidance on first aid for schools' – www.dcsf.gov.uk/firstaid

DCSF/Home Office 'School security: dealing with troublemakers' – www.dcsf.gov.uk/schoolsecurity/dwthome.shtml

DCSF video 'Can you see what they see?'

DCSF 'Code of practice on LA–school relations' – www.dcsf.gov.uk/lea/

DfEE 'Guidance on Standards for School Premises' (ref DfEE 0029/2000)

DCSF/CEDC 'Safe keeping: a good practice guide for health and safety in study support'

(Source: ref DfEE 0197/2000, www.teachernet.gov.uk/wholeschool/healthandsafety/responsibilities/visitsresponsibilitiessection4/)

Task 9.6 **HEALTH AND SAFETY**

Consult the DCSF and their guidance on health and safety. Now revisit the Learning Outside the Classroom list of 20 hubs of potential activity that could involve external organisations and visits. Select one of these and review what health and safety issues might pertain, and what procedures you might need to undertake before planning and undertaking such activity. Use the lesson planning and scheme of work sheets in Chapter 7 in this volume, together with Appendix 2 'Citizenship and special educational needs: key resources and guidance' and QCA's *Citizenship and PSHE: Working with external contributors – guidance for schools* and devise a Scheme of Work of four to six lessons that you think would introduce a strong element of 'active participation' into citizenship.

Task 9.7 **CITIZED: THE NETWORK FOR INITIAL TEACHER EDUCATION IN CITIZENSHIP**

CitizED is a major organisation that offers wide-ranging support for teachers of citizenship (www.citized.ac.uk). For more practical ideas on developing your lesson plans and scheme of work see: 'Play your part: a new active citizenship toolkit for teachers' (2 September 2008). The Academy for Sustainable Communities (ASC) and Community Service Volunteers (CSV) have developed an online active citizenship toolkit that supports teachers to encourage pupils to play an active role in community projects – http://citizenship.ascskills.org.uk/.

The 'Play your part' website includes ideas, resources, activities and teaching aids designed to raise awareness of sustainable communities, inspire young people to play a part in improving their communities and develop the skills, knowledge and understanding needed to devise and run successful citizenship projects.

The site includes four main areas:

*   What makes a good community?
*   What can we do to improve our communities?
*   Planning and carrying out an active citizenship project.
*   Celebrate and evaluate.

The toolkit can be downloaded free of charge and used to support citizenship, drama, geography and PSHE lessons.

Review these materials at www.citized.ac.uk (and follow links), integrating one or more aspects of any of their resources into a practical teaching activity.

SUMMARY AND KEY POINTS

This chapter has provided some background to the historical and contemporary relationship between democracy and education, and the wider relationship between politics and pedagogy. It has highlighted the ways in which these relationships are of direct relevance to the teaching of citizenship and, specifically, to the encouragement of active participation in citizenship. The chapter has also argued that the use of external organisations can substantially enrich pupils' citizenship through experiential learning, also highlighting the need for teachers to be aware not only of the health and safety of pupils/students in these contexts but also, as with citizenship generally, of any potential for biased political or other influences.

FURTHER READING

Ajegbo, K., Kiwan, D. and Sharma, S. (2007) *Diversity and Citizenship Curriculum Review*, London: DfES.

An important review of citizenship in relation to religion, community cohesion and diversity, though its view on British history is arguably flawed and overly contemporary.

Arthur, J., Davis, I. and Hahn, C. (2008) *The SAGE Handbook of Education for Citizenship and Democracy*, London: SAGE.

This is an excellent scholarly resource, to be highly and unreservedly recommended.

Crick, B. (1998) *Education for Citizenship and the Teaching of Democracy in Schools: Final report of the Advisory Group on Citizenship*, London: QCA.

This is essential reading, forming as it does the basis for the introduction of National Curriculum Citizenship in England.

Osler, A. and Starkey, H. (2006) *Education for Democratic Citizenship: Research policy and practice 1995–2005*. London: British Educational Research Association.

This is a first rate, accessible, yet authoritative overview of research in citizenship.

chapter 10

DEVELOPING ACTIVE PARTICIPATION IN CITIZENSHIP

Ralph Leighton

INTRODUCTION

Active participation is not only central to the citizenship curriculum, it is an essential component of one of the three key aims of the National Curriculum – making 'a positive contribution to society' (QCA 2007: 7) cannot be a passive process. In specific relation to the Citizenship National Curriculum, teachers are enjoined to ensure that their pupils are able to take informed and responsible action based on research and investigation, and to analyse the impact of their actions. This is not simply because it is an effective teaching and learning strategy, which it undoubtedly is. As Kolb wrote, 'Experiential learning . . . offers the foundation for an approach to education and learning as a lifelong process' (1984: 3) and 'Learning is the process whereby knowledge is created through the transformation of experience' (1984: 38); thus, presenting pupils with opportunities to learn from their experiences will enable them to continue to learn from them as active and responsible (but not necessarily compliant) citizens.

A major concern regarding both the meaning and significance of active participation is highlighted by Peterson and Knowles (2007) where they indicate a polarisation of citizenship student teachers' perception of active citizenship as a concept and whether that concept has a shared meaning. If this is the case for specialist teachers in training, there is a great danger that it could be equally true for those already trained and those teaching the subject without specialist training. As Peterson and Knowles indicate, the guidelines on active participation are clear and freely available, but this does not equate with regular access and shared understanding.

It is clear from the National Curriculum that the purpose of active participation is not simply to get pupils to 'do' things, but to enable them to be creative and reflective about the activities in which they become involved. If such activities are performed simply because a teacher says they must be, or only in order to fulfil public examination requirements, they are unlikely to have any longstanding positive impact; indeed, the opposite is more likely. If you want to encourage lifelong participation and involvement, you will have to ensure pupils' learning experiences are positive. You must also, therefore, ensure that active citizenship is a learning experience.

The QCA (2007) emphasises that active participation, often also referred to as active citizenship, should be both informed and responsible. This requires creativity, research, negotiation and, at times, resistance. The activity itself is not the purpose of active citizenship, but a means through which pupils can learn how to become involved and consider the impact of such involvement on themselves and others around them. If pupils are not given the opportunity to reflect upon their actions but simply to do something, tick a box and move on, with no consideration of impact and no thought to potential improvements or developments, they are not being active citizens and a vital opportunity will be missed.

OBJECTIVES

At the end of this chapter you should be able to:

▪ understand and act upon the differences between carrying out citizenship-related activities and being an active citizen;
▪ identify opportunities in school for pupils to become active citizens;
▪ identify opportunities beyond the school for pupils to become active citizens;
▪ enable your pupils to critically reflect upon their roles as active citizens.

WORTHY ACTS AND ACTIVE PARTICIPATION

Experience as a GCSE examiner has provided me with many examples of pupils carrying out activities that their teachers present to them as active citizenship but which are nothing of the sort. These activities are typified by being decided upon and organised by teachers, with scant regard for the interests and involvement of their pupils and with little attention paid to the requirements of the examination boards' specifications and assessment criteria. Such events can be collectively described as 'worthy acts' rather than 'active citizenship' as they appear to lack the essential opportunity to 'involve, engage and empower pupils' (Arthur and Davison 2003: 21).

It is important to understand that 'work experience' does not, of itself, constitute active participation or active citizenship. Lockyer indicates the conflation of the US concept of 'service learning' with the UK notion of work experience, with the vital difference that service learning 'involves students engaging in, and reflecting upon, voluntary service in the community . . . the experience must involve reflection and deliberation' (2003: 12). The most cursory examination of public examination specifications for Citizenship Studies, and the examination papers and mark schemes that derive from them, will clearly indicate to you that there is much more to active participation than working in a preschool nursery for a week or spending time in an office or other working environment. Adding in a requirement that pupils carry out a health and safety check does not move such experiences much closer to what is expected. Active participation requires pupils to take action on problems and issues in order to achieve clearly identified outcomes in relation to them. Pupils have to research and plan actions, try to bring about or resist change, offer critical assessments and reflections; these are skills and processes that rarely, if ever, feature in work experience diaries. Events and activities that do not allow pupils to demonstrate and develop these skills, no matter how worthwhile such events and activities might be, are not examples of active participation.

Task 10.1 **THE SPEED AND NATURE OF SOCIAL CHANGE**

1 List the changes in politics, technology and other aspects of society that have taken place during your lifetime.
2 Now identify those from the last ten years that were significant to you.
3 Finally, try to predict what changes might take place locally, nationally and globally during the lifetime of a Year 7 pupil.

(Developed from Palmer and Garrett 2003)

You will not be working with your pupils to get them to perform 'worthy acts' but to equip them with the skills and insights necessary for a lifetime of social and political engagement. As the outcomes of Task 10.1 are likely to indicate, we have all witnessed and experienced myriad changes in the long and short term – many of them changes that nobody could have predicted with any certainty and, if you compare your thoughts with those of colleagues, you will find some common ground, but also observations that indicate different perceptions and different interests. It follows from this that you are not in a position to predict what future events will matter to your pupils nor, therefore, exactly what skills and knowledge they will need. Thus there is no point in planning for the specific; you have to enable your pupils to develop insights and understanding that will enable them to engage with whatever changes occur, in whatever ways they feel most appropriate.

None of this is to derogate good deeds. Helping the disadvantaged, fundraising and recycling waste or unwanted goods are all activities to be praised and encouraged. If the planning and organisation of these activities are conducted by the pupils, if they have decided on the activity and its beneficiaries, if they analyse what went well and how to improve those aspects that were less effective than they hoped or expected – then there is at least a vestige of active participation. If, however, there is an imposed task about which pupils have little say and in which they have no interest or personal investment, then there is only a worthy act; a short-term good at the expense of long-term engagement.

In order for your pupils to understand and reflect upon the activities in which they have been or will be involved, to move these activities from worthy acts to active participation, you should build in opportunities for them to complete a self-assessment form such as the one shown in Box 10.1. To prepare them for this, you should consider what their learning objectives will be, and make sure your pupils know and understand what these objectives are. Such objectives could include:

- working with others to plan an activity;
- being aware of and accepting the consequences of your actions, intended or not;
- constructively assessing your performance and the performance of others;
- providing and accepting relevant feedback;
- setting and reviewing targets for your future participation.

Box 10.1 **SELF-EVALUATION OF ACTIVE PARTICIPATION**

What was the activity? ....

What was my role in it? ....

Why did I take on this role? ....

....

What skills did this role involve? ....

....

....

What went well with my role? ....

....

....

What went well with the activity? ....

....

....

What could have been done differently? ....

....

....

How would this have improved the activity or my role in it? ....

....

....

PREPARATION AND PLANNING

As with all aspects of teaching and learning, preparation and planning are the keys to success. In relation to active participation this not only means that specific activities themselves have to be carefully planned, and that there should be opportunities for reflection and self-assessment as referred to above, but that it is necessary to ensure that pupils are enabled to develop skills and interests throughout their programme of study. There is no requirement for active participation to be world altering or on a global scale. For many pupils the immediate environment is of more concern and interest and therefore presents opportunities for engagement in a secure context to which they can relate. The learning that takes place within this environment can then be applied to wider contexts when your pupils are ready.

For many of your pupils there is the likelihood that they will consider a task or activity to be an end in itself. If they realise that you are more interested in the process than the outcome it will help them focus on what is important in the longer term, as well as relieving pressure to 'succeed'. Ensuring that your pupils are also aware of the self-assessment process rather than a teacher-allocated grade could also help them to concentrate on understanding processes and developing skills.

Task 10.2 **PLANNING FOR OPPORTUNITIES FOR ACTIVE PARTICIPATION**

Consider a lesson you have planned, or intend to plan, in relation to the Key Stage 3 Citizenship Programme of Study. Think about challenges or questions that your pupils might offer, for example, 'Why spend all that money on defence?' 'Why can't we have a better voting system?' 'Why do they want to build an incinerator near us?':

1   Does your lesson plan give your pupils the opportunity to raise such questions?
2   Does it give them the opportunity to find the answers for themselves?
3   Do they have an opportunity to consider alternative solutions and to think about the repercussions of these?

If you are able to answer 'yes' to the questions in Task 10.2 then you are already building active participation into your lessons. If your answer to one or more was 'no' then you need to consider how to give your pupils such opportunities. By asking questions and seeking answers, your pupils will be preparing themselves for active participation on a larger scale; they will also be giving you pointers for future lessons as they will have indicated those things about which they care or have an interest. Your planning for discrete and explicit active participation should be informed by such expressions of interest and you will have supported your pupils in acquiring the skills that will be further developed. Remember: every time one of your pupils questions the status quo, argues in favour of a particular action or event, suggests another (not necessarily 'better') way of doing something, says they will 'do it differently next time' and can begin to justify the change – they are demonstrating some of the skills of active participation.

ACTIVE PARTICIPATION IN SCHOOL

While it is important that the ideas, planning, conduct and evaluation of activities are managed by your pupils, they are unlikely to be able to operate at their best in a vacuum. Being able to offer some ideas and issues will start them off, particularly if you make it clear that these are prompts rather than a prescriptive list and if they derive from previous lessons (see Task 10.2). A very secure context for your pupils should be their school – they experience it on an almost daily basis, they know the informal as well as formal structures, they will have some awareness of its purpose and aims and how it goes about addressing these. This could, therefore, present a safe and relevant learning environment within which to develop their skills of active participation.

Some of the opportunities for such participation will arise outside the citizenship classroom and can provide a useful point of reference, for example, during school council elections. Why people decide to stand/not stand, why they decide to vote/not vote, how effective the council is or could be, whether they are more influenced by stylish campaigns or realistic campaigns – all of these issues involve the Key process 2.3 'Taking informed and responsible action' described in the National Curriculum for both key stages. Task 10.3 will help you to identify and consider further examples.

Task 10.3 ACTIVE PARTICIPATION IN SCHOOL

Make a list of aspects of your school that could provide pupils with opportunities to take action as described in the National Curriculum (Key Stage 3, p. 31; Key Stage 4, p. 45). For example: reviewing a school policy on bullying, then making representation to the school management team based on their findings.

Take one thing from your list and consider what the key citizenship learning outcomes should be.

If you adapt Task 10.3 to a consideration of the opportunities for pupils to actively participate provided by the National Curriculum for Citizenship, you will find them in abundance. Throughout the Key Concepts, Key Processes, Range and Content, and Curriculum Opportunities, and in the explanatory notes, which provide commentary and expansion, your attention should be drawn to terms such as 'engage with', 'communicate', 'represent', 'reflect on'; the message you should take from this is that, if you are delivering the National Curriculum for Citizenship as it should be delivered then your pupils are engaged in active participation.

Many other subjects offer pupils the opportunity for active participation. All National Curriculum subjects have shared aims – that young people become successful learners, confident individuals and responsible citizens. They are also, within 'Curriculum Opportunities', required to make links with other subjects. Active participation is one aspect of the National Curriculum for Citizenship that lends itself to cross-curricular work. Examples of this from Key Stage 3 include: art involves pupils taking risks and learning from mistakes; English requires pupils to make informed choices about effective means of communication; in mathematics they have to make sense of others' findings and judge their value in the light of evidence; in physical education there is a requirement that pupils can be clear about what they want to achieve and what they have achieved. Cross-curricular activities can, therefore, mean that your pupils will be developing the appropriate skills and knowledge elsewhere, which you can 'tap into', and that there is an opportunity to collaborate with your teaching colleagues and to clarify with them the role and relevance of citizenship education within their curriculum areas.

ACTIVE PARTICIPATION IN WIDER COMMUNITIES

One common approach to active involvement within wider communities is to require pupils to volunteer to work with, or on behalf of, others. An inherent problem within this is the oxymoron of compulsory volunteering. As with other worthy acts, there is nothing necessarily bad, and much to be applauded, when people choose to support, work with, help and/or understand others; to make this compulsory is to remove the notion of choice implied by the term 'volunteer'. Those of your pupils who freely decide that volunteering is something they want to do are already embarking upon active participation; if they are encouraged and enabled to reflect upon why there is a need for their involvement (for example, the lack of appropriate facilities), the intended and unintended consequences of that involvement (for example, impinging on the employment opportunities of others), the skills they have developed and the effects of their involvement on themselves and others, then their active participation is more secure and their learning from it more substantial. Many of your pupils might already be involved in such activities without your awareness and, with sensitivity, that involvement could become something from which they develop learning about themselves, their skills and the nature of active participation. But volunteering in this sense is not for everyone.

As you are required to take a creative approach to active participation, and to engage your pupils' experiences and imagination, it is advisable to take a creative view of the concept of communities. All of your pupils will be members of a range of communities, perhaps feeling allegiance to some more than others, and they are much more likely to be willing and able to engage with these than with communities about which they have not heard or which they do not think relate to them.

Just as some of your pupils might not engage with volunteering, others might be reluctant to take on the whole world. Kolb (1984) points out that learning is best conceived as a process rather than in terms of outcomes, and that it is the continuous process of creating knowledge. It is therefore advisable to concentrate your pupils' attention on the process and to enable them to recognise new processes and new knowledge, building their awareness, confidence, self-esteem and critical understanding of the world around them.

Task 10.4 **OPPORTUNITIES FOR ACTIVE PARTICIPATION IN WIDER COMMUNITIES**

1   Make a list of all the categories of community to which your pupils might belong, for example, faith, geographical, virtual.
2   Then make a separate list of perceptions of community needs, for example, to have leisure time, to have a pleasant environment.
3   Working your way through your first list, identify opportunities for active participation that address the issues in your second list.

By completing Task 10.3 you will create an extensive list of active participation opportunities for your pupils. When trying to get them to identify areas of participation in which they would be interested, it might be helpful to get them to perform a similar task. Offer examples and encourage them to think creatively and laterally, concentrating on what they think would be worthwhile trying to do rather than worrying about what can be achieved. It is improbable that your pupils will eradicate world poverty and its associated problems, but that does not mean they cannot plan events to raise funds and public awareness about some of those problems – and doing that through a virtual environment might be more appealing than shaking a collection box and selling leaflets.

ENSURING REFLECTION AND EVALUATION

A self-evaluation form such as the one shown in Box 10.1, adapted to meet the needs of your pupils and the learning objectives you have for them, should be part of the process of their reflection and evaluation. Throughout your delivery of the National Curriculum for Citizenship, build in opportunities for pupil planning, for stage-by-stage evaluation; encourage your pupils to keep planning diaries and to keep brief notes of meetings and events. Regularly and positively refer to prior or ongoing participatory activities to emphasise lessons learned and progress made. Identify the skills and knowledge they have developed and ensure you encourage their consistent use and further development.

Whatever activities your pupils embark upon, it is your responsibility to ensure that they have opportunities to be involved, engaged and empowered by them. To say that they have to be involved in all stages of planning, conducting and evaluating the activities is not to say that any teacher should abrogate their responsibility to plan and guide pupil learning. You cannot be absolutely certain what your pupils will learn as they go through the process of active participation and as they build on those experiences year on year, in citizenship and in other subjects, but you can be fairly certain what they will learn about. It is also essential that your pupils recognise what they have learned, and how to apply that knowledge and those skills in the future.

SUMMARY AND KEY POINTS

You must be clear about the National Curriculum requirements for active participation, and the many learning opportunities that they provide – not only in citizenship but in all other subjects. It is essential that you enable your pupils to move beyond worthy acts in order to enable them to become active participants in society now and in the future, rather than simply being involved in an event for its own sake or through compulsion. It behoves you as the teacher to be creative, supportive and demanding of your pupils, to ensure that they see beyond each activity and recognise their own worth and the skills and knowledge that they develop. Whatever strategies you employ in the classroom and beyond, your focus must be to involve, engage and empower your pupils for lifelong learning – to realise that they are political beings and that they can make a difference.

FURTHER READING

Ajegbo, K., Kiwan, D. and Sharma, S. (2007) *Diversity and Citizenship Curriculum Review*, Nottingham: DfES.

The recommendation by 'The Ajegbo Report' that 'Identities and diversity: living together in the UK' should become a new strand of the Citizenship National Curriculum was accepted and acted upon. The report offers many strategies – subject-specific and cross-curricular – to support pupils and teachers in making this an effective and exciting part of the citizenship programme. The report itself is worth reading for this and many other reasons and can be found at: http://publications.teachernet.gov.uk/eOrdering Download/DfES_Diversity_&_Citizenship.pdf.

Arthur, J. and Davison, J. (2003) 'Active citizenship and the development of social literacy: a case for experiential learning', www.citized.info/pdf/commarticles/Arthur_Davison.pdf.

Palmer, J. and Garratt, D. (2003) 'Active Citizenship Reconsidered – the Challenge for Initial Teacher Training', www.citized.info/pdf/commarticles/Dean_Garratt_Janet_Palmer.pdf. There is a wealth of very useful reading relating to active participation and most other aspects of citizenship available through the CitizEd website. Of particular relevance here is research by Jon Davison and James Arthur which concludes that '[e]xperiential learning in the community offers a tangible and valid way for developing pupils' social literacy that will actively involve, engage and empower pupils' (p. 21). Another useful article presents suggestions and recommendations for designing the curriculum to incorporate activities that would enable pupils to see the point of active participation. Rather than making such activities an imposition in isolation from pupils' needs, wants and experiences, Palmer and Garratt offer structured approaches that can be adapted by teachers and which foster a positive attitude to active participation without pupils having to leave the classroom.

In particular relation to Key Stage 4, public examination specifications for Citizenship Studies offer insights and advice on the possible nature and structure of active participation. These can be followed or adapted irrespective of whether your pupils will be studying or entered for any of these examinations. There could be copies in your school; alternatively, specifications are available from:

To order from AQA https://secure.aqa.org.uk/GCSESupportMat/registerSpec.php.

The Edexcel specification www.edexcel.org.uk/VirtualContent/67791.pdf.

The OCR specification www.ocr.org.uk/Data/publications/key_documents/GCSE_Citizenship_Spec.pdf.

THE CITIZENSHIP CURRICULUM DE-SCHOOLED

Tony Rea

INTRODUCTION

This chapter is written in three parts. First, I make a case for learning outside the school. I situate this argument within the theoretical context of postmodernism and de-schooling society and try to show how informal learning outside the school brings about benefits for young people and relates to what I see as the discourse of citizenship as well as to a de-schooled citizenship curriculum. Then, I illustrate how informal learning outside the school can be achieved, with practical suggestions of activities citizenship teachers might wish to engage in with their pupils. Finally, I take a slightly light-hearted look at those arguments that will undoubtedly be encountered when you attempt to take young people outside the school.

OBJECTIVES

By the end of this chapter you should be able to:

- understand why outdoor informal learning might be important;
- articulate some 'authentic' citizenship experiences;
- identify and plan worthwhile citizenship projects outside the school;
- provide arguments in favour of outdoor learning.

PART 1 WHY LEARN OUTSIDE SCHOOL?

I will start by considering what learning is, or, more precisely, what it might be. Although academics have been studying learning for many centuries, and teachers have been tasked with realising children's learning for just as long, not very much is known about learning. There are a number of models and theories that attempt to explain learning. Behaviourist, cognitivist, developmental-psychological, constructivist and experiential models perhaps summarise the main ideas in the field. The existence of so many widely divergent theories vying for consideration is evidence of a high degree of uncertainty.

Stables (2005) has proposed that learning is 'a theoretical concept'. Stables suggests that learning is something quite different to teaching. Teaching can be looked at as an embodied activity, or social practice; you can observe it being done, or you can participate in it as a teacher or as a pupil/student. According to Stables, learning has a different status. It cannot be seen, touched or felt; it is not tangible in the same sense. Accepting Stables' idea means thinking of learning as something without tangible reality. Instead, it is better thought of as what people collectively understand it to be and is subject to change in time and place (which helps to explain the competing theories and models mentioned above).

Now I will summarise two recently proposed models of learning. First, Stables goes on to propose that 'making meaning from experience' might be a more useful term. If you accept this definition (even for the time it will take you to continue reading this chapter) then you must also accept that children (people) can make meaning from any and all experiences and not just those provided in schools. In fact, there is a great deal of evidence to suggest that much of the more important life-long learning 'lessons' people encounter take place informally, outside schools. This point is most important to understand and retain, as it forms the essence of what I call the power of informal learning.

Second, Wenger (2008) argues that the twenty-first century will be the century where learning is seen in terms of *changed identity* rather than of knowledge acquisition. This is because information and knowledge have become commodities that can be traded; part of consumerism. As Wenger has said, 'If we want to know something we simply Google it!' I will consider the concepts of identity and multiple-identities later.

Having considered learning, having suggested it might be a theoretical concept and without substance, and having suggested two recent models of learning (making meaning from experience and identity change) I will now turn to consider schools, which are, in many ways, the most tangible of realities.

What might be wrong with schooling?

My argument in favour of informal learning of citizenship outside school is based first and foremost on critiques of schooling. Critiques of schooling are multifarious, but I will outline some of what I consider the more important ideas in this area and explain why they are an important part of my argument.

There is a body of literature that sees schools as so conservative that they actually hinder learning. For example, Illich (1970) argued, broadly, for the abolition of compulsory education and of publicly funded schooling. This was not because he was against learning, or against education, but because he saw schools as the new form of social control in secularised Western societies. The writings of the French post-structuralist Michel Foucault help to explain how this works. Foucault sees schools as a technology of social control by the state and its vested interests. The French postmodernist philosopher Jean-François Lyotard (1984) suggested that schools only impart the knowledge and skills necessary to preserve and enhance the operational efficiency of society, rather than encouraging plurality of thought, innovation, imagination and creativity. Part of my argument is that informal learning and some approaches to outdoor learning could provide greater opportunity for more innovative and creative thinking.

Neill (1953), a progressive thinker and founder of the Summerhill School, made a case against compulsion and authority in education, arguing that children only learn when they are ready. Out-of-school learning, which can be much more informal than schooling, might engage young people more and help to make them ready to learn.

A group of US academics (Seely Brown *et al.* 1989) helped to develop the engagement argument by maintaining that the best that schools can provide are *ersatz*[1] experiences, which are the poor relations of the authentic experiences of real life. I have many problems with this *ersatz*–authentic binary, but the notion is useful as it forces policy makers, school leaders and teachers to reconsider the strengths and weaknesses of schooling, and so I will retain it in this chapter.

Task 11.1 **AUTHENTIC EXPERIENCES IN CITIZENSHIP**

What do you think are authentic experiences in citizenship? Perhaps you will ponder this question while reading on, and will return to it later. Make a list of all the authentic citizenship experiences you can think of, dividing the list into in-school and out-of-school.

Having summarised some of the problems with schooling, I will now turn to learning outside the school.

What is outdoor learning?

Many things to many people is the short answer. We could perhaps think of a continuum, stretching from the use of school grounds and the local community on the one side, to adventurous activities in wild and desolate places on the other. In between would be trips and visits to museums, farms, local councils, environmental and sustainability projects, and so on. A group of researchers at the National Foundation for Educational Research (NFER), funded by the Field Studies Council, undertook a review of research in this area of education in 2004 (Rickinson *et al.*) in which they divide out-of-school opportunities into three areas: school grounds and local community, trips and visits, outdoor adventure activities. I have used their framework in the next section.

The historical context of informal learning outside

Moving on from these critiques, learning outside the school can be seen as both an antidote to schooling and an attempt to come closer to authentic experience. I will now present a very short historical overview of learning outside, in a number of contexts.

First, I shall consider how school grounds have been used. In nineteenth-century Germany, Friedrich Froebel founded nursery gardens where children were encouraged both to play and learn outside. Children in Froebel's 'Kindergarten' were given small plots of land to tend and nurture, and were encouraged to observe the growing plants, thus stimulating awareness of the natural world. They were also places where children would exercise and play using songs, dances and movement games to help develop healthy activity. In Britain, a century later, Susan Isaacs recognised the power of gardens for developing both spiritual and scientific learning and Margaret McMillan advocated the use of small, natural outdoor spaces to promote the health of children from underprivileged urban environments.

Froebel also took children on excursions into the surrounding countryside; but urban environments also provide prime learning opportunities for children. Many subjects, for instance science, geography and art, have at their heart observations of the outside environment. Children have regularly been taken outside to learn about them. Visits might also be made from the school to councils, museums, galleries and theatres, so expanding our definitions of teaching outside the classroom.

Outdoor adventurous activities are yet another example of outdoor learning opportunities. These include climbing on rocks or over obstacles, building dens, going on some kind of expedition, perhaps going in, on or near water, and working together in a team to solve problems in a physical, experiential way. Such activities have a long tradition in the British educational system. They have been influenced by Lord Baden-Powell, who founded the scouting movement, and the theories of Kurt Hahn, the originator of Outward Bound. Central to the thinking of Baden-Powell and Hahn is the idea that, by experiencing challenge and overcoming it, character is developed. There is a lot of recent research that suggests properly planned and managed outdoor adventurous activities can encourage a growth in self-confidence and self-esteem (for example, Rickinson *et al.* 2004). This is not to suggest that thrusting children into the mouths of raging storms on open mountainsides could boost their self-concept; rather, that safely managed outdoor adventurous activities are certainly worth considering as an essential part of children's learning.

The benefits of learning outside

There is a wealth of research and literature claiming great benefits from outdoor learning opportunities, so much so that I will not cite any of it (but see Rickinson *et al.* 2004, for an excellent overview). I will, however, summarise some of the claims in a general way. Learning outdoors can help to improve the self-concept of the child, for example, self-confidence, self-esteem and self-efficacy have been shown to increase following participation in outdoor programmes. It has been shown that information, knowledge and understanding gained outdoors is retained better than when the same 'content' is learned in the classroom. Specifically targeted outdoor programmes have successfully re-engaged disengaged young people, and have improved the SATs scores of some younger pupils. My own research (Rea, in progress) shows that the differences between outdoor education centres and schools are important in constructing the identity of the child through a process known as 'positioning'. My thesis is also very relevant to the argument being developed here, that outdoor and informal learning is important to citizenship. To understand this more fully you need to understand something about identity, positioning and discourse.

Identity, positioning and discourse

You will recall that Wenger suggested that the twenty-first century will be the century where learning is seen in terms of changed identity, not the acquisition of knowledge. Important questions here are what is identity and how does it change?

Identity is not the same as personality. It is a sociological, rather than a psychological concept. Identity is how we position ourselves, how others position us, and how we are positioned by discourses. Discourse crops up again later, so here is a definition. To me a discourse is a system of statements that, together, produce or construct a particular version of events, in other words a narrative. Discourses position us all; that is, they help to construct our identities. Because there are many discourses available to us, present in some social contexts and not in others, so we have multiple identities. You will be totally familiar with this concept of multiple identity; you are a teacher, you were a pupil; you were, or are, somebody's offspring, you might be a partner or a parent. You might be British (or English, Scottish, Irish, Welsh) or you could be another nationality, but at the same time might be European (or defiantly not so). You might not, however, have thought about the discourses that position you. For example, females are positioned as Miss, Ms or Mrs, and the competing discourses of gender, marriage, conformity, feminist assertiveness and motherhood are all at work in positioning women into one or other of these classifications.

According to Davies and Harré (1990) we all have some agency over this positioning (and thus our identity). We exert this agency by using discourses to our own advantage; but we can only use those discourses available to us. This is manifestly important to my argument about outdoor learning and why it is so potent.

Discourses of schooling, citizenship and the outdoors

When I write about discourse I foreground the concept of a 'hidden curriculum' in schools. This hidden curriculum stands beside (and, perhaps, opposed to) the visible, overt, public curriculum. It was Illich who raised the possibility of a hidden curriculum in schools; which is one of institutionalised order and control. This hidden curriculum is implemented by what Foucault would call 'normalising' technologies of the school; the authority of the teacher, the structure of year groups, classes, curriculum subjects, timetables, bells. Added to this are the effectiveness/accountability discourses that have led to rationalised inspection regimes; over-testing and the publication of results. These are the discourses of schooling prevalent in the UK and many other Western societies.

A problem lies in the tensions between these discourses of schooling and the ethos (discourses) of the citizenship curriculum. For example, part of the citizenship discourse is about human rights, freedoms and democracy. Yet society compels most of our children into schools 'for their own good' and severely limits their choice of what to learn and how to learn. Another tension is the citizenship discourse of community involvement and community service, which challenges the schooling discourse that locks the community out and children in, for their safety.

Outdoor learning (and likewise, I maintain, informal and out-of-school citizenship learning) can make available to children new discourses that they do not encounter in schools or in their homes. These discourses might include risk taking, self-sufficiency, overcoming personal challenges, exposure to and care for the environment.

Having considered some quite complex and slippery ideas that relate to learning, schooling and discourses, I now turn to a consideration of what citizenship teachers can do to counter some of the problems and issues raised. I will make reference to some of the theoretical background as I proceed.

PART 2 CITIZENSHIP AND OUT-OF-SCHOOL LEARNING

First, what answers did you find to the question, what are authentic experiences (Seely Brown *et al.* 1989) in citizenship? Debating, arguing, participating in elections, representing others, campaigning, advocating, serving the community: I am sure you came up with all of these and many others besides.

Now, a more taxing question. Which of these experiences are best delivered in schools and which might be better delivered outside the school?

Wenger, who talked of learning as identity, also talked about learning as practice (Wenger 1998). Following this, where do you think it might be better to practise citizenship? In the school or in the local community?

One of my critiques of the *implementation* of the citizenship curriculum is that it positions many teachers to devise *ersatz* experiences in lieu of more authentic ones. Community service is a fine example. Many schools have community service activities that are confined to the school itself, such as improving the facilities or surroundings, providing peer support for other children or acting as school prefects.

Task 11.2 **AN ECO-SCHOOLS PROJECT**

Citizenship encompasses environmental education and conservation issues and can be very engaging for children of all ages. Schools might choose to become eco-centres involving their pupils as active custodians of their local environment; 'Eco-warriors!'. Visit the website www.eco-schools.org.uk/ and consider how the projects outlined there could be incorporated into the school where you are working. How might a school's ethos affect the likelihood of its adoption of Eco-school? and how might Eco-school change a school?

Peer mentoring schemes encourage pupils to work alongside each other addressing important issues (more information is accessible at www.teachernet.gov.uk/teachingandlearning/socialandpastoral/peermentoring/).

Without doubt, useful learning opportunities can be provided through such routes; but might this learning be better achieved in the community? The main problem I have with this is that the 'hidden curriculum' (the discourse) strongly at work here is that the school community and the wider community are separate. Why not demand the children do their community service in the local (or wider) community?

Citizenship projects outside school

I am now going to provide two examples of community projects, each developed from the Duke of Edinburgh's Award. The award was founded in 1956 with the aims of providing young people (aged 14–25) with an enjoyable, challenging and rewarding programme of personal development. Information is readily available on their website (www.theaward.org).

The award operates at three levels, bronze, silver and gold, and contains four (five at gold level) elements:

1   a service in the community;
2   the acquisition of a new skill (a hobby, skill or interest), or the development of an existing one;
3   physical recreation (sport, dance or fitness);
4   an expedition (on foot, cycle, horseback, or water);
5   a residential experience (at gold level only) which needs to be an enterprise with people not known to the participant.

EXAMPLE 1

All secondary school pupils in England are obliged to participate in an active citizenship project. This could also be the community service aspect of the Duke of Edinburgh's Award, at a number of levels. Some schools are entering their Year 10 and 11 pupils in a GCSE short course in Citizenship Studies and are using a written report of the Duke of Edinburgh's Award community service as one piece of coursework, with the second piece (a critical commentary on two or more articles) coming from English or history. This seems to be an excellent way of accrediting pupils' work and maximising their achievement by engaging them in holistic learning.

EXAMPLE 2

It is widely accepted that the power of authentic experiences offered by the exploration part of the expedition has great potential and there is no reason why this could not be a citizenship exploration. For example, a group of teenagers might organise an expedition to Auschwitz, or to the Somme battlefield, or another historical site with humanitarian overtones, and undertake some form of exploration there. Then there is the personal and social (citizenship?) learning that comes from living with others for a week; dealing with the tensions that inevitably arise. This is learning based on 'real' situations and genuine personal engagement and has much to commend itself to schools that can make the commitment.

Political literacy in and outside school

Schools' councils, elections to them and mock elections are now commonplace in schools (information can be found at www.schoolcouncils.org/secondary/index.shtml).

Local and general elections offer opportunities for parallel mock elections in school with parties, candidates and electoral officials; but there are also opportunities to get children into the community.

There are also opportunities to link with local councils. In a school where I once taught, a citizenship project was organised where members of the school's councils received some training from officers of the local district council and followed this with a visit to the district council offices. Benefits in terms of the pupils' understanding of council procedures and the role of the council, and councillors' increased understanding of the perceptions of young people, their perspectives and ideas were evidenced (Rea and Rutter 2003).

International opportunities for informal citizenship

The European and global dimensions offer great possibilities for links between schools, and citizenship is a fertile ground for linking projects. The Government has set a target that by 2012 every school in England will have at least one international link and the British Council offer funding for such partnerships. This supports a range of school partnerships that enable pupils, students and staff from across Europe to work together on joint projects. Schools might simply form relationships through the web (*ersatz?*), but they might also arrange visits.

Older pupils can become involved with their peers from all over Europe through the European Youth Parliament, formed in 1987, where they can debate real issues in a challenging and enjoyable adult environment (information at www.eypej.org/?go=1).

The Model United Nations, as its name suggests, engages pupils in replicating sessions of the United Nations Organisation, again for older pupils (information at www.nmun.org/).

PART 3 SOME GOOD REASONS WHY YOU SHOULD KEEP CHILDREN INSIDE THE SCHOOL (AND THE COUNTER ARGUMENTS)

1   *Inside is safe*: outside they could get attacked or abducted by a stranger. Stranger danger is largely a myth (read Furedi 1997 for a discussion of this and related phenomena). The number of children harmed or murdered by strangers is very low indeed and has not changed for many years. Children are more likely to be harmed by people they know (close relatives).

Additionally, inside is *not* safe. There is some evidence linking sedentary, indoor lifestyles with physical and emotional problems such as obesity and depression. So arguments premised on the risks of taking young people outside must be balanced by assessments of the risks associated with keeping them inside.

2   *They might get knocked down by a car*: yes, they might, but again it is unlikely. Children also need to learn how to make practical risk assessments and become competent pedestrians. If adults see children out and about they are likely to drive accordingly.

3   *Inside is cheap*: so is battery-produced chicken, and we all know how good for us that is.

4   *They will miss out on so much curriculum time*: Good! It is all *ersatz*. Get them doing something authentic!

Task 11.3 **THE ARGUMENTS FOR OUTDOOR LEARNING**

There are opponents of informal, out-of-school learning opportunities and you are almost bound to encounter them in school. You will be well advised to consider what arguments you might use. Though slightly tongue in cheek, the above points might be useful starting points for your counter arguments.

Consider and rehearse the arguments you might use to defend outdoor learning opportunities from opponents in your school.

SUMMARY AND KEY POINTS

I have outlined some of my main concerns regarding the problems of schooling that may be summarised thus: the high degree of conservatism that leads to lack of creativity and innovation; their general unawareness of, or inability to respond to, the pupil's readiness to learn; the dominance of *ersatz* activities in schools.

I have outlined the benefits and potential power, on the other hand, of informal learning opportunities outside the school, and I have given some examples of possibilities teachers could adopt.

These are ideas, and they will need to be thought through, recontextualised in terms of the school in which you work and the design of the citizenship curriculum there. There is work to be done to achieve progress in the areas I have outlined; much work. I am convinced of the potential benefits to young people's engagement in learning through the kinds of programmes and activities I have mentioned and urge you to be a champion of outdoor and informal learning in citizenship.

NOTE

1   *Ersatz*: a German word, which I translate and understand as meaning artificial or fake.

FURTHER READING

Cooper, G. (1998) *Outdoors with Young People*, Lyme Regis: Russell House Publishing.
Although a little dated and possibly in need of a revised edition, this book provides a really excellent introduction to the problems and practicalities of taking pupils outside, and many ideas for what can be done with them in numerous outdoor environments.

Eco-schools: www.eco-schools.org.uk/.
Eco-Schools is an international award programme that guides schools on their sustainable journey, providing a framework to help embed these principles into the heart of school life. It is now easy for Eco-Schools across the world to get in touch and explore ways of working together on environmental issues. Once registered, schools follow a simple seven-step process that helps them to address a variety of environmental themes, ranging from litter and waste to healthy living and biodiversity.

Rickinson, M., Dillon, J., Teamey, K., Morris, M., Choi, M.Y. and Sanders, D. (2004) *A Review of Research on Outdoor Learning*, Shrewsbury: NFER/Field Studies Council.
This is a thorough review of the literature in English about the efficacy of outdoor learning. It divides outdoor learning into three types, outdoor adventurous activities; trips, visits and field studies; and the use of school grounds and local community spaces. It is a very useful quick guide to published research and evidence from the findings of that research.

PART IV

CITIZENSHIP ACROSS THE CURRICULUM

CHAPTER 12

CITIZENSHIP MAKING LINKS WITH ENGLISH

John Moss

INTRODUCTION

This chapter argues that there are profound reasons for English and citizenship to work together. It suggests that, while the aims of English are complex and contested, its most recent and current official definitions in the National Curriculum and public examination specifications underline the scope for productive working with citizenship.

It is a relatively straightforward point to make that the key processes that English seeks to develop, that is, speaking and listening, reading and writing, underpin many of the activities that take place in citizenship, but it might be less obvious to you that principled practice in teaching language and literature, as well as drama and the media, which many English departments are responsible for, can address key citizenship objectives.

Having established this point, the chapter will go on to argue that the concept of critical literacy can provide a bridge, not only between English and citizenship, but one from them both to other subjects, through the kind of reconceptualisation of curriculum organisation that the 2007 National Curriculum for England calls for, and which is anticipated, for example, by the Australian 'New Basics' curriculum.

OBJECTIVES

At the end of this chapter you should be able to:

- relate the aims and objectives of English to those of citizenship;
- identify key focuses of English that can enhance citizenship and vice versa;
- take practical steps to develop the links between English and citizenship in different contexts;
- understand how the key priorities of English and citizenship can be incorporated in an integrated curriculum underpinned by critical literacy.

THE KEY SKILLS OF ENGLISH

To outsiders, English often appears more a process-focused than content-focused subject. It is evident that its key processes, speaking and listening, reading and writing, are used as learning tools across the curriculum, and, for this reason, English has often been thought of as a service subject by the teachers of other subjects. However, 'language across the curriculum' initiatives and distinctions between English and literacy have been used in recent years to suggest that the development of skills in the key literacy processes is a cross-curricular or whole-school responsibility, and while functional skills are now explicitly embedded in the National Curriculum for English, it is recognised that all subjects provide opportunities to develop them (all references to the 2007 National Curriculum are to http://curriculum.qca.org.uk).

English has a core content, which its teachers will defend with a passion, including the study of language, literature and other texts, and, to different extents in different schools, drama and media education. As a result, departments are unlikely to respond favourably to approaches made on the basis that citizenship can usefully provide meaningful content for English to develop its processes studying. In later sections of this chapter, it will be suggested that an increasing focus in English on the social and political contexts in which language is used, and texts are written and read, provides the basis for much richer links between the subjects.

However, English and citizenship do have shared interests in developing particular approaches to, and aspects of, the processes of speaking and listening, reading and writing. This becomes apparent by mapping how some of the key processes of citizenship at KS3 can most obviously be enacted through key processes of English.

■ **Table 12.1** Subject processes in English and citizenship

Subject processes		English		
KS3		Speaking and Listening	Reading	Writing
Citizenship	Critical thinking and enquiry	Exploring topical and controversial issues	Evaluating sources	Undertaking enquiries into issues
	Advocacy and representation	Expressing opinions Representing others	Researching different viewpoints	Using persuasive arguments
	Taking informed and responsible action	Negotiating or taking action to bring about change	Analysing policies and position statements	Using evidence to support arguments

Source: based on extracts from the 2007 National Curriculum

The particular expertise that English teachers bring to the collaborative development of activities linking these two sets of key processes includes knowledge and understanding of:

- the *processes* used in speaking and listening, reading and writing to achieve successful learning and competent 'productions' in speech and writing;
- the key features of the *genres* that it is appropriate for pupils to read and produce (pupils learn about genre by exploring and developing a wide repertoire in the English classroom) and how to help pupils incorporate them in their work;
- the importance of a sense of *audience* and how to develop this in pupils (English will engage pupils with speaking to, and writing for, a range of audiences for a wide range of purposes);
- strategies that will develop the appropriateness of the *language register* and *technical accuracy* of pupils' spoken and written productions.

Task 12.1 **CITIZENSHIP KNOWLEDGE AND PROCESSES**

Make a list of the key areas of knowledge and understanding in which you would bring expertise as a citizenship teacher to collaborative work with an English teacher on the key learning processes and activities outlined in Table 12.1 above.

While a focus on the differences in the expertise citizenship and English teachers can bring to collaboration on shared learning objectives is a good starting point, considering the fundamental aims the subjects have in common can provide a basis for much richer joint working.

TOWARDS CRITICAL ENGLISH AND CRITICAL CITIZENSHIP

Ever since English emerged as a discrete curriculum subject in the late nineteenth century, most attempts to define and redefine it have recognised that it has a key role in the formation of citizens: what has been contested has been the kind of citizen that it seeks to develop.

The Cox Report, which defined the first National Curriculum for English, argued that in most English teachers' practice five different views of the subject could be detected to varying extents, and that they all merited a place in the curriculum, although as you will see in Box 12.1 commenting on these, the views imply quite different aspirations for pupils' citizenship (DES, 1989).

The 2007 National Curriculum for English re-presents these five views as four Key Concepts underpinning the curriculum: competence, creativity, cultural understanding and critical understanding. If you read the explanatory notes on these terms, you will find much that echoes the Cox Report in the definitions of competence, creativity and critical understanding.

However, the explanatory note on cultural understanding is more inclusive than earlier definitions of cultural analysis: it calls for the reading of a diversity of texts from different *cultures*, and from the *traditions*, rather than the tradition, of English

---

Box 12.1 NOTIONS OF CITIZENSHIP IN THE ENGLISH CURRICULUM

Cox Report View of English	Broad notion of pupil citizenship
Cross-curricular: English provides the skills of speaking and listening, reading and writing that are needed elsewhere in the curriculum.	English serves other subjects' views of the citizen rather than its own.
Adult needs: English provides the language-related skills that are a toolkit for functioning as an adult in society.	English sees the citizen as a competent, well-equipped worker.
Personal growth: English is about fostering creativity, imagination and personal development for the individual.	English sees the citizen as a creative and fulfilled contributor to society.
Cultural heritage: English is about inducting pupils into the cultural values promoted by a 'canon' of great novels, poems and plays.	English sees the citizen as a patriotic upholder of a particular moral and cultural tradition.
Cultural analysis: English provides the tools needed to analyse cultural artefacts in which language has a significant place (media texts and other non-literary material as well as literature).	English sees the citizen as a confident critical evaluator and user of language, especially the language of persuasion.

---

literature. It also speaks of the need to study linguistic *heritages*, *ideas* of cultural excellence, the *groups* in which pupils participate, and *questions* of local and national identity, referring to regional and global *variations* of English as an example of an appropriate topic for investigation.

The emphasis on plurality evident in the plurals I have italicised, underpinned by the promotion of an investigative approach to culture, society and identity, characterises a view of English that is gaining strength, and which makes available as an outcome from the subject, a learner who is a critical global citizen, who has come to understand how his or her experience of language and culture, mediated by English, relates to that of those in other local, regional, national and international communities, especially, but not only, those who use English as a medium of communication. The rest of this chapter proposes that the most significant developmental links between English and citizenship will occur when teachers with a view of English centred on cultural and critical understanding work with citizenship teachers who hold similar aspirations for their pupils' development as critical global citizens.

In the next part of the chapter, you will be asked to consider how English teachers' objectives in the study of language, literature, drama and the media, respectively, relate to those of citizenship.

Task 12.2 **ASPIRATIONS FOR THE CITIZENSHIP CURRICULUM IN ENGLISH**

Print a copy of the statement about the importance of English and the definitions of its Key Concepts in the 2007 National Curriculum and annotate it to identify the statements that most and least reflect your aspirations for citizenship education.

LANGUAGE STUDY

The promotion of cultural and critical understanding embedded in the 2007 National Curriculum for English can be traced through to its detailed guidance on language study. Significantly, in the sections of this guidance that define the range of content for English, the requirements for language study are listed under the heading 'language structure and *variation* [my italics]'. This emphasis on variation is exemplified by the requirement that pupils should study: 'the ways in which language reflects identity through regional, social and personal variation and diversity'. In turn, this requirement is further glossed as including the study of 'accent, dialect, idiolect, lexical change, varieties of standard English such as Creole, occupational variation, and differences in language use according to age and gender'; focuses that encourage learners to explore the relationships among language, culture, identity and society.

These statements invite teachers, more than any previous version of the National Curriculum for English has done, to offer a programme of language study that is constructed from the principles, articulated particularly well in a famous set of professional development materials that were strongly influenced by Halliday's functional theories of language, that language:

- is used primarily for social purposes;
- is dynamic and varies according to who is using it, the context and time;
- embodies social and cultural values and more specific meanings related to each user's identity;
- is closely connected in use to the definitions users make of social power, culture and gender;
- is systematically organised, but constantly changing as users negotiate and renegotiate meaning.

(Adapted from LINC 1992)

The case study in Box 12.2 shows that teaching language with these principles in mind requires teachers to engage with at least one key citizenship topic, 'Identity and diversity in the UK', and at least one key citizenship knowledge base, key UK institutions and their place in the sociopolitical system.

Box 12.2 **CASE STUDY: 'THIS IS THI SIX A CLOCK NEWS'**

In Tom Leonard's poem 'This is thi six a clock news', a speaker, whose broad Glaswegian accent is represented by phonetic spelling in the text, comments on the fact that, in late twentieth-century Britain, the news is always read in a 'BBC accent', because, he or she suggests, the BBC's view is that its audience would not find the news credible if read in regional accents (Leonard 1984).

For English, studying this poem to promote critical and cultural understanding should involve considering:

- the poem's representation of different users of the English language;
- the origins of the 'BBC accent' and its relationship to Received Pronunciation.

To do this effectively, teachers will need to draw on knowledge and understanding of:

- the status of the BBC as a public broadcasting corporation including its charter and formal responsibilities at the time the poem was written;
- the significance of the use of the word 'British' in its title;
- the extent of its independence as an organisation;
- the extent and character of its aspirations to freedom from bias.

In other words, to meet the objectives of English effectively, pupils should investigate matters that are so central to the citizenship curriculum that objectives of citizenship will also be met.

LITERARY THEORY AND THE STUDY OF TEXTS

The promotion of cultural and critical understanding in the teaching of literature and other texts is supported by the ideas available to English teachers from a plethora of critical and literary theories. Broadly speaking, literary theories are concerned to different extents with providing a means to think about:

- the writers and readers of texts, who they are and what they do;
- texts themselves, how they work and how they relate to other texts;
- the social, historical and cultural contexts in which texts are written and read;
- the systemic factors that influence who writes, reads and interprets texts, and how.

Very many of these concerns focus on the relationships between texts and society, and, in particular, the ways in which writers, texts and readers offer a selective view of, and/or make choices about, how particular societies, and the relationships between individuals and societies, are represented. For example, the overlapping concerns of new historicism and Marxism are with the social contexts in which texts are written and the relationship between these contexts and the textual representation of power. The focuses of at least some versions of feminism, postcolonialism and queer theory are on the relationships between the meanings of texts and the status of particular groups of people writing them, referred to in them, and/or reading them (for a more detailed discussion, see Davison and Moss 2000).

These contemporary theories all encourage English teachers to explore fundamental questions, such as those about power and values, inclusion and exclusion, voice and identity, that are also central to citizenship, and which citizenship's knowledge base, with respect to political, legal and social systems and their operation can usefully inform.

These concerns are now firmly embedded in the curriculum, for example, in the current assessment objectives for A-level English Literature, which include: 'show understanding of the contexts in which literary texts are written and understood'; and 'evaluate the significance of cultural, historical and other contextual influences on literary texts and study' (Literature assessment objectives from http://curriculum. qca.org.uk).

Box 12.3 **CASE STUDY: *THE TEMPEST***

In Shakespeare's *The Tempest*, an exiled Duke, Prospero, magically controls the island he occupies with his daughter Miranda. He uses his powers to control Caliban, a prior inhabitant of the island, and through his management of the events in the play, engineers a marriage for Miranda.

Study of *The Tempest* will typically include considering:

- through a feminist critique, the extent to which the relationship between Prospero and Miranda fails to challenge the view of patriarchal authority conventional in Shakespeare's time;
- through a postcolonial critique, the extent to which Prospero's attitude to Caliban fails to challenge an imperialist presentation of him as an alien in what is nevertheless his homeland.

See, for example, Brett (2005).

A well-informed understanding of the relevant sociopolitical contexts is essential for a reader to be able to make judgements on these matters with any degree of reliability. Key objectives of the citizenship curriculum can be met through this course of study.

Task 12.3 **ASSESSING CITIZENSHIP IN LANGUAGE AND LITERATURE WORK**

Review the case studies of 'This is thi six a clock news' and *The Tempest* above. To the extent that you agree with the claims made above, identify the *assessable* objectives of citizenship that could be met through the approach to teaching the texts proposed.

DRAMA

The example of *The Tempest* above points towards some of the more obvious connections between drama and citizenship that teachers can exploit. Many plays, of course, have the experience of citizenship as an explicit or implicit theme. The presentation of this theme, especially in workshops, rehearsals and performances, where it is enhanced by direct human representation, makes theatre an especially powerful medium for this purpose. As *The Tempest* case study suggests, citizenship's knowledge base can enrich understanding of matters such as the differences in the conventions of society when a play was written and when it is performed, helping a reader to interpret it more reliably.

It is also the case that pupils studying drama, particularly at KS4 and above, are taught to use theoretical frameworks derived from the work of 'theatrical practitioners' to interpret drama, and that some of these are especially concerned with the relationships between drama and citizenship. For example, Brecht's theoretical writings focus on the ways in which theatre can explicitly set out to encourage an audience's engagement in active citizenship after watching a play, through the use of a series of conventions that draw attention to the decisions made both by characters and by the director, actors and technical crew (Brecht and Willett 1978).

What might be less apparent is that current drama teaching and learning strategies can make a powerful contribution to the meeting of the objectives of citizenship. The drama workshop is a place in which the conditions of active participation in society are intensively 'rehearsed', frequently both within the dramatic fictions pupils create and participate in, and, at another level, in the educational processes they experience. The current orthodox pedagogy for drama, developed by Neelands, involves pupils in learning a repertoire of 'conventions' for exploring and developing dramatic fictions, and, as they become more experienced, in taking increasing collaborative responsibility for making choices from this repertoire to develop their work (Neelands 2004). Citizenship issues are explored *within* the processes of a number of the conventions, such as those defined below, and active citizenship processes, especially democratic decision making, are experienced in the choices pupils make from the repertoire of conventions available to them.

Like English teachers, specialist drama teachers will bring a particular set of expertise to collaborations with citizenship teachers. This will include knowledge and understanding of:

- the drama workshop *processes* which, over time, extend the capacity of a class to develop their work democratically;
- the repertoire of drama *conventions* that most effectively provide for the enactment of citizenship issues;
- the drama-specific *theoretical frameworks* that facilitate the analysis of citizenship-related issues in dramatic texts and performances.

Box 12.4 **DRAMA CONVENTIONS AND CITIZENSHIP**

Convention	Description and link to citizenship
Choric speaking	Pupils prepare and present a commentary on a text that is being used to create a dramatic fiction, representing the response of a particular group of people (who may formally be citizens) to the action: the 'commentary' might consist of the way lines are divided, allocated and spoken and/or the addition of new text by the pupils.
	Theatrical reference: the choruses in Greek tragedy that provide the views of the citizenry on the actions of the protagonist.
Hot-seating	Characters are interviewed in role by other members of a class, who could also be in role as, for example, the police, legal advisers, journalists or historians, whose questions help to deepen understanding of the relationships between the individual character and the social conventions operating in his or her context.
	Theatrical reference: Becket's interviews with his four tempters in Eliot's *Murder in the Cathedral*.
Meetings	Members of the group meet in role in the context of a formal meeting operating within the social and cultural context in which the dramatic fiction has been set. This draws out the significance of decisions made by characters and the range of responses to them, which are likely from members of the community.
	Theatrical reference: trial scenes, for example, in Miller's *The Crucible*.

(Developed from Neelands 2004)

Task 12.4 **TEACHING CITIZENSHIP THROUGH DRAMA**

Identify a citizenship topic that you could teach making use of each of the drama conventions in Box 12.4. Consider how you would plan a lesson to introduce pupils effectively both to the topic and the skills involved in using the convention.

MEDIA EDUCATION

The case study of Tom Leonard's 'This is thi six a clock news' above points towards some connections between citizenship and media education. Studying this poem should provide some coverage of most of the areas of knowledge that pupils are required to explore in GCSE Media Studies, as demonstrated in Table 12.2.

■ **Table 12.2** Areas of knowledge in media education

Area of knowledge required in GCSE Media Studies	Issues raised by Leonard's poem
How media forms, codes and conventions create meanings	The conventions that enable us to recognise a programme as a news broadcast
Representation in the media	The status given to people with different accents in the media
Contexts of media production, distribution and consumption	Ownership and control of the news media
How different audiences/users respond to and interact with media products and processes	The reception of the same news broadcast by different regional audiences
Media products, concepts and contexts	Expectations of news (for example, reliability and how this is represented) in relation to viewing figures
Media technologies	The 'reading' of the news from a script invisible to the audience written by invisible authors (as against the spontaneity of the voice in the poem)
A minimum of three different media (including at least one print and one audiovisual-based form)	Editorial control of national television news in contrast with that of national newspapers

Source: GCSE Media Studies requirements from http://curriculum.qca.org.uk

Table 12.2 shows how the concepts of media education mediate the concerns of English in relation to this poem, which are primarily with matters such as how social attitudes, cultural viewpoints and power are expressed and represented through *language*, and those of citizenship, which are primarily with the relationships between *the individual* and the institutions of *society*.

It is worthy of note that new technologies and the forms and genres of communication that are used in them, such as blogs, wikis and the pictures taken on cameras incorporated in mobile phones, respectively, facilitate the democratisation of access to public audiences, knowledge and understanding, and the capture and presentation of news. As a result, they provide particularly good focuses for work that bridges citizenship and English through the most important concerns of media education.

Specialist media education teachers will bring a particular set of expertise to collaborations with citizenship teachers. This will include knowledge and understanding of:

- media *forms* and *technologies, codes* and *conventions*;
- the theory underpinning key media concepts such as *narrative* and *representation*;
- the relationships between the media and society, including *media organisations*;
- the pedagogy that will help pupils to use *media processes and genres* with a sense of *audience* to make media products of high technical quality.

> ## Task 12.5 ASSESSING CITIZENSHIP IN MEDIA EDUCATION WORK
>
> Review the areas of knowledge required for GCSE Media Studies in the table above. Consider what *assessable* objectives of citizenship could be met by studying these topics.

ENGLISH AND CITIZENSHIP IN AN INTEGRATED CURRICULUM

The 2007 National Curriculum encourages us to rethink the structure of the curriculum from first principles. Determining what we are trying to achieve in terms of overall curriculum aims, including the kinds of learners, individuals and citizens we are setting out to produce, our aspirations for pupil wellbeing and development, and the knowledge and understanding, skills, attributes and attitudes we seek to promote in them, provides the complex context in which questions about the organisation of learning now have to be answered. We are also asked to reconsider how and where learning experiences should take place, what teaching and learning strategies should be used, what over-arching themes should be taught across the curriculum, and what statutory outcomes pupils are expected to meet, when we think about how we group and organise subjects (see the overview of the National Curriculum at http://curriculum.qca.org.uk).

Schools face an extremely demanding task in interpreting the new curriculum, which challenges all kinds of orthodoxies and vested interests, and for this reason, teachers developing project-based learning and integrated curriculum models, especially at KS3, are turning to international sources of inspiration.

Since 2003, The Australian State of Queensland has been developing a 'New Basics' integrated curriculum in which the interests of English and citizenship are strongly represented. The New Basics 'curriculum organisers' (the term used instead of 'subjects') are: Life pathways and social futures, Multiliteracies and communications media, Active citizenship, and Environments and technologies. The focus on, and perceived connections among, language, society and citizenship are immediately apparent from these titles, but their operational integration in the project is dependent on 'productive pedagogies' that generate 'rich tasks' assessed when 'students display their understanding, knowledge and skills through their performance in transdisciplinary activities that have an obvious connection to the wide world' (Queensland 2004). In Table 12.3, a Rich Task that foregrounds the integration of work on Multiliteracies and communications media with Active citizenship is described.

What is of particular interest about this approach is that the thinking at different levels, from curriculum design to task planning, is not controlled or limited by considerations about the relative importance of conventional curriculum subjects such as citizenship and English. Indeed, among the 'targeted repertoires of practice' for the task is included: 'acquiring a broad range of knowledge – literary, historical, philosophical, scientific, linguistic' (Queensland 2004).

■ Table 12.3 Opinion-making oracy: a Rich Task

Years 7–9	Opinion-making oracy
New Basics referents	Multiliteracies and communications media • Making creative judgements and engaging in performance • Communicating using languages and intercultural understandings • Mastering literacy and numeracy Active citizenship • Interacting within local and global communities • Operating within shifting cultural identities • Understanding the historical foundation of social movements and civic institutions
Rich Task	• Select an issue that has national/international importance and personal interest • Analyse influential speeches by leaders in such fields as politics, social movements, humanitarian causes and spirituality • Research the chosen issue and three different forums in which a speech on the issue could be presented • Prepare, polish and present the speech to the proposed national or international audience

Source: adapted from Queensland 2004

CRITICAL LITERACY

The theoretical basis for the linking of English and citizenship in the Queensland curriculum can be found in 'critical literacy', a concept originating in the work of Paulo Freire, who taught adults literacy in South America with the specific aim of empowering them to bring about change through cultural action (Freire 1972, 1975).

The concept was developed for the Australian school context by Colin Lankshear among others, in texts such as 'Critical social literacy for the classroom: An approach using conventional texts across the curriculum' (Lankshear *et al.* 1997), where he sets out the fundamental questions about any text with which critical literacy is concerned. These are as follows:

1 What version of events/reality is foregrounded here?
2 Whose version is this? From whose perspective is it constructed?
3 What (possible) versions are excluded?
4 Whose/what interests are served by this representation?
5 By what means – lexical, syntactic, and so on – does this text construct its reality?
6 How does the text position the reader? What assumptions about readers are reflected in the text? What beliefs, assumptions, expectations (ideological baggage) do readers have to entertain in order to make meaning from the text?

Lankshear also suggests how any topic, including those that we would recognise as falling within the boundaries of citizenship, should be investigated:

1   Locate (for a range of curriculum subjects, for example, history, geography, science) a range of texts relevant to [the topic].
2   Ensure that among them the texts reflect different perspectives.
3   Identify and describe key differences in the perspectives, in terms of their underlying theories, the questions or issues with which they are most concerned, their key assumptions, whose standpoint they most reflect, where you would locate them on a continuum.

(Lankshear 1997: 52)

These key questions and approaches provide a powerful organisational driver for collaborations among teachers of English, citizenship and other subjects. However, the potential impact of the emphasis on empowerment and the tackling of controversial issues in critical literacy practices should not be underestimated. In *None But Our Words* Chris Searle describes the impact of his adoption of critical literacy practices in a range of educational contexts in England. His definition of the principles of critical literacy is as follows:

> **creation** . . . the mobilization of words and the imagination in response to a certain situation . . . **consideration** . . . acts of individual and collective thinking . . . **consciousness** . . . thoughts freshly forged, newly expressed . . . **confidence** . . . both in the creative self and others who have worked in collaboration . . . **consolidation** [leading to] the determination . . . for cultural action . . . [which may involve] **crossover** of culture.
>
> (Searle 1998: 10, original emphasis)

His book records the outcomes of his work, describing how, for example, the publication of *Stepney Words*, an anthology of pupils' work about the community they lived in, against the wishes of the school governors, led to his dismissal and a strike by pupils. As the case study that follows shows, determining what critical literacy practices will be supported by those with power in the education system remains a topical issue.

Task 12.6 **CRITICAL LITERACY IN PRACTICE**

Consider the implications of the discussion of critical literacy and the case study on 'Education for leisure' for your own practice. If possible do this in discussion with an English teacher.

Box 12.5 **CASE STUDY: 'EDUCATION FOR LEISURE'**

In Carol Ann Duffy's poem 'Education for leisure', the narrator, an unemployed person, describes a series of events that culminate in going onto the streets with a breadknife (Duffy 2006).

The poem was included in a 2005 Examination Board Anthology for GCSE English. Following 'public concerns' the Board removed it, on the grounds that some teachers might be uncomfortable with the poem and that it might 'affect some readers adversely'. The Board's officer wrote to schools:

> I am sure you will understand the tension between facilitating and encouraging teachers to help young people think about difficult but important topics and the need to do this in a way which is sensitive to all the influences upon young people today, including prevailing social issues and public concern.
>
> (AQA 2008: 39)

Alison Smith notes that some teachers have used the poem, the Board's letter and media texts about the controversy for teaching, consciously or unconsciously adopting Lankshear's three critical literacy principles for topic investigation. She quotes a pupil's response as follows:

> To remove the poem is nothing more than an attempt to cover up the reasons for knife crime. The poem allows young people to see into the mind of a killer and understand what motivates someone to want to kill, which is something we need to do in order to discuss knife crime.
>
> (Smith 2008)

SUMMARY AND KEY POINTS

English and citizenship share obvious interests in the development of key functional skills in speaking and listening, reading and writing. However, when we ask what the purpose of developing these skills is, it becomes apparent that a more fundamental shared objective, to develop critical global citizens, will be more effectively met when the expertise English teachers have in relation to language and literature study, drama and media education, can be combined with the expertise of citizenship teachers. Radical curriculum models and the concept of critical literacy provide a rationale for this partnership that can cut through the potentially limiting interests of the two subjects seen discretely, and offer a challenging vision for pupil empowerment. The possibilities of this approach are being newly explored in England in integrated curriculum projects, but as new teachers, readers of this book have a key role in further developing practice and the curriculum structures that support it.

FURTHER READING

In addition to further reading mentioned in the text and listed in the references, the following are recommended:

Buckingham, D. (2000) *The Making of Citizens*, London: Routledge.
    A book-length study of the relationships among young people, news and politics that mediates the concerns of English and citizenship through a media education focus.

Claire, H. and Holden, C. (eds) (2007) *The Challenge of Teaching Controversial Issues*, Stoke: Trentham.
    This book includes chapters by a range of authors covering policy issues and whole school perspectives as well as the curriculum, and includes useful chapters on drama, literature and racism among other topics.

Klages, M. (2006) *Literary Theory: A guide for the perplexed*, London: Continuum.
    A readable introduction to literary theory from Plato to postmodernism, the second half of which deals entirely with contemporary literary theories that have particular relevance for citizenship.

Patel Stevens, L. and Bean, T. (2007) *Critical Literacy Context, Research and Practice in the K-12 Classroom*, London: SAGE.
    A study offering a definition of critical literacy from the perspective of US academics with a useful analysis of the history and application of the concept including its role in teacher education.

CHAPTER 13

CITIZENSHIP MAKING LINKS WITH HISTORY

Andrew Peterson

INTRODUCTION

The purpose of this chapter is to explore the nature of links between citizenship and history. The term 'history' is used broadly to refer both to the development of a historical dimension within citizenship lessons and the making of cross-curricular links to citizenship within history lessons. Making links with history holds a great deal of potential for citizenship teaching. When taught well, connections can serve to enhance pupil learning in both subjects, and this chapter sets out the foundations that are likely to underpin such positive practice. The relationship between citizenship and history is not, however, unproblematic. You will need to think very carefully about how particular topics and themes covered in lessons can enable pupils to achieve learning outcomes that incorporate both a citizenship and a historical dimension. For this reason, the chapter also raises some critical issues that you are likely to face when establishing cross-curricular links.

While the aims of the National Curriculum carry the expectation that all curriculum subjects should be concerned with producing 'responsible citizens who can make a positive contribution to society', many have identified the links between citizenship and history as being particularly fruitful (Kerr 1993; Davies and John 1995; QCA 1998; Wrenn 1999; Davies 2000; Arthur *et al.* 2001; Crick 2001; Phillips 2002). In presenting their case for citizenship education, the Advisory Group (QCA 1998: 22) recommended that 'schools consider combining elements of citizenship education with other subjects' adding that 'combinations of citizenship and history have obvious educational merit'. More recently, the QCA *Innovating with History* online resource (www.qca.org.uk/history/innovating/index.htm) has supported such links from the perspective of history teachers, contending that:

> [M]uch of the knowledge, concepts and skills acquired by pupils through their study of history is highly relevant to their development as informed, active and engaged citizens. Equally, citizenship can add a new dimension to history

teaching helping pupils make more sense of the world in which they live through an understanding of the past.

As this statement suggests, the building of a relationship between citizenship and history is likely to serve, both at the local level of the school and at the wider national level, to redefine the nature of both citizenship and history as subjects.

The chapter is comprised of five main sections. Following the objectives, the first section establishes the basis of connections between citizenship education and history. The second section considers the place of a historical dimension within citizenship lessons, while the third reflects on the extent to which citizenship themes can be meaningfully explored within history lessons. The fourth section deals with the potential commensurability of the citizenship and historical skills. There is a great deal of potential benefit for citizenship in building effective links with history, and these need to be thought through carefully. When reading this chapter you should consider how your understanding of citizenship education permits a historical dimension.

OBJECTIVES

At the end of this chapter you should be able to:

■ understand the basis of links between citizenship and history;
■ recognise that there are a number of critical issues regarding the nature and form that links between citizenship and history might take;
■ critically reflect on your own perceptions of the validity of making links between citizenship and history;
■ make links between the focus of this chapter and your school experiences.

ESTABLISHING CONNECTIONS

Before considering the nature of the links between citizenship and history education, it is worthwhile considering the logically prior question of why you might want to establish such links at all. Given the diversity of citizenship and history provision across schools in England, this is a complex question to answer, with responses ranging from theoretical thinking to practical teaching arrangements and expertise within individual schools. In broad terms, there are a number of positive reasons for the cooperative working of citizenship and history teachers, and these include the following:

• Citizenship and history are concerned with similar key concepts, such as power, democracy and freedom.
• Citizenship and history seek to develop similar skills within pupils, such as enquiry, communication and empathy.
• Through citizenship learning pupils are able to make meaning from key historical issues and processes.

- Through historical learning pupils are able to make sense of the present-day institutions and practices central to citizenship.
- Citizenship requires pupils to consider the nature of the local, regional, national and global communities to which they belong. This can only be achieved through an understanding of the historical roots of such communities.
- Citizenship is likely to gain acceptance and status within schools if it is aligned with a subject such as history. Such links can also help to develop a distinctive pedagogy of citizenship teaching.
- The inclusion of a citizenship dimension within history lessons affords citizenship essential time within an overcrowded secondary curriculum.

These reasons provide you with a basis for the positive close-working of citizenship teachers with the history departments of their schools. Central to this cooperative relationship must be an acceptance that links are likely to succeed where collaboration is symbiotic. In other words, links between citizenship and history will be compromised if connections are forced.

A useful starting point in establishing links between citizenship and history education is to compare curricular documents, such as units of work, in order to identify connected areas of study. On the basis of this, a mapping document can be produced that shows how a particular school covers elements of the citizenship Programmes of Study in both citizenship and history lessons. Mapping documents are at their most useful when it is clear where the contribution of history complements pupil learning in citizenship lessons. For Key Stage 3, such a document might contain information similar to that outlined in Table 13.1.

Task 13.1 ANALYSING CROSS-CURRICULAR MAPPING DOCUMENTS

During your contrasting school experiences, obtain copies from each school of cross-curricular citizenship mapping documents. Consult these, using the following questions as prompts:

- Through which processes were the documents produced? Who identified the need for a document? Who coordinated the document and who was involved in its composition? Who was it distributed to?
- How useful are the documents in supporting teachers and pupils in understanding how the citizenship curriculum is being addressed within history lessons?
- Do the mapping documents act as a working tool that is reflected upon and revised at regular intervals? If so, who is responsible for this?
- What impact have the revised curriculum Programmes of Study for citizenship and history had on the mapping documents?

When you have completed this task, you should consider how you would go about constructing your own curriculum mapping document.

■ **Table 13.1** Mapping document showing how history complements citizenship learning at KS3

Example elements of citizenship KS3 PoS	Coverage in citizenship Units of Work	Complementary coverage in history Units of Work	Assessment of citizenship learning
Legal and human rights	Y7: The UN Declaration of Human Rights and the Rights of the Child Y9: Human rights in the UK and around the world	Y7: *Medieval realms – King John and the Magna Carta* Y8: *Black peoples of America: from slavery to equality?* Y9: *Decolonisation and the fight for independence*	Citizenship: Pupils produce a chart that evidences the rights of the child and gives examples of breaches of this today. History: Pupils compare the UNDHR with the Magna Carta looking at change and continuity, and what both tell us about different societies and different times.
Parliament	Y8: What is parliament? How does parliament work?	Y8: *The making of the UK* Y9: *Politics and protest*	Citizenship: Pupils produce a leaflet/guide to parliament. History: Pupils produce a power graph/timeline of the changing powers of parliament through the period of the English Civil War. This includes times when the king was strongest and when parliament was gaining strength.
Democracy and voting	Y7: What is democracy? Why do people vote?	Y8: *The franchise: why did it take women so long to get the vote?* Y9: *Politics and protest*	Citizenship: Pupils undertake structured discussion regarding the importance of voting. History: Pupils consider and evaluate the methods of protest used by the Luddites, Chartists and Suffragettes, considering short- and long-term successes.
Resolving conflict	Y8: Conflict in the world	Y9: *Divided Ireland: Why has it been so hard to achieve peace in Ireland?*	Citizenship: Pupils present visual PowerPoint presentation on a conflict in the world today. History: Pupils construct a short narrative history from two different perspectives in Ireland and then provide an account of why interpretations differ and how this affects the resolution of conflict.
Global community	Y8: The UK and Europe Y9: The UN and the Commonwealth	Y8: *Major twentieth-century conflicts* Y9: *Empire and Commonwealth*	Citizenship: Pupils produce an essay presenting either arguments for or arguments against the UK joining the euro. History: Pupils sort reasons for the development of Empire into the categories of 'trade', 'exploration', 'Christianity' and 'war'. Pupils consider the nature of colonialism in India, and determine which of the features was the most dominant.

While the value of a cross-curricular mapping document should not be underplayed, you should regard it only as the first step in developing positive links between citizenship and history. According to Counsell (2002: 2; cf. Brett 2002) 'cross-referencing an extra column in a workscheme cannot take the place of serious theorising and creative reflection'. More important to how you understand cross-curricular connections between citizenship and history are the nature and form that such learning takes.

DEVELOPING HISTORICAL THEMES WITHIN CITIZENSHIP LEARNING

The manner in which historical themes are included within citizenship learning will largely be determined by individual schools and school departments, as it is within these that the content of the National Curriculum is interpreted into units of work and learning activities for pupils. This raises difficult choices for those involved in designing the curriculum within schools. As a teacher you will be involved in selecting which citizenship topics and themes require historical understanding and, on the basis of this, in helping to set out the nature that such historical learning might take. There are three central issues which, with colleagues, you will face in reaching these decisions.

First, you must decide which citizenship topics and themes require some level of historical understanding. Some areas of the citizenship curriculum explicitly require pupils to understand their historical basis. The Citizenship Order (1999: 15), for example, requires that at Key Stage 4 pupils are taught about 'the origins and implications of the diverse national, regional, religious and ethnic identities in the United Kingdom'. Similarly, the revised Programmes of Study for citizenship at Key Stage 4 (http://curriculum.qca.org.uk/) require that the study of citizenship should include 'the development of, and struggle for, different kinds of rights and freedoms in the UK'. In both cases, the idea of historical development is clearly referenced. In addition to this there are some areas of the curriculum where it would seem likely that pupils would be asked to consider historical issues. The understanding of human rights required at Key Stage 3, for instance, is likely to involve pupils in considering certain historical events or processes in order that they can fully understand their importance and application in the present-day global context. While teachers and observers might disagree about the precise examples to use, it would seem relatively unproblematic to suggest pupils' understanding of these themes is enhanced by the elucidation of the central historical connections. There are other areas of the citizenship curriculum, however, where connections with the past become more difficult for citizenship teachers. For example, you will have to think very carefully about whether pupil learning about national identity, diversity and the United Kingdom's relationship with the Commonwealth should be underpinned by a respective knowledge of Empire. If you decide that it should, then you will be faced with the thorny issue of how Empire might be addressed with pupils in a balanced, yet critical, way. In examples such as Empire, the establishment of historical links within citizenship lessons becomes more problematic and sensitive.

Second, and equally integral to establishing effective historical contexts within citizenship lessons, are the decisions that you will need to make in selecting *which* historical events and issues will be employed in order to develop pupils' comprehension of citizenship. Recourse to the published materials in support of citizenship teachers highlights some commonalities in the events and issues selected. For example, the Holocaust is often utilised in order to frame and inform pupils' contemporary thinking about prejudice, persecution and human rights. Similarly, the development of the franchise and the suffragette movement are frequently employed to shape the study of democracy and voting today. There is a need, though, for you to think carefully about the historical topics and examples that you will use to enhance pupil understanding in citizenship. For example, you might want a lesson on human rights to adopt a global focus, and draw on the 1948 United Nations Declaration of Human Rights or the 1989 United Nations Convention on the Rights of the Child. Alternatively, you could take on a domestic focus and reference the Criminal Justice and Public Order Act of 1994 or the Human Rights Act of 1998.

Third, and more critically, you will need to consider how the historical themes encountered in your citizenship teaching develop historical understanding. This begins with recognition that simply citing and drawing upon events in the past does not, in itself, constitute historical learning. While such references are likely to inform pupils' understanding of the present in important ways, it is essential that teachers of citizenship do not misinterpret either the past or the character of historical knowledge and skills. In other words, when citizenship learning adopts a historical dimension, you will need to think carefully about core historical concepts and processes, such as causation, interpretation, chronology and significance. With regard to this, Lee and Shemilt (2007: 16) usefully draw our attention to what Wineburg (2001: 19) has termed the danger of *presentism*. Wineburg (2001: 90) contends that: '[J]udging past actors by present standards wrests them from their own context and subjects them to ways of thinking that we, not they, have developed. Presentism . . . must be overcome before one achieves mature historical thinking.' This reminds us that pupils should be encouraged not to lose sight of the context of historical events and processes, and that these might be radically different from the present-day contexts that inform citizenship learning. Moreover, it helps us to recognise the need to remember the importance of *context* when asking pupils to investigate and reflect on the actions of other cultures, both past and present. For this reason, links within citizenship to history need to be thought through and then sensitively mediated by the teacher.

In considering how historical understanding might better inform understandings of diversity and British identity, the *Diversity and Citizenship Curriculum Review* in 2007 (known commonly as the Ajegbo Report) makes reference to the idea of pupil learning in citizenship being underpinned by historical foundations. One of the recommendations of the Ajegbo Report (DfES 2007: 97) includes the view that: '[W]hile it is important for young people to explore these issues [diversity and identity] as they affect them today, it is equally important that they understand them through the lens of history.' The term 'the lens of history' requires some critical attention, and our appreciation of its implications for citizenship teaching is likely to develop as the term attracts more reflection. However, teaching citizenship through the lens of history is likely to include the following:

- clear identification of the topics, concepts and themes within the citizenship curriculum that require some historical understanding;
- careful and thoughtful selection of historical events that enlighten and inform the study of these contemporary citizenship topics, concepts and themes;
- the delineation of appropriate learning objectives which, either individually or as a collective set, make reference to both citizenship and historical themes;
- explicit reference to relevant historical knowledge and skills within citizenship lessons;
- support for pupils in understanding why and how historical knowledge and skills impact on their comprehension of citizenship themes;
- assessment of pupil learning that places citizenship at its core, while recognising and drawing on a historical dimension.

Task 13.2 **BRITISH IDENTITY**

A key debate within discourse upon citizenship education is the extent to which, and how, the curriculum should include a component of learning about 'Britishness' and 'British Identity'. Using *Diversity and Citizenship Curriculum Review* (DfES 2007) as a starting point, produce a four-lesson unit of work, with supporting resources under the title of 'British Identity'. Within the lessons you should look to include a historical aspect in a way that takes into account the bullet points above. You might like to produce a short commentary alongside the unit of work that explains the focus and sets out the reasoning behind the focus and learning activities selected.

DEVELOPING CITIZENSHIP THEMES WITHIN HISTORY LEARNING

Taught well, the stand-alone or discrete provision of citizenship lessons within the curriculum of a school should be supported by its cross-curricular development. Similarly to the development of a historical dimension within citizenship lessons, it is appropriate that teachers of history consider how they can meaningfully incorporate a citizenship aspect within their work with pupils. While this brings challenges for teachers, the integrated emphasis of the revised secondary curriculum is only likely to make more widespread the need for teachers to tackle seriously the cross-curricular nature of pupil learning about and for citizenship. Within your own practice, you might be faced with teaching elements of the citizenship curriculum through discrete history lessons or working closely with history specialists in order that they may do so.

Clearly, it would be very difficult for history teachers to be responsible for delivering all elements of the citizenship Programmes of Study. However, according to Crick (2001: xviii–xix), of all the other subjects within the curriculum, history 'may have (should have) overall the greatest role to play' in the 'delivery of parts of the [citizenship] order through other subjects'. Data collected by the National Foundation for Educational Research's (Kerr *et al.* 2007: 21–2) ten-year citizenship longitudinal study evidences recognition of such links within the practice of schools, with history the third most favoured subject (after PSHE and Religious Education) identified by school leaders as supporting the cross-curricular teaching of citizenship. Understood simply, as Arthur *et al.* (2001: 75) explain, 'closing the gap between history and citizenship education may be a matter of bringing the past "up-to-date" by legitimate analogies with the present or a demonstration of the lineage of ideas, concepts and institutions into the present'. Despite the drawing of potentially fruitful connections to citizenship, there has been some consternation and debate among history educators concerning the potential impact of citizenship education upon the teaching of history. Within the history community positions range from those who see the integration of a citizenship dimension as a way of ensuring history teachers make greater representation of the present within their subject (Kerr 1993; Davies and John 1995; Davies 2000; Arthur *et al.* 2001; Phillips 2002) to those who remain suspicious of the impact that either citizenship or moral/social education could have upon historical learning (Elton 1991; Kinloch 1998).

Task 13.3 CITIZENSHIP AND HISTORY: CRITICAL PERSPECTIVES

Read and critically reflect on the following two articles that consider the nature of history education.

N. Kinloch (1998) 'Learning about the Holocaust: moral or historical question?', in *Teaching History* 93: 44–6.

A. Wrenn (1999) 'Build it in, don't bolt it on: history's opportunity to support critical citizenship', in *Teaching History* 96: 6–7.

They present rather different views on the place of moral and social aspects of historical learning, and hold different implications for the development of citizenship themes within history lessons. Are any of the views expressed replicated by history teachers within your school experience settings? How do these compare with your own perceptions of the place of citizenship within history education?

Lee and Shemilt (2007: 15) present three models of the relationship between citizenship and history from the perspective of history educators. You will need to consider how these three models may be replicated in practical terms within your experience schools and, significantly, the processes that have brought them about. First, history can be seen as acting as a *cornucopia* for citizenship. That is, history education already incorporates a citizenship dimension and therefore requires no particular change to the current provision of schools and departments in order to meet the challenge of delivering key aspects of the citizenship curriculum. Second, history might act as a *carrier* for citizenship. Central to this model is the belief that most of the citizenship Programmes of Study could be covered rigorously within history lessons if teachers were to make certain adjustments of content and, more importantly, of focus.

In the third model, which from the perspective of citizenship teachers is the most positive, history acts as a *complement* to citizenship learning. This third model recognises the areas of overlap between the two subjects, while also appreciating the uniqueness of each. As such, links are made within history lessons to citizenship themes in a way that supports pupil learning in both subjects. There are a number of practices that are likely to feature in schools and departments that adopt a complementary approach and which, in turn, can work toward ensuring the meaningful inclusion of a citizenship dimension within history lessons:

- explicit citizenship learning objectives and learning opportunities that are signposted and explained to pupils;
- the recognition and celebration of citizenship themes as an integral part of (rather than as a temporary add-on to) history lessons;
- clear links between historical knowledge and skills and their relation to present-day citizenship topics and themes;
- explicit recognition and development of citizenship skills and processes, such as enquiry and participation, as related to, but differentiated from, historical skills and processes;
- the assessment of citizenship understanding within the wider historical learning;
- the establishment of connections made between citizenship learning within history and learning within discrete citizenship lessons.

A positive practical example that incorporates a number of these practices is provided by Upton (2004). Reflecting on a sequence of lessons entitled 'Holocaust and human behaviour', Upton (2004: 35) evidences how the use of historical case studies 'enriched student' citizenship education'. Through engaging with historical examples provided by the Facing History and Ourselves organisation, pupils investigated and explored the citizenship issues of identity, membership and community. The careful planning of the connections between history and citizenship in this example established a platform through which pupil learning in both areas could be assessed. Crucially, in undertaking this work citizenship learning was embraced alongside the historical.

DEVELOPING CITIZENSHIP AND HISTORICAL SKILLS

Up to this point, this chapter has focused predominantly on knowledge-based links between citizenship and history. However, when developed in the context of knowledge and understanding, *skills* also form an essential part of both citizenship and history learning. It is important, therefore, that you give consideration to the extent to which the skills that form the basis of pupil learning in citizenship can benefit from links with those within history.

At the base of both citizenship and historical learning is a set of equally essential skills founded upon a commitment to critical thinking and enquiry. As Winch *et al.* (2005: 9) suggest, '[T]he proper study of history includes a critical rationality about human affairs in the past when a critical rationality about the present is central to civic education.' In citizenship, the current Programmes of Study require that pupils learn to 'think about political, spiritual, moral, social and cultural issues', to 'analyse information', to 'justify opinions' and to 'contribute to group and exploratory class discussions', while the revised Programmes of Study add that pupils should be able to 'research, plan and undertake enquires' and 'represent the views of others'. Similarly, the current history Programmes of Study ask that pupils should be taught to 'identify, select and use a range of sources of information', to 'recall, select and prioritise and select historical information', and 'communicate their knowledge and understanding of history, using a range of techniques', while the revised Programmes of Study add that pupils should be able to 'identify and investigate . . . specific historical questions' and 'reflect critically in historical questions and issues'. In other words, a central strand of both citizenship and history is to develop within pupils a proclivity to undertake and engage in critical enquiry.

It is important, however, that you think deeply about whether the type of critical enquiry undertaken by the pupil of history is of the same nature as that which you would want to develop within citizenship. On one level, the critical enquiry likely to be undertaken in both subjects adopts a similar form. Pupils will be involved in selecting and analysing information, in communicating and justifying decisions reached, and in listening to and seeking to understand the views of others. On another level, however, pertinent differences between the skills of citizenship and history materialise. Two examples can help to clarify this point. First, consider the analysis and evaluation of sources. The revised Programme of Study for citizenship at Key Stage 3 requires that pupils 'analyse and evaluate sources used, questioning different values, ideas and viewpoints and recognising bias'. Similarly for history, the revised curriculum requires that pupils should be able to 'identify, select and use a range of historical sources' and that they should 'evaluate the sources used in order to reach reasoned conclusions'. In both subjects pupils will be faced with analysing and evaluating a range of source types through considering factors such as provenance, authorship, motivation, intended audience, genre and language in order to assess validity and reliability. The crucial distinction here lies in the purpose of this analysis and evaluation. In citizenship, pupils are likely to be seeking to identify different opinions in order to justify or challenge a particular point of view. In addition, pupils might be using the sources as a model from which they will seek to replicate the particular form of the media under consideration. Conversely, in history pupils will be fundamentally concerned with how the sources can help them to build a picture of the past and an ability to understand decisions made by key figures at the time. On this basis, the type of information source valued by the pupil in history might be rather different to that valued by the pupil in citizenship.

Second, consider the development of empathy. The current Programmes of Study for citizenship at Key Stages 3 and 4 require pupils to 'use their imagination to consider other people's experiences'. Imagination is, however, a problematic concept, which in history education is understood as lacking in rigour in comparison to critical empathy. Within history lessons pupils are likely to be discouraged from imagining personal narratives and life stories of others without an associated knowledge and understanding of historical context and meaning. As such, there is a danger that, in its practical expression, imagination within citizenship education could become confused with something more akin to sympathy. Again, the central purpose to which the skill of empathy is aimed within history concerns the building of an understanding of a particular picture of the past and an ability to understand decisions made by key figures at the time. In citizenship, the development of a robust approach to empathy is more likely to be aimed at pupils understanding the interests of others from the perspective of others in order that they can meaningfully engage with them through democratic and discursive processes. In both examples, while the skills share some common elements, the purposes to which they are put and the outcomes to which they lead are differentiated. An awareness and understanding of such differences does not render links between citizenship and history meaningless. On the contrary, they serve to provoke further thought as to how pupil learning in citizenship and history can effectively complement each other. Viewed positively, the relationship could result in rewarding collaboration. As Davies (2000: 144) suggests in relation to interpretation:

> If pupils can come to understand that different judgements have been developed at particular points in history, then it may be possible not only to develop greater tolerance but also to recognise the forces that act upon citizens as they create specific forms of society.

Task 13.4 **SKILLS COMPARISON AND ANALYSIS**

During your time in your school experience, take the time to consult units of work, lesson plans and resources for both citizenship and history. Consider the processes through which pupils are encouraged to undertake enquiry-based learning, analyse and evaluate sources and use empathetic activities in order to understand the perspectives of others. Can you identify any commonalities and/or differences in the way in which these skills are approached in citizenship and history lessons? What are the reasons for this?

Also of importance in considering the potential links between citizenship skills and history is the extent to which historical learning can help pupils to undertake community involvement. Effective practice in this area is likely to commence with involving pupils in coming to understand the historical basis of community which, in turn, will allow them to understand the historical contingency of identity. As Maylor *et al.* (2007: 35) suggest: '[H]istory (or, at least, particular *constructions* of the past) is very important in identity formation and maintenance.' This reminds us that historical understandings and interpretations of community identity are essential to pupil learning in citizenship, and that these can play a significant role in informing community involvement. In other words, comprehension of the historical nature of community is likely to engender and permit deeper community involvement for pupils.

Practical guidance concerning how citizenship and history learning might come together to engage pupils in learning for community understanding and involvement is, at present, scarce (Brett 2002). A good model for such activities is provided by Clemitshaw (2002) in his work with Year 8 and 9 pupils focusing on a derelict cemetery in Sheffield, which is subject to planning request. Clemitshaw details pupil learning through a sequence of lessons that build upon pupils' historical investigation and enquiry in order, in the final lesson, to inform participation and responsible action through role play. In this final lesson, pupils were asked to adopt the role of a key stakeholder (either the Friends of the General Cemetery, Sheffield City Council or the property development company) and to employ their historical research to inform their political discussions and decision making in a present-day context. Through the activities described by Clemitshaw, pupils are likely to have engaged with issues such as civic pride, community identity and community belonging in a way that informed their decision making. You might like to consider the manner in which citizenship participation and action projects undertaken by pupils in the locality of your experience schools either are, or could be, usefully underpinned by historical investigation.

SUMMARY AND KEY POINTS

The establishing of clear and meaningful links between citizenship and history is still in a developmental stage. This chapter has sought to provide an overview of where practice and thinking currently stands. It has suggested that with careful considera-tion, citizenship teaching and learning can benefit a good deal the recognition and implementation of cross-curricular links. Adopting a critical appreciation of such cross-curricular work, the chapter has also offered some areas for further consider-ation and investigation. Most importantly, it has suggested that a complementary approach that recognises a meaningful relationship between citizenship and history, while celebrating the unique contributions that citizenship and history have to make, is essential in furthering pupil learning.

FURTHER READING

Arthur, J., Davies, I., Wrenn, A., Haydn, T. and Kerr, D. (2001) *Citizenship through Secondary History*, London: RoutledgeFalmer.
   A core academic yet accessible text that considers how citizenship education links with history. Leading thinkers in the field set out and debate a range of issues, while positively identifying the key place of history in supporting the citizenship curriculum.

Davies, I. (1999) 'Citizenship and the teaching and learning of history', in J. Arthur and R. Phillips (eds) *Issues in History Teaching*, London: Routledge, pp. 137–47.
   An interesting article which, from a positive perspective, establishes the challenges for those wishing to develop citizenship themes within their teaching of history.

DfES (2007) *Diversity and Citizenship Curriculum Review* (The Ajegbo Report), London: DfES. (Available online from publications.teachernet.gov.uk/eOrderingDownload/DfES_Diversity_&_Citizenship.pdf).
   A review of the teaching of diversity and citizenship within secondary schools that promotes the role of a historical dimension within citizenship to further pupil

understanding of identity. The report advocates the teaching of citizenship through 'the lens of history' and includes some example units of work in its appendices.

Lee, P. and Shemilt, D. (2007) 'New alchemy or fatal attraction? History and citizenship 14–19', in *Teaching History*, 129: 14–19.
Considers the place of citizenship learning from the perspectives of history teachers, and introduces three potential models for the relationship between citizenship and history.

CITIZENSHIP MAKING LINKS WITH RELIGIOUS EDUCATION

CHAPTER 14

Liam Gearon

INTRODUCTION

Citizenship has often been regarded by its political and educational proponents to be a largely secular domain. National and international initiatives in citizenship education have thus, historically, tended to neglect the role of religion. Explanation for citizenship's prior neglect of religion lies with complex historical relationships between religion, politics and education. Yet one of the increasingly evident changes in the nature and content of citizen education is a reversal of this trend. This chapter examines national and international developments in the fields of citizenship and religious education and tries to place these educational developments into historical and political context.

OBJECTIVES

By the end of this chapter you should:

- ■ have some grounding in theoretical perspectives on the historical relationships between religion, politics and education;
- ■ have a range of practical ideas and tasks to apply in the secondary school classroom.

RELIGION, POLITICS AND EDUCATION: FOUR CRITICAL CONTEXTS

Four critical contexts provide some insight into the complex historical relationship between religion, politics and education in the modern era. I argue that these contexts can also help to elucidate the contemporary and changing relationships between citizenship and religious education.

Critical context 1: religion and politics

If the role of religion in public and political life has been historically underplayed since the European Enlightenment, there is now increasing evidence of the importance of religion in post-Cold War public and political life. Often, though not exclusively, this centres on issues of human rights, including freedom of religion or belief. This trend has been highlighted by a number of theorists of religion: Berger *et al.* (2008); Burleigh (2006, 2007); Casanova (1994); Davis *et al.* (2005); de Vries and Sullivan (2006); Fox and Sandler (2006); Gearon (2002, 2006, 2008); Hanson (2006); Harpviken and Roislien (2005); Haynes (2006); Himmelfarb (2004); Hoelzl and Ward (2006); Jackson (2002, 2004); Jackson *et al.* (2007); James (2006); Juergensmeyer (2005); Runzo *et al.* (2004); Smart (1969, 1989); Swaine (2006); Trigg (2007); Ward (2003); Woodhead *et al.* (2002).

UNPACKING CRITICAL CONTEXT 1

In modern European history, separation of the powers of Church and State arguably originates within the sixteenth-century Reformation, in a Europe in which the intellectual authority of the Church had already been challenged by many developments of Renaissance Humanism (Chadwick 1990; MacCulloch 2005). In many European countries (though patterns varied enormously between and within them) the Reformation and Counter-Reformation radically reshaped the notion of the political and ecclesiastical authority of Christendom: from Luther's alliances with the German princes to Henry VIII's establishment of the Church of England to the theocratic vision of Calvin's Geneva (Chadwick 1990; MacCulloch 2005). The political and religious violence that resulted was in part resolved by the 1648 Treaty of Westphalia (http://fletcher.tufts.edu/multi/texts/historical/westphia.txt).

The Reformation and Counter-Reformation, then, and the religious feuding that accompanied both, did much to weaken the political remit of religious authority, and, with the Renaissance, laid the groundwork for the European Enlightenment (Burleigh 2006, 2007; Himmalfarb 2006). The European Enlightenment began a period of marginalisation of religion from the arts and humanities, from philosophy as much as public life but also increasing presumptions of a liberal secularism within social and political life, a modern polity, linking citizenship to human rights under nation states professing liberty in belief and religious practice, nowhere better encapsulated than in Thomas Paine's *Rights of Man* (1985 [1791/2]). Paine's *Rights of Man* showed how the political and religious freedom spanned the Atlantic: it is both a philosophy of, and testimony to, late eighteenth-century American and French Revolutions.

The post-Enlightenment separation of Church and State presented the groundwork for a wider marginalisation of religion in public life, often defined as 'secularisation'. Secularisation thesis presented in varying forms an expectation of the decline in the public role of religion, and its marginalisation to the private sphere. When this intellectual tradition has been combined with totalitarian political power, such states have tended towards a militant atheism (Arendt 2004 [1951]; Burleigh 2006, 2007; Gray 2007; Talmon 1961 [1952]).

Against the expectations of this (until recent decades, often uncontested) secularisation thesis, religion seems to have retained a role in public governance, something noted early by Smart (1969) and elaborated by scholars in subsequent decades (for instance, Casanova 1994; Haynes 2006; Trigg 2007; Ward 2003), and to the extent that some claim we now inhabit a 'post-secular world' (de Vries and Sullivan 2006). Indeed, some time before 11 September 2001 religion had increasingly served as a wider political barometer. For example, in the US the 1998 International Religious Freedom Act made it a requirement for the US Secretary of State to publish an annual report on religious freedom worldwide, the US Department of State making freedom of religion a measure of a country's respect for other fundamental rights. The report provides comprehensive worldwide accounts of religious freedoms and infringements of freedom (www.internationalrelations.gov, and links), though the study and its selective use of rights such as freedom of religious above other human rights has not been without its critics (cf. Marshall 2000; cf. Shattuck 2003).

Task 14.1 **FREEDOM OF RELIGION OR BELIEF**

There are a number of independent indicators that highlight the importance of freedom of religion or belief as a barometer of wider democratic freedoms, such as the Center for Religious Freedom, http://crf.hudson.org. Its database not only presents worldwide and comprehensive independent guidance on freedom of religion or belief but also invaluable quick reference to key geopolitical context, including some reference to educational contexts. The Freedom House database presents information on religious freedom *by area* and *by tradition*.

Visit the Center for Religious Freedom website. Using guidance provided here, plan a lesson or series of lessons to introduce pupils to the topic of religion and politics. Relate your plan to the appropriate key stage, GCSE or Advanced Level syllabus. Share devised lesson plans and/or Schemes of Work with the whole group.

Critical context 2: religion and the United Nations (UN)

The UN system incorporated and defined freedom of religion or belief since the 1948 Universal Declaration of Human Rights but the early history of the UN tended to downplay religious and ideological diversity. After a long neglect (or low-level treatment) of religion explicitly, the UN system from the late 1970s and particularly with the Declaration on the Elimination of All Forms of Intolerance and Discrimination Based on Religion or Belief (1981) began to recognise the international significance of religion for a stable world order: Ayton-Shenker (1995); Bennett and Finnemore (2004); Bowles (2004); Forsythe (2000); Harpviken and Roislien (2005); Jackson *et al.* (2007); Krasno (2004); Lerner (2000); Shattuck (2003); Trigg (2007); UNESCO (2006, 2006a).

UNPACKING CRITICAL CONTEXT 2

The 1948 United Nations' Universal Declaration of Human Rights includes a number of articles of relevance to freedom of religion and belief. These include Article 2 (forbidding prejudicial distinctions of any kind, including those related to religion), Article 26 (on the rights to a particular religious education) and Article 29 (on responsibilities and proscription against limitations of proclaimed rights). Pivotal, though, is Article 18 of the Declaration, which states that:

> Everyone has the right to freedom of: thought, conscience and religion; this right includes freedom to change his [*sic*] religion or belief, and freedom, either alone or in community with others and in public or private, to manifest his [*sic*] religion or belief in teaching, practice, worship and observance.

As Lerner (2000) comments, Article 18 was influential in regional treaties and the 1981 Declaration, and integral to several international instruments, notably:

- The Arcot Krishnaswami Study (1959).
- The International Covenant on Civil and Political Rights (1966).
- The International Covenant on Social, Economic and Cultural Rights (1966).
- The Declaration on the Elimination of All Forms of Intolerance and Discrimination Based on Religion or Belief (1981).

Though religion featured in numerous general UN covenants and declarations, until the UN Declaration on the Elimination of All Forms of Intolerance and Discrimination Based on Religion or Belief (1981), in its own right religion received relatively low-level treatment. Thus the 1981 Declaration marks a phase of growing recognition about the international significance of religion for a stable world order. During the 1990s – in a post-Cold War world of newly emergent nationalisms and struggles over religious, cultural and ethnic identities – religion gained unprecedented prominence, for instance:

- Declaration on the Rights of Persons Belonging to National or Ethnic, Religious and Linguistic Minorities (18 December 1992).
- Oslo Declaration on Freedom of Religion or Belief (1998).
- World Conference against Racism, Xenophobia and Related Forms of Discrimination (September 2001).

(Visit www.unhchr.org, and follow links)

The notion of freedom of religion was itself extended to freedom of non-religious (for example, humanistic) worldviews in the 1981 and 1998 Declarations, the 'or belief' in both being significant.

This, in turn, has had the effect of linking in a fairly direct way rights of 'freedom of thought, conscience and religion' to 'third generation' rights of 'human solidarity', concerned with specific groups – women, children, indigenous peoples, religious traditions – rather than generic 'civic and political' ('first generation') or 'cultural and economic' ('second generation') rights (Wellman 2000). Most notable is the linking of religious intolerance to the ending of racism, xenophobia and discrimination more broadly. For example, the 1981 Declaration on the Elimination of All Forms of Intolerance and of Discrimination Based on Religion or Belief was followed just over a decade later by the UN Declaration on the Rights of Persons Belonging to National or Ethnic, Religious, and Linguistic Minorities (1992). While a post-September 11 context has further highlighted the issue of potential violence in and over conflicts in (religious and/or ideological) worldviews, this potential fissure between universal rights and particular cultural, especially religious traditions, has been a live one for many years (Ayton-Shenker 1995).

Task 14.2 RELIGION AND THE UNITED NATIONS

The United Nations has a Special Rapporteur for Freedom of Religion or Belief, mandated:

* to examine incidents and governmental actions in all parts of the world that were inconsistent with the provisions of the Declaration on the Elimination of All Forms of Intolerance and of Discrimination Based on Religion or Belief, and to recommend remedial measures for such situations;
* to apply a gender perspective in the reporting process, including in information collection and in recommendations;
* within the terms of his mandate and in the context of recommending remedial measures, to take into account the experience of various States as to which measures are most effective in promoting freedom of religion and belief and countering all forms of;
* to continue to bear in mind the need to be able to respond effectively to credible and reliable information that comes before him, to seek the views and comments of the Government concerned on any information that he intends to include in his report, and to continue to carry out this work with discretion and independence.

Visit the United Nations and/or the visit the United Nations High Commission for Human Rights, respectively, at www.un.org and www.unhchr.ch, and follow links for the Rapporteur.

Create a small group forum to interrogate critically the role of religion in the UN. Assign a chair to the discussion, a secretary and a reporter to feed into a whole-group session (adapt this as numbers and circumstances allow). Here are some possible questions for each group:

* Does freedom of religion or belief require particular protection and why?
* In what ways does the Special Rapporteur on Freedom of Religion or Belief promote and protect such rights in the international community?
* Are there notable occasions when freedom of religion or belief (Article 18) seems to conflict with freedom of expression (Article 19)?

There is, now, no denying that issues of religion have increasingly come to the fore in a United Nations previously cautious about explicit reference to religion. This has been most recently reiterated by the twenty-fifty anniversary of the 1981 Declaration commemorated in Prague in November 2006. Debates on freedom of religion or belief and, more widely, religion in global governance can be found through the listed UN site (www.un.org), with links to the UN Special Rapporteur on Freedom of Religion or Belief.

Critical context 3: religion in citizenship education

The role of religion in citizenship education (and related curricula areas such as civics and human rights education) has been underplayed. Reflecting broader global trends there is now increasing recognition of the importance of religion in citizenship and human rights education, although the recognition of the importance of teaching about religion remains, arguably, less strong in civic or citizenship education than in religious education: Ajegbo *et al.* (2007); EPPI (2005); Gearon (2004); Heater (2004); Huddleston and Kerr (2006); Lindholm *et al.* (2003); McLaughlin (1992, 2000); NFER (2007); Osler and Starkey (2006).

UNPACKING CRITICAL CONTEXT 3

International reviews of citizenship education (Kerr 2003) reveal national education systems subject to similar issues and challenges of global change, including:

- the rapid movement of people within and across national boundaries;
- a growing recognition of the rights of indigenous peoples and minorities;
- the collapse of existing political structures and the fledgling growth of new ones;
- the changing role and status of women in society;
- the impact of the global economy and changing patterns of work and trade on social, economic and political ties;
- the effects of the revolution in information and communications technologies;
- an increasing global population and the consequences for the environment;
- the emergence of new forms of community and protest.

(Kerr 2003: 9)

Interestingly Kerr's assessment neglects any explicit reference to the role of religion in the modern world as contributing to any challenges to notions of citizenship.

If the reasons for the current prominence of citizenship are notable, definitions of citizenship education itself are equally wide-ranging, and, as the following indicates, equally neglectful of the role of religion:

- Arnot and Dillabough (2002) – emphasise feminist perspectives.
- Audigier (1998: 13) – emphasises the necessity of citizenship education to be socially and politically all inclusive, nothing of what is experienced in society should be foreign to democratic citizenship.

- Crick (2000) – emphasises the all-importance in citizenship of political knowledge.
- Davies (2007) – emphasises the need for pedagogical pragmatism, on enabling pupils to become citizens.
- Heater (2004) – emphasises the educational-political aspects of citizenship in historical contexts through the ages, from the Greek city state onwards.
- Isin and Wood (1999) – emphasise citizenship as part of a search for identity.
- Osler and Starkey (2006) – emphasise the need to move away from narrow national perspectives to a global and cosmopolitan citizenship.

(adapted from Davies 2007: 1–8)

Citizenship education can be said, then, to be a conscious pedagogical response to the challenges of social and political change but often one that has neglected the place of religion (cf. Gearon 2003, 2003a, 2007). National reviews of citizenship education in England show this neglect is well embedded:

- EPPI (2004, 2005) www.eppi.ioe.ac.uk (and follow links to citizenship).
- Gearon (2003) www.bera (and follow links to Professional User Reviews).
- House of Commons Report (2007) www.gov.uk (and follow links to House of Commons, 2007).
- NFER (2007) www.nfer.ac.uk (and follow links to citizenship).
- Osler and Starkey (2006) www.bera (and follow links to Academic Reviews).

Such a pattern is equally evident in Europe and internationally:

- Eurydice (2008) www.eurydice.org/portal/page/portal/Eurydice (and follow links to citizenship).
- UNESCO (2008) http://portal.unesco.org (and follow links to citizenship).
- United Nations http://ap.ohchr.org/documents (and follow links to the International Decade of Human Rights Education, 1995, 2004).

In England, however, the Ajegbo Report *Citizenship and Diversity* (2007) in reviewing citizenship made a number of recommendations, one of which was the inclusion of another strand in the citizenship curriculum, 'Living together in the UK'. This did appear in the new National Curriculum (2007). There remains, though, an absence of systematic consideration of religion within citizenship education, as the reviews of research literature noted above indicate (Arthur *et al.* 2008; EPPI 2005; Gearon 2004, 2006, 2007; cf. Osler and Starkey 2006;).

Critical context 4: citizenship in religious education

The political has been underplayed in religious education, and contentious historical contexts sidestepped, including notions of citizenship. Yet the exponential growth of civic or citizenship education around the world has forced religious education to consider the political and historical, a matter itself forced upon education by manifold

Task 14.3 **RESOURCES FOR RESEARCH**

1   Review one or more of the following websites:

British Educational Research Association (BERA): The BERA website contains downloadable reviews of citizenship research, including Gearon (2003) *How Do We Learn to Become Good Citizens?: a professional user review of UK research* and Osler and Starkey (2006) *Education and Democratic Citizenship* 1995–2005, visit www.bera.ac.uk (and follow links).

CitizED: www.citized.info (and follow links) provides a major source of current information on citizenship for schools and universities, including links to the Citizenship Foundation and Institute for Citizenship, and other agencies responsible for promoting citizenship education.

Citizenship Foundation: The Citizenship Foundation is a well-established and important resource for citizenship education, www.citizenshipfoundation.org.uk.

Council of Europe: The Council of Europe is a human rights focused organisation of over 50 member state countries of Europe. The Council of Europe dedicated 2005 as the European Year of Citizenship through Education and its website provides a Europe-wide resource of recent research in Education for Democratic Citizenship, www.coe.org.

European Union: The European Union has, like the Council of Europe a considerable interest in harmonising notions of European identity, and thus prioritising notions of citizenship across its member states; http://europa.eu.int (and follow links for citizenship).

Eurydice: This hub provides excellent empirical resources for citizenship education across Europe. Visit www.eurydice.org (and follow links).

Institute for Citizenship: The Institute for Citizenship is a well-established and important resource for citizenship education, www.citizen.org.uk.

National Foundation for Educational Research (NFER): This is a major funder of educational research generally with a considerable interest and track record in empirical research in citizenship. Visit www.nfer.ac.uk (and follow links).

United Nations: The United Nations offers a wealth of sources for all issues in citizenship, including economics, environment, global terrorism, and human rights, www.un.org (and follow links).

United Nations Educational Scientific and Cultural Organisation: UNESCO is a highly useable resource, with much specific work on citizenship education, www.unesco.org (and follow links).

2   Create a small group forum to analyse whether you think religion continues to be marginalised within citizenship education. Divide into groups, assign a chair to the discussion, a secretary and a reporter to feed into a whole-group discussion (adapt this as numbers and circumstances allow).

Box 14.1 **THE EQUALITY AND HUMAN RIGHTS COMMISSION**

The Equality and Human Rights Commission is an important source of legal and related information about all aspects of equality and human rights within the UK, www.equalityhumanrights.com. Here is what you will find on its website relating to religion and belief:

- Under human rights and anti-discrimination legislation, you have the right to hold your own religious beliefs or other philosophical beliefs similar to a religion. You also have the right to have no religion or belief.

- Under the Equality Act 2006, it is unlawful for someone to discriminate against you because of your religion or belief (or because you have no religion or belief):

  - in any aspect of employment
  - when providing goods, facilities and services
  - when providing education
  - in using or disposing of premises, or
  - when exercising public functions.

  There are, however, some limited exceptions when discrimination might be lawful. You can find out more about these in this section of the site.

- Under British anti-discrimination and human rights legislation, you are also entitled to practise your religion or belief, express your views and get on with your day-to-day life without experiencing threats or discrimination.

The web pages for religion and belief also include short definitions of key terms, for example:

- What is a religion?
- What is a belief?
- What is religious discrimination?
- When and where could discrimination take place?
- When does the law allow religious discrimination?
- What does the law say?

changes in the world in which we live: Ajegbo *et al.* (2007); de Souza *et al.* (2006); de Souza *et al.* (2010, forthcoming); Gearon (2006, 2007, 2008); Jackson *et al.* (2007); Lindholm *et al.* (2003); Ofsted (2007); Osmer (2003).

UNPACKING CRITICAL CONTEXT 4

For Christian religious communities already divided by the Reformation, the European Enlightenment gave birth to an unprecedented onslaught of scepticism from innumerable philosophical and political quarters. One of the effects of this onslaught of scepticism was an increased marginalisation of religion from philosophy and politics and, indeed, wider aspects of public life. Ironically, the Enlightenment also made religion a matter of serious study, with many pioneering scholars from the late eighteenth and nineteenth centuries onwards trying to accommodate religion with this new light of reason (Burleigh 2006). In Britain, the groundbreaking work of Ninian Smart and the Department of Religious Studies at Lancaster University is a good example of this in practice, pioneering ways for religions to be studied in the university system in their own right, without the need for a particular religious commitment or faith perspective (Smart 1969, 1989). Such academic developments had many implications for religious education. It is a long and contested history (Copley 2005, 2009). In Britain at least, despite actually subtle differences in pedagogy, this meant that from the 1970s onwards religious education emerged as a subject given to the study of world faiths, and aiming to encourage tolerance and understanding between religious traditions in an open, plural democracy (Grimmitt 2000; Stern 2006).

Ironically, though, this religious education has tended to emphasise precisely the positive aspect of religion in order to justify its place in contributing to harmonious living together with diversity. In some early articles, I tried to elaborate how far cognisance was needed of the negative and even dystopian aspects of religious traditions by religious educators (Gearon 2002). Arguably, though, in a context where tolerance, and related positive *utopian* attributes of religious education, are often the focus (cf. Grimmitt 2000; Osmer 2003; Stern 2006), educators need to take seriously *dystopian* global realities of which religions, often through ethnic and cultural identity, play a part (Amor 2001; Gearon 2004, 2006; Harpviken and Roislien 2005; Jackson *et al.* 2007; Runzo *et al.* 2004; Rushton 2004; Trigg 2007).

There is an emergent dividing line between those who suggest the differences of politics and culture are irresolvable, 'the clash of civilizations' (Huntington 2002), and those pluralist thinkers, at the instigation of, and under the banner of, the United Nations, who opt for a more conciliatory tone of 'the alliance of civilizations' (UN 2008). Debates around the resolution of potential and actual conflicts through education remain unresolved. Arguably the great struggle here is in the need to reconcile the (often secular citizenship/human rights) values of international law and the traditional moral teaching of religions (de Souza *et al.* 2006; Jackson *et al.* 2007; de Souza *et al.* 2010, forthcoming).

Box 14.2 SOURCES ON RELIGION AND POLITICS

- The International Association for Religious Freedom presents some useful and accessible case studies on the repression of religion in political contexts at www.iarf.net (and follow links).
- Among the oldest established networks for scholarly research on religion and politics is the *Journal of Church and State* (since 1949). It provides regular updates on the relationship between religion and politics worldwide, see www.baylor.edu (and follow links, especially to 'Church-State Notes').
- The charitable foundation, PEW, has a useful 'Forum on Religion in Public Life', see http://pewforum.org/religion-human-rights (and follow links).
- The Norwegian Ministry of Foreign Affairs funded international consultancy on religion in international diplomacy at the International Peace Research Institute, Oslo (PRIO), see www.prio.no (and links, especially links to Harpviken and Eggen Roislien 2005).
- The annual report on religious freedom by the US administration, at www.house.gov/international_relation (and follow links).
- Shattuck's (2003) keynote paper to a Harvard Conference on Religion, Democracy and Human Rights entitled 'Religion, Rights and Terrorism'; www.law.harvard.edu (and follow links).

Task 14.4 CLASH OF CIVILIZATIONS?

1   Visit the site of the United Nations Alliance of Civilizations www.unaoc.org (and follow links). Compare and contrast its underlying positive message with Huntington's more conflictual model. Which position has more justification?

2   Visit the QCA website at www.qca.org.uk, and follow the links for citizenship. Use 'Compare', the facility here that allows you to make comparisons between subjects, for example, on the importance of a subject, its key concepts, and so forth. For either Key Stage 3 or 4, compare and contrast citizenship and religious education. Create a group forum to interrogate critically how links might be made between the two subjects. Box 14.3 is an example of two statements on the importance of citizenship and religious education.

Box 14.3 THE IMPORTANCE OF CITIZENSHIP AND RELIGIOUS EDUCATION

Explanatory notes

The importance of citizenship: This reflects the three principles of effective citizenship education set out by the Advisory Group on Education for Citizenship and the Teaching of Democracy in Schools. These are that citizenship should develop social and moral responsibility, community involvement and political literacy.

The importance of citizenship

Education for citizenship equips young people with the knowledge, skills and understanding to play an effective role in public life. Citizenship encourages them to take an interest in topical and controversial issues and to engage in discussion and debate. Pupils learn about their rights, responsibilities, duties and freedoms, and about laws, justice and democracy. They learn to take part in decision making and different forms of action. They play an active role in the life of their schools, neighbourhoods, communities and wider society as active and global citizens. Citizenship encourages respect for different national, religious and ethnic identities. It equips pupils to engage critically with and explore diverse ideas, beliefs, cultures and identities and the values we share as citizens in the UK. Pupils begin to understand how society has changed and is changing in the UK, Europe and the wider world.

Citizenship addresses issues relating to social justice, human rights, community cohesion and global interdependence, and encourages pupils to challenge injustice, inequalities and discrimination. It helps young people to develop their critical skills, consider a wide range of political, social, ethical and moral problems, and explore opinions and ideas other than their own. They evaluate information, make informed judgements and reflect on the consequences of their actions now and in the future. They learn to argue a case on behalf of others as well as themselves and speak out on issues of concern.

Citizenship equips pupils with the knowledge and skills needed for effective and democratic participation. It helps pupils to become informed, critical, active citizens who have the confidence and conviction to work collaboratively, take action and try to make a difference.

The importance of religious education

Religious education provokes challenging questions about the ultimate meaning and purpose of life, beliefs about God, the self and the nature of reality, issues of right and wrong, and what it means to be human. It develops pupils' knowledge and understanding of Christianity, other principal religions, other religious traditions, and other worldviews that offer answers to these challenging questions. It offers opportunities for personal reflection and spiritual development. It enhances pupils' awareness and understanding of religions and beliefs, teachings, practices and forms of expression, as well as of the influence of religion on individuals, families, communities and cultures.

RE encourages pupils to learn from different religions, beliefs, values and traditions, while exploring their own beliefs and questions of meaning. It challenges pupils to reflect on, consider, analyse, interpret and evaluate issues of truth, belief, faith and ethics and to communicate their responses.

RE encourages pupils to develop their sense of identity and belonging. It enables them to flourish individually within their communities and as citizens in a diverse society and global community. RE has an important role in preparing pupils for adult life, employment and lifelong learning. It enables pupils to develop respect for and sensitivity to others, in particular those whose faiths and beliefs are different from their own. It promotes discernment and enables pupils to combat prejudice.

SUMMARY AND KEY POINTS

This chapter has provided some grounding in theoretical perspectives on the historical relationships between religion, politics and education. It has developed the notion of 'four critical contexts' in order to provide a framework for understanding the complex relationships between religion, politics and education, and as a backdrop for understanding some of the issues that affect citizenship and religious education. The chapter has also presented a wide range of national and international resources for the multifaceted relations between religion, politics and education. It has also included a number of practical ideas and tasks for making links between citizenship and religious education for general debate in your initial teacher education context and for practical application in the secondary school classroom.

NOTE

The chapter is a largely updated version of work published in *Learning to Teaching Religious Education in the Secondary School* edited by Barnes *et al.* (2008), with this current chapter containing entirely new activities that will help to explore the relationship between citizenship and religious education. It develops ideas originally delivered in germinal form at a presentation given at the Nobel Institute, Oslo, Norway. In addition to drawing upon published sources (Gearon 2002, 2003, 2003a, 2004, 2006, 2007, 2007a, 2008, 2008a), this report also draws upon some of my recent work with UNESCO in religious, citizenship and human rights education, and my contribution to a working consultation on *UNESCO Guidelines on Intercultural Education*, UNESCO Headquarters, Paris (Published November 2006, Paris). UNESCO have also formally published a precise record of our deliberations as *Expert Cultural Meeting on Intercultural Education Report, UNESCO Headquarters, Paris, 20–22 March 2006* (Published November 2006, Paris). The four critical contexts were presented (November 2006) for a UNESCO-funded International Symposium on Intercultural Understanding and Human Rights

Education, at the UNESCO Asia-Pacific Centre of Education for International Understanding, Seoul National University, Republic of Korea, and subsequently published in the *Journal of Religious Education* (an Australian-based international journal) in autumn 2006 as 'Between tolerance and dissent: religious, citizenship and human rights education' (*Journal of Religious Education*, 54(3): 54–62). A CitizED lecture on totalitarianism delivered in February 2005 formed the basis of some resource materials on the CitizED website (www.citized.info). The work was also the subject of a short Japanese lecture series (December 2006) at Kobe University, Aichi University of Education, Nagoya, and Sophia University, Tokyo, and presented at the European Forum of Teachers of Religious Education. I am grateful to all peer-review and other, less formal feedback from colleagues.

FURTHER READING

Arthur, J., Davies, I. and Hahn, C. (2008) *The SAGE Handbook of Education for Citizenship and Democracy*, London: SAGE.
This is an excellent overview of current scholarship and research in citizenship.

Burleigh, M. (2006) *Earthly Powers: Religion and politics in Europe from the Enlightenment to the Great War*, London: Harper Perennial.
A popular but scholarly work of history, highly informative.

Burleigh, M. (2007) *Sacred Causes: The clash of religion and politics from the Great War to the War on Terror*, New York: HarperCollins.
Another popular but scholarly work of history, and again highly informative, originally this and Burleigh (2006) were designed as a single volume.

Morgan, M.L. (ed.) (2005) *Classics of Moral and Political Theory*, 4th edition, Cambridge: Hackett.
A rich and accessible reader of important works in political philosophy.

PART V

RESEARCHING CITIZENSHIP

Local, national and international contexts

LEARNING FOR COSMOPOLITAN CITIZENSHIP

Theoretical debates and young people's experiences

Audrey Osler and Hugh Starkey

INTRODUCTION

Since citizenship is a contested concept, education for citizenship is also a site of debate and controversy. This chapter explores the limitations of education for national citizenship, and reflects on the deficit models of young people that are often presented in justifying citizenship education. Extending political theorist David Held's model of cosmopolitan democracy, the authors propose the term 'education for cosmopolitan citizenship'. They explore the features of education for citizenship in the context of globalisation, noting that citizenship education addresses local, national, regional and global issues. Such a perspective is critical in preparing young people to live together in increasingly diverse local communities and an interdependent world. The authors report on research carried out with young people living in multicultural communities in Leicester, UK, to explore understandings of community and levels of civic engagement. They explore the multiple identities and loyalties of these young people and identify sites of learning for citizenship in homes and communities. Drawing on these findings, the chapter concludes that a reconceptualised education for cosmopolitan citizenship needs to address peace, human rights, democracy and development, equipping young people to make a difference at all levels, from the local to the global.

OBJECTIVES

The objectives of this chapter are to:

▪ explore the limitations of education for national citizenship;

▪ reflect on the deficit models of young people used to justify citizenship education;

▪ argue the case for adopting a model of cosmopolitan democracy and, in secondary schooling, the term 'education for cosmopolitan citizenship';

▪ report on research carried out with young people living in multicultural communities in Leicester to explore understandings of community and levels of civic engagement;

▪ argue that a reconceptualised education for cosmopolitan citizenship needs to address peace, human rights, democracy and development, equipping young people to make a difference at all levels, from the local to the global.

Task 15.1 **SITES OF LEARNING FOR CITIZENSHIP**

To what extent do you agree that teachers of citizenship need to understand 'home and community sites of learning for citizenship'?

Make a list of the kinds of knowledge and skills relating to citizenship that young people might gain from involvement with, for example, religious organisations such as churches or mosques; sports clubs; political campaigning; meeting relatives and friends from around the world.

AIMS OF CITIZENSHIP EDUCATION

Education for citizenship is one response to the political and social realities of globalisation. Global migration, both of specialised labour and of individuals and groups displaced by war, political instability or dire economic conditions, has produced cosmopolitan societies across the world. Simultaneously, political movements based on ethnic, religious and narrowly nationalist ideologies threaten democracy and challenge existing political and social structures. In this context, education in general and education for citizenship in particular, provide the mechanism for transmitting the core shared values on which just and peaceful democratic societies may be built.

Citizenship, in a legal sense, is anchored in the rights and responsibilities deriving from sovereign nation states. However, it also has broader meanings deriving from international law. Migration requires individuals and groups to develop multiple loyalties and identities. This reality calls into question the idea of citizenship as having a unique focus of loyalty to a particular nation state. The tensions between competing views of citizenship are the site of much stimulating debate. In this chapter we confront some of these theoretical perspectives with the realities experienced by young people from a cosmopolitan urban area of Europe. This leads us to propose a reconceptualisation of education for citizenship so as to build on, rather than deny, multiple loyalties.

Since citizenship is a contested concept, education for citizenship is potentially a site of debate and controversy. In cosmopolitan societies, namely those characterised by a high degree of cultural diversity, one crucial area for debate is how citizenship education responds to this diversity and, in particular, the extent to which it addresses the formal and informal barriers to citizenship faced by minorities. Our contribution to the debate is to propose a model of citizenship education that draws on theories of cosmopolitan democracy. This has the advantage of acknowledging local, national and global contexts and the wide variety of experiences that learners might bring to their education.

Debates about citizenship and education are not the sole purview of academics. The fact remains that young people are rarely given opportunities to contribute and yet, as important stakeholders in education and in society, young people have much to contribute to such debates and to the formulation of a relevant and effective education for citizenship. Therefore, we set out to explore with young people in a cosmopolitan city in England their feelings about community and how they negotiate their multiple identities and sense of belonging within multi-localities. Through analysing data from interviews and workshop activities with these young people, we identify key sites of learning for citizenship within their communities (Osler and Starkey 2001a).

An understanding of home and community sites of learning for citizenship can inform teachers, curriculum planners and policy makers responsible for citizenship learning in schools. We argue that this understanding is critical if we are to build effectively on learners' experiences and develop a comprehensive and sustainable programme of education for cosmopolitan citizenship.

Here, preparation for citizenship is a key task of all state education systems. Whether through the whole curriculum or through specialised programmes, education provides socialisation into what has been termed the 'imagined community' of the nation (Anderson 1991). A major objective of education for national citizenship is to ensure that young people understand their present and future roles within the constitutional and legal framework of the state in which they live. They are expected to learn about and identify with the legal, political, religious, social and economic institutions of the country in which they are being educated (Torney-Purta *et al.* 2001). In democratic states, citizens are constitutionally entitled to equal rights to participate in, and to influence, government. However, in practice, this formal equality is undermined by discriminatory practices and public discourses that exclude minorities or which marginalise them within the imagined community of the nation. In such discourses the nation is often portrayed as having a homogeneous cultural identity into which minorities are expected to integrate.

In this respect, education for national citizenship often fails to engage with the actual experiences of learners, who, in a globalised world are likely to have shifting and multiple cultural identities and a sense of belonging that is not expressed first and foremost in terms of the nation (Alexander1996; Osler 1997; Hall 2000). Moreover, we suggest that such education tends to prepare young people for future citizenship without acknowledging their experiences and their existing citizenship rights. Young people are frequently presented as citizens-in-waiting (Verhellen 2000) and youth is often portrayed as threatening yet politically apathetic (Griffin 1997; Osler and Vincent 2003). Citizenship education programmes that build on these assumptions can, unintentionally, serve to alienate and exclude. Young people are likely to feel alienated by programmes that overlook their experiences and sites of learning for citizenship within communities. Where public discourse and discriminatory practices serve to undermine the citizenship rights of minorities, education for national citizenship can be doubly exclusionary.

Task 15.2 DISCOURSES OF SINGLE AND PLURAL IDENTITIES

Try to identify or find examples of political discourses (what ministers, MPs or commentators say) that encourage the notion of British people as having a single or predominant identity or characteristics.

What other discourses can you find in the media of plural identities held by British people?

CONTEXT

Current international interest in citizenship education stems from a number of political developments. First, there is the emergence of recently democratised states, such as South Africa and those of Central and Eastern Europe and Latin America. Citizenship education is essential to enable populations to understand democracy and its basis in human rights. Second, governments in established democracies, concerned at an apparent crisis of confidence in formal, established political processes including elections, see citizenship education as a means of restoring confidence in democracy. Third, globalisation has led to increased migration and consequent demographic changes. In urban areas in particular, school populations are characterised by increased cultural diversity and by the presence of refugees and asylum seekers. Citizenship education is intended to enable young people from different backgrounds to live together.

It is the issue of civic disengagement, analysed by writers such as Putnam (2000), that most concerns governments in the longer established democracies. As a consequence, the programmes of citizenship education in England, for example, are based on a view of young people that assumes that they are apathetic because they fail to understand the political basis of the state and they are ignorant of their responsibilities and their rights (Crick 2000). We have noted that this deficit model, which defines young people as less good citizens, can lead to compensatory programmes that are unlikely to engage them (Osler 2000; Starkey 2000; Osler and Starkey 2000). We therefore propose that education for citizenship be explicitly recognised as education for cosmopolitan citizenship. We develop this notion below, but note here that it implies learning to imagine the nation as a diverse and inclusive community. This appears to be an essential precondition for the renewal of democracy in a globalised world.

COSMOPOLITAN DEMOCRACY AND LEARNING FOR CITIZENSHIP

A number of political theorists argue that we need to rethink democracy in the context of our increasingly interdependent world. Held (1995, 1996) proposes a model of 'cosmopolitan democracy', challenging the notion that the nation state is the only locus for democracy and that the state alone has the power to guarantee the rights of its citizens. Processes of globalisation and increased interdependence mean that no one, wherever they live in the world, can remain completely isolated within a single nation. All human lives are increasingly influenced by events in other parts of the world. One of the most visible manifestations of this is that local communities have become more diverse. If democracy is now conceptualised as cosmopolitan, then the actors within the democracy are, by extension, cosmopolitan citizens. We have characterised education for cosmopolitan citizenship as incorporating the local, national, regional (for example, European) and global dimensions of citizenship education (Osler and Vincent 2002). The concept of cosmopolitan citizenship, currently the focus of considerable academic debate and discussion (see, for instance, Gilroy 1997; Hutchings and Dannreuter 1999; Kymlicka 2001), provides us with a theoretical construct that informs our analysis of education for citizenship.

Citizens now find themselves belonging to what Held (2001) calls 'overlapping communities of fate': local, regional, national, international and, increasingly, virtual. Even though they might have very different cultures and beliefs, their interests are tied up with others, not because they share a common national citizenship, but because they might be members of a diasporic group, have a common faith or political agenda, or live in a particular neighbourhood.

These changes provide opportunities for the development of new forms of inclusive democracy and democratic decision making. Held argues for the building of human rights into the constitution of states and for the democratisation of continental and global institutions. The Human Rights Act 1998, which incorporates the European Convention on Human Rights into UK law, is one example of the ways in which national institutions are voluntarily subjecting themselves to international standards. The setting up of an International Criminal Court is an illustration of a new supra-national institution, created in the image of those operating at national level. As Habermas notes:

> Even if we have a long way to go before fully achieving it, the cosmopolitan condition is no longer merely a mirage. State citizenship and world citizenship form a continuum whose contours, at least, are already becoming visible.
>
> (Habermas 1996: 515)

Doubts have been cast on whether changes such as these, in fact, constitute democratisation, given that international institutions are invariably intergovernmental and that it is unelected NGOs that take the lead in trying to influence decision making at a global level (Miller 1999; Kymlicka 2001). Despite these limitations and the lack of an institutional locus for the cosmopolitan citizen, the concept of cosmopolitan citizenship is helpful insofar as it recognises the existence of transnational and diasporic communities composed of individuals entitled to, and aware of, their human rights (Gilroy 1997).

DEFINING EDUCATION FOR COSMOPOLITAN CITIZENSHIP

Drawing on UNESCO's (1995) framework, we have identified some characteristics of the educated cosmopolitan citizen (Osler and Vincent 2002). We suggest that educated cosmopolitan citizens will be confident in their own identities and will work to achieve peace, human rights and democracy, within the local community and at a global level, by:

- accepting personal responsibility and recognising the importance of civic commitment;
- working collaboratively to solve problems and achieve a just, peaceful and democratic community;
- respecting diversity between people, according to gender, ethnicity and culture;
- recognising that their own worldview is shaped by personal and societal history and by cultural tradition;
- respecting the cultural heritage and protecting the environment;
- promoting solidarity and equity at national and international levels.

(Adapted from UNESCO 1995)

Task 15.3 **PROGRAMMES OF STUDY**

To what extent do the Programmes of Study for the National Curriculum for England for Citizenship provide opportunities to explore each of these dimensions?

YOUNG PEOPLE AND CITIZENSHIP PROGRAMMES

Young people are not usually invited to contribute to the process of formulating programmes of citizenship education and yet it is axiomatic in other areas of policy that user groups be consulted before key reforms are put in place. Young people's interests might be overlooked because they are perceived as citizens-in-waiting rather than as citizens in their own right and thus they are seen as lacking equal status with other stakeholders. Since most young people of school age are not entitled to vote in elections for local or national representatives, politicians are not directly accountable to them. It is also often assumed that as non-voters they are not involved or engaged in political processes. Consequently, little attempt is made to build on their existing political knowledge or experience and to use this as a foundation for citizenship learning in school. Disengagement from formal political parties is equated with widespread apathy, ignorance and complacency, despite evidence to suggest that many young people are finding alternative routes to political action (Roker *et al.* 1999). It is rarely acknowledged that, among those aged 18-plus, a decision not to vote could reflect a lack of confidence in politicians or in the efficacy of formal political processes.

Young people from minority ethnic backgrounds in postcolonial societies might be even more harshly judged. They might be subject to labelling and stigmatising on the basis of appearance (Jenkins 1996) and be considered as second-class citizens. Assumptions might concern nationality, residence status, language skills, capacity to operate effectively in society, religious affiliations and the compatibility of religious beliefs with social norms as defined by the majority community. Visible minorities are exposed to 'everyday racism' (Essed 1991) and 'street racism' (Parekh 2000). When those working in the police and in other public sector services make assumptions about members of ethnic minority groups on the basis of name or appearance (Banton 1997: 16), this amounts to 'institutional racism' (Macpherson 1999). Research from Canada confirms the findings of earlier ethnographic studies in English schools (for example, Wright 1986 and 1992) that teachers are not immune from such discriminatory judgements: '[In the school being studied] skin colour and its related physical traits serve perhaps more than any other characteristics to mark students. . . .Teachers often adjust their expectations of students on the basis of the latter's physical appearance' (Ryan 1999: 86).

As a consequence, and as we have previously demonstrated, those responsible for developing programmes of education for citizenship assume that young people from ethnic minorities require extra instruction in national citizenship and even special programmes not required by the majority (Osler 2000; Osler and Starkey 2001b). They fail to appreciate that these young people are likely to bring considerable insights to their citizenship learning.

THE RESEARCH PROJECT

We set out to explore with young people living in Leicester, a multicultural city in England, their sites of learning for citizenship. In particular we wished to gain insights into the opportunities they have to experience rules, rights, responsibilities and institutions. We recognise that: 'People learn to be responsible citizens not only in schools, but in the family, neighbourhood, churches and many other groups and forums in civil society' (Kymlicka 2001: 293).

The research project involved some 600 young people aged 10–18, from four schools in the city, who responded to a questionnaire. We also collected further data from volunteers who took part in two workshops we ran at each school. Here we draw on data from pupils in Year 9 (aged 13–14 years) attending school in two contrasting inner-city areas. Ours was an opportunity sample, but the demographic composition of the schools is in many ways typical of inner-city schools in Europe. For instance, in School A the vast majority of the pupils (87.3 per cent) described themselves as Indian, around 5 per cent from other Asian backgrounds, 4 per cent as white and 3.5 per cent as being of mixed descent. The school has a relatively stable pupil population. More than 80 per cent of our sample had lived in Leicester for 12 years or more, that is, for all or most of their lives. Many of the parents of these pupils were formerly pupils at the same school, and for many families this is the third generation living in Leicester, their grandparents having migrated to Britain from East Africa during the late 1960s and 1970s.

By contrast, School B has a very mobile school population; 77.8 per cent of our sample had lived in Leicester for four years or less. Around one-third had lived in the city for less than two years and had therefore joined the school since Year 7. A significant proportion of these had arrived in Britain from overseas, many of them as refugees and asylum seekers. There was greater ethnic diversity within the school population with 60 per cent of the pupils describing themselves as Indian, 11 per cent as Pakistani, 6.7 per cent as Bangladeshi and 4.3 per cent as from other Asian backgrounds. Some 4 per cent described their heritage as African, 3 per cent as Caribbean and around 3 per cent as white. A further 3.6 per cent described themselves as being of mixed descent. The self-descriptors of these pupils indicate considerable heterogeneity within each of these broad groupings.

At school A all those participating in workshops were members of the school council who volunteered to participate in the project. They had therefore worked together before and knew each other quite well. In school B workshop participants were selected and invited to participate by senior teachers. We asked for a group who would be at ease working with two 'unknown' adults. The young people were representative of the wider school population, in that they were drawn from a variety of religious and ethnic backgrounds, with some relatively new to the school. They did not all know each other well, although each pupil knew at least one other, being from the same tutor group.

YOUNG PEOPLE'S IDENTITY AND COMMUNITY

Seven of the eight pupils taking part in the workshops at the more settled school A, mentioned Leicester when writing about where they came from. Only two out of the seven pupils at school B mentioned Leicester. All but two of the total sample identify with other places as well as Leicester, even when it is the only place they have lived. For example, Ranjit, said he was: 'born and bred in Leicester. Parents from India and Africa'.

Abdul had recently returned to Leicester after his family fled from Malawi. He had lived in the city for less than a year, after growing up in East Africa:

> I am from Malawi and I was born in Leicester in the General Hospital. My father and mother are from Malawi and my grandmother is from India. We left Malawi because almost every day people were getting shot in their houses and one of them was my neighbour.

Changes in family circumstances, particularly parental separations, often meant a change of home:

I was born in Dominica (the Caribbean) but I came to England when I was only three. First I lived in Highfields with my mum and dad, then they split up and I lived with my dad in Beaumont Leys.

(Thabo)

I was born in Manchester and [lived there] until I was six months old. I moved from Manchester because my mum and dad had a divorce. My mum, dad and granddad are from Africa and my grandma is from India.

(Asha)

Many of the young people had strong affective ties with other countries and places. This was true whether they had lived most of their lives in Britain or were relatively new arrivals. International travel and visits to family overseas were often mentioned as particularly significant events in their lives.

I was born in England. I grew up with my parents. The place I lived in [in Pakistan] was a very nice place, it was very quiet and the neighbours we had were really kind and friendly. What I liked most is the sun always used to shine and how it was really hot.

(Rehana)

I was born in Keighley in West Yorkshire. I lived there for nine years and moved to Leicester when I was in Year 5. My parents are both from Bangladesh and I visited Bangladesh in 1995 and moved to Leicester in 1996.

(Najma)

These young people already identify with a range of places, beyond Leicester and the UK, giving them the potential to see themselves and to develop as cosmopolitan citizens.

Task 15.4 **SELF-DEFINITIONS**

What response would you personally give to the questions posed to the young people in this research, namely:

- Where do you come from?
- How do you define yourself in terms of ethnicity, culture, colour or race?
- What are the main communities where you live/study?

SELF-DEFINITIONS

The pupils were invited to write about how they defined themselves in terms of ethnicity, culture, colour or race. A number stressed their bilingualism. Many chose to explain their values, sometimes drawing on religious beliefs. Some chose to explain that theirs was an interfaith family. For example, after her parents' divorce, Asha continued to live with her mother, a Sikh, but she herself was brought up a Hindu. Asha identified with her religion, but was not uncritical, emphasising her opposition to the caste system.

For many, religion was an identifier, even when they professed to be 'not very religious':

> I am Hindu, born in Leicester and proud of being a Hindu.
>
> (Wayne)

> I believe in God. I am a Hindu, my language is Gujarati and I like my religion. I HATE people who are RACIST! I don't have a problem with people who have a different culture than me, I mix with other religions. I am a very strong believer in God.
>
> (Nadeera)

> I'm Asian and my religion is Islam. I live in a multicultural area with Christians, Sikhs, Muslims and Hindus.
>
> (Najma)

> I am Methodist. Don't really believe in God.
>
> (Ayleen)

Some chose to identify themselves without reference to religion, or by stressing they drew inspiration from a number of religions, but these were a minority. Rehana, for instance, refers to language and to the country of origin of her parents, but omits any reference to religion:

> My parents and my grandparents are both from Bangladesh. And we speak Bengali. I have been to Bangladesh and it is a nice place with a beautiful countryside.

CONCEPTS OF COMMUNITY

When asked in the questionnaire to name the main communities in Leicester, only a very few pupils from either school (about 3 per cent) named a geographical location such as their neighbourhood. Although a third of the pupils failed to respond to the question, perhaps implying that they were unclear of a meaning for the word 'community', over half the pupils responded unequivocally by naming religious or ethnic groups.

In the workshops, pupils were invited to create an exhibition of photographs illustrating themselves in their communities and to write descriptive captions. Their pictures were largely of friends, family, home and their neighbourhood. Although many lived within a few minutes walk of the city centre, only a few pupils chose to take photos there. The captions reveal much about their sense of community and belonging.

Rehana, for instance, sees community in terms of what she sees from her house and in her street. This includes the public facility of a park and two places of worship. This is a community in which she feels at ease, where she recognises people to be friendly. She gets a sense of occasion from crowds attending religious services:

This is St Peter's Church. I see lots of people go. I see weddings, funerals.

This is the big mosque in St Peter's. Lots of people go there every Friday to pray. The mosque is just behind my house. When it's a big day, I always go up in the attic to see people and I get a very good view.

I quite like my community where I live because I get a good view of everything. I have very good neighbours – they are very friendly. At the bottom of my street I have a small park and pond. Old people go there for a walk, it's a small pond. In the summer little kids go there to play.

Morgan, too, feels at ease in the cosmopolitan neighbourhood where he lives. He is proud of the cultural diversity he experiences, and he identifies with his place of worship as providing a focus to his week and a sense of historical continuity. The other key institution in his neighbourhood is the community centre, which he associates with leisure and relaxation:

My church is a very important place for me. I am not very religious but I love going to pray every Sunday. It's a really old building and on its other side there is our community centre. At my community centre is where people go and relax and chill. At the same centre there are clubs, karate, drama etc. I do karate at this centre and it is good fun.

My street is called G. It's in Highfields, there are many people living there, people of many cultures, religions and race. I like my street people and these many cultures which are fascinating and you can learn more in life with many cultures surrounding you.

Many of the young people had been involved in campaigns to save a local school and had been engaged in fundraising efforts for earthquake victims in Gujarat. They were clear about how they would improve their city: in general they were concerned about other neighbourhoods that were perceived to be dangerous because of 'bullies' and 'racists'. They wanted more cinemas, fewer racists and fewer gangsters, whom they explained spoiled their own neighbourhoods, smoking drugs and hanging about in groups, extorting money and ruining parks.

In general they had considerable sensitivity to injustice, although they were more likely to understand how to respond politically to local issues, than to injustices or inequalities in other parts of the world. The major response was to give charitably, and schools tended to support this approach. In the school with the relatively stable population there was significant hostility to refugees and asylum seekers, although some young people were aware that their own grandparents had arrived in Leicester as refugees and some were willing to defend the rights of current refugees and asylum seekers. There was an open approach to discussion on this issue and a willingness to engage in dialogue.

SITES OF CITIZENSHIP

As well as demonstrating strong affective ties, either to their immediate locality or to the city of Leicester, these young people identified a number of facilities within the city that they valued. These included public spaces such as parks, schools, shopping centres, community centres and libraries. They provided examples of experiences, such as visits to hospitals, housing and social security offices, and dealings with police and immigration officers, which enabled them to gain an understanding of services and procedures. These young people were often supporting and sometimes interpreting for an adult; on these occasions they were often required to present a case or act as an advocate. Individuals were gaining and practising skills for citizenship and these examples, together with others where young people gave informal help to neighbours and family members, illustrate sites of learning for citizenship in homes and community.

DISCUSSION

As we have argued, citizenship requires a sense of belonging (Osler and Starkey 1996). To neglect the personal and cultural aspects of citizenship is to ignore the issue of belonging. Cosmopolitan citizens have learnt to be confident in their own identities and schools can usefully provide learning opportunities to explore and develop these. Evidence from these young people suggests that they are engaging as citizens and learning the skills for cosmopolitan citizenship within their homes and communities.

The majority of young people we worked with identified strongly with their city and/or their local neighbourhood. Cosmopolitan citizenship does not mean asking individuals to reject their national citizenship or to accord it a lower status. Education for cosmopolitan citizenship is about enabling learners to make connections between their immediate contexts and the national and global contexts. It is not an add-on but rather it encompasses citizenship learning as a whole. It implies a broader under-standing of national identity. It also requires recognition that British identity, for example, may be experienced differently by different people.

Cosmopolitan citizenship implies recognition of our common humanity and a sense of solidarity with others. It is insufficient, however, to feel and express a sense of solidarity with others elsewhere if we cannot establish a sense of solidarity with others in our own communities, especially those others whom we perceive to be different from ourselves. The challenge is to accept shared responsibility for our common future and for solving our common problems. It implies dialogue and peer collaboration to address differences of opinion, as illustrated in the example of young people's discussion about the position of asylum seekers.

SUMMARY AND KEY POINTS

The young people in our research demonstrated multiple and dynamic identities, embracing local, national and international perspectives. An education for national citizenship is unlikely to provide a sufficiently comprehensive context for them to integrate their own experiences and identities.

We suggest that citizenship education requires reconceptualising in the context of globalisation. Our research suggests that education for cosmopolitan citizenship will enable all young people to perceive themselves as citizens with rights and responsibilities. It is not a process that can be realised exclusively at school. Learning is taking place beyond the school and the school needs to build on this learning and to encourage learners to make connections between their experiences and learning in the school and in the community. This implies that teachers need to be aware of sites of citizenship learning beyond the school.

We have argued that education for cosmopolitan citizenship addresses peace, human rights, democracy and development. It is about equipping young people with the knowledge, skills and attitudes to enable them to make a difference. It is orientated towards the future, preparing young citizens to play an active role in shaping the world, at all levels, from the local to the global. The processes of globalisation make this a critical task.

Task 15.5 COSMOPOLITAN CITIZENSHIP

How does Osler and Starkey's concept of cosmopolitan citizenship extend beyond notions of global citizenship found in the curriculum, and in textbooks and other resources?

FURTHER READING

Crick, B. (2000) *Essays on Citizenship*, London: Continuum.
    An authoritative collection from the late Sir Bernard Crick, one of the leading contemporary influences on citizenship education in England.

Kymlicka, W. (2001) *Politics in the Vernacular: Nationalism, multiculturalism and citizenship*, Oxford: Oxford University Press.
    Cutting-edge analysis from a leading social and political theorist

Habermas, J. (1996) *Between Facts and Norms*, London: Polity.
    A useful entry point to advanced theory, from a leading contemporary philosopher whose writings have been influential across a number of subject domains and disciplines.

Osler, A. and Vincent, K. (2002) *Citizenship and the Challenge of Global Education*, Stoke: Trentham.
    A more detailed exposition of cosmopolitan citizenship, by one of the authors of this chapter.

RESEARCH IN CITIZENSHIP

International, European and national

David Kerr

INTRODUCTION

The last decade has seen citizenship education move rapidly up the policy agenda for national governments and supranational organisations, such as the Council of Europe. This has been in response to a number of drivers. They include: concern about weakening political and civic engagement in society, particularly among the young; increased movement of peoples within and across countries and the pressures on community cohesion and intercultural relations; enlargement of supranational entities such as the European Union (EU); the impact of global events, particularly 9/11 and the London, Madrid and Mumbai attacks; and concerns about combating terrorism and extremism.

The result has been considerable growth of, and focus on, developing effective policies and practices for citizenship in the twenty-first century at national, European and international levels. The growth of policies and practices has been matched by increasing research in citizenship at international, European and national levels. The aim of this chapter is to introduce you to some of the key research in citizenship and to encourage you to think about how you can make best use of it in your practice. In short, everyone involved in citizenship should be interested in what research is telling us, and everyone has the opportunity to add to the evidence base.

OBJECTIVES

By the end of this chapter you should be able to:

- understand why research in citizenship is important;
- be aware of the key issues under investigation in citizenship research;
- recognise and find the major research studies in citizenship;
- be aware of what some of the research studies are telling us;
- consider how you can make use of citizenship research findings.

WHY RESEARCH IN CITIZENSHIP?

There are four main reasons for research in citizenship:

1   Citizenship is a new and developing area of growing importance at national, European and international levels with much scope for research.
2   There is much that remains unknown about the most effective policies and practices in citizenship.
3   Practitioners and policy makers can use research findings to improve their practice.
4   Research findings can help to frame further research.

Now, we look at each reason briefly, in turn.

A new area

Unlike other areas, there is not a long tradition of citizenship in schools and communities in England, and elsewhere. Accordingly, there is not a long track record of research in this area, particularly concerning citizenship in schools and colleges. Therefore, the foundations upon which policy and practice are built are not as extensive as in other areas.

Much still to be researched

There is plenty still to explore and understand about citizenship and much work for researchers. As Gearon notes in his review of citizenship education (2003: 20):

> It cannot be emphasised too strongly that citizenship education research, like the National Curriculum, is in a very early stage of development. Nevertheless this is also an exciting time for researching an area of developing importance in a devolved UK context, within Europe, and in wider international context.

Researchers have responded to this challenge, and there is now a growing body of evidence available about citizenship education in England, as well as in Europe and internationally. The grey areas of understanding are rapidly being investigated and the research and knowledge map for citizenship education is being filled in.

Central to reflecting on and improving practice

It is not sufficient to research for research's sake. There need to be clear aims and goals to the research that is carried out in citizenship. Many of these aims and goals concern encouraging policy makers, practitioners in schools and young people to reflect on the outcomes of research in relation to their own practices in order to make those practices more effective. Research in citizenship is therefore vital in laying the foundations for more effective policies and practices.

A help in framing further research

The findings from citizenship research can help to generate further research, both through sharpening up existing research questions and stimulating new ones. It is important to continually review and link up emerging research findings in order to build a stronger empirical base for citizenship.

Task 16.1 **WHY RESEARCH IN CITIZENSHIP?**

Consider the reasons given for *Why Research in Citizenship?*

- How far do you agree with them?
- Using the information in this chapter and in the Further reading section draw up a list of the main reasons why research in citizenship can be useful to you and your practice.
- Compare your list with tutors and fellow student teachers.

WHAT ARE THE KEY RESEARCH ISSUES AND STUDIES IN CITIZENSHIP?

The majority of research in citizenship, whether at national, European or international level, addresses some aspects of three related sets of research issues:

1 Issues concerning the *aims and organisation of citizenship programmes in schools and colleges*:
   - status, goals, priorities and reach, instructional principles, influence on identity development and conflict resolution.
2 Issues that focus on *pupils*:
   - definitions and understandings, rate of development, extent of participation opportunities, and impact of gender and socioeconomic differences.
3 Issues that focus on *teachers and teaching* and on *schools and colleges*:
   - teaching approaches, classroom practices, effectiveness of training and impact of school organisation.

The focus of citizenship research at all levels is influenced by the overall context of renewed interest in this area and by the moves in many countries to include citizenship as a new or revised part of the school curriculum. This is certainly true of the current research context in England. Because policy for citizenship is new and practices are still evolving, there is a particular focus in citizenship education research on the:

- nature of the policy-making process:
  - particularly of cross-national comparison

- state and effectiveness of emerging practices concerning:
  - active citizenship and participation
  - citizenship in the curriculum
  - citizenship in the school culture
  - citizenship in the wider community
- establishment of baseline data concerning policy, practice and attitudes:
  - particularly the attitudes of young people, teachers and school leaders
  - at international, cross-national and national levels.

This focus is reflected in recent citizenship research at international, European and national levels. The main studies of which you should be aware are introduced, in brief, below. The list is not exhaustive but provides a sound starting-point for raising your awareness of research in citizenship. The key findings from some of these studies are examined later in this chapter.

International

The main focus has been on cross-national comparison of pupil attitudes and experiences of citizenship in classrooms, schools and communities. This has been driven by the need to provide policy makers and practitioners with a stronger evidence base to inform the making of policy and development of practice. It is reflected in the leading international study:

IEA Civic Education Study (CIVED) – this remains the largest and most important international study of citizenship. It was conducted between 1996 and 2002 and involved 28 countries, including England, 24 of which were European. The main goal was to examine, in a comparative framework, the ways in which young people are prepared to undertake their role as citizens in democracies. The study provided the first large-scale evidence base for policy makers concerning the development of citizenship education in schools and communities across the world (Torney-Purta *et al.* 1999, 2001; Steiner-Khamsi *et al.* 2003).

European

The main focus has been on cross-national comparison in establishing a baseline concerning:

- nature of the policy-making process;
- state and effectiveness of emerging practices concerning:
  - citizenship education in schools
  - citizenship education in the curriculum
  - citizenship education and participation in school and community life;
- nature and measurement of citizenship outcomes.

This focus is reflected in the three leading European research initiatives:

Council of Europe All-European Study on Education for Democratic Citizenship (EDC) Policies – this study sought to provide a systematic description of EDC policies across Europe. The study looked to: identify the current policies on EDC in all European countries (including the UK – England, Northern Ireland, Scotland and Wales); map the concrete measures taken by governments to ensure the effective implementation of these policies; collect the views of a sample of practitioners and stakeholders on the implementation of EDC policies in their country. The outcomes included a detailed synthesis (Birzea *et al.* 2004) and five regional studies (Froumin 2004; Kerr 2004a; Losito 2004; Mikkelsen 2004; Pol 2004).

Eurydice Survey Citizenship Education at School in Europe – an overarching survey of the provision of citizenship education in schools in 30 European countries. The survey provides the most up-to-date overview of approaches and challenges in citizenship education (Eurydice 2005).

European Commission initiative to develop programmes and indicators for civic competence and active citizenship – an initiative linked to the 2000 Lisbon Objectives in education and training where eight key competencies were identified that Europeans need to acquire by 2010 if Europe is to respond to globalisation and the shift to knowledge-based economies. Among these eight key competencies is *social and civic knowledge* linked to the capability to be an active citizen. The outcomes include a framework to develop indicators for active citizenship and attempts to measure and map active citizenship in Europe (Hoskins 2006; Hoskins *et al.* 2006).

National (England)

Research in England has followed the policy initiative to introduce citizenship into schools, colleges and local communities. Research has focused on:

- state and effectiveness of emerging practices concerning:
  - active citizenship and participation
  - citizenship in the curriculum
  - citizenship in the school culture
  - citizenship in the wider community
- establishment of baseline data concerning policy, practice, attitudes and research concerning:
  - what research tells us to aid policy and practice
  - the attitudes of young people, teachers and school leaders to citizenship education
  - and how England compares at international and cross-national levels.

There are differing types of research on citizenship in England. They include comparative/baseline research, literature reviews and research studies.

COMPARATIVE/BASELINE RESEARCH

The main comparative studies are explored under International and European above and provide details of how policies, practices and attitudes in England compare to those in other countries. Such information affords a broader canvas on which to compare and contrast national developments. It has the potential to provide fresh insights concerning citizenship practice in schools, colleges and communities.

IEA CIVIC EDUCATION STUDY (CIVED) (KNOWN AS THE IEA CITIZENSHIP EDUCATION STUDY IN ENGLAND)

As noted above, this remains the most important, and largest, international study of citizenship education ever undertaken. England was one of 28 countries that participated. In England, 3,043 14-year-olds, 384 teachers and 118 head teachers, drawn from a representative sample of 128 schools, participated in the study. England's findings provided a baseline for citizenship education prior to the introduction of statutory citizenship in schools (Kerr 1999; Kerr *et al.* 2002; Kerr 2004b).

LITERATURE REVIEWS

Literature reviews are helpful in summarising the state of current research evidence and knowledge concerning aspects of citizenship education. They enable a snapshot to be provided at a given point in time and the identification of gaps in knowledge and understanding that further research should address. The most recent literature reviews concerning citizenship are those by EPPI and BERA.

EVIDENCE FOR POLICY AND PRACTICE INFORMATION AND CO-ORDINATING CENTRE (EPPI-CENTRE)

The EPPI-Centre was established in 1993 to address the need for a systematic approach to the organisation and review of evidence-based work on social interventions. The EPPI-Centre has carried out two systematic reviews of evidence about citizenship education: the first concerning the impact of citizenship education on the provision of schooling, and the second on the impact of citizenship education on pupil learning and achievement (Deakin Crick *et al.* 2004a, 2004b).

BERA REVIEW ON EDUCATION FOR DEMOCRATIC CITIZENSHIP 1995–2005

The British Educational Research Association (BERA) has commissioned a series of reviews to investigate historical and current developments in particular areas. They have conducted two such reviews of citizenship (Gearon 2003; Osler and Starkey 2006). The latest review examines developments in education for democratic citizenship during the decade 1995 to 2005. The review identifies key themes in citizenship research and gaps in the research literature. It concludes by setting an ongoing agenda for citizenship research (Osler and Starkey 2006).

RESEARCH STUDIES

There are a growing number of research studies under way in citizenship education at a range of levels from individual classroom to national. There is only space here to highlight the largest study.

CITIZENSHIP EDUCATION LONGITUDINAL STUDY (CELS)

The *Citizenship Education Longitudinal Study (CELS)* has been commissioned by DfES (now DCSF) and is being carried out by NFER. The study is groundbreaking in its duration and scope. It began in 2001 and runs through to 2010 and is the largest study of its kind in the world. It is tracking a cohort of young people (from age 11 to 18) who entered secondary school in September 2002 and are the first pupils to have a continuous statutory entitlement to citizenship. The overarching aim of the study is to 'assess the short-term and long-term effects of citizenship education on the knowledge, skills, attitudes and behaviour of pupils'.

The research design of the study is based on three interrelated components:

- four cross-sectional surveys of Year 8, 10 and 12 pupils, their schools and their teachers;
- a longitudinal survey of a cohort of Year 7 pupils tracking the whole Year 7 group through Years 9 and 11 and 13 (or equivalent when they are aged 18), their schools and their teachers;
- twelve longitudinal school case studies.

The CELS study has, to date, produced six annual reports and a number of literature reviews (Kerr *et al.* 2003, 2004; Kerr and Cleaver 2004; Cleaver *et al.* 2005; Whiteley 2005; Ireland *et al.* 2006; Benton *et al.* 2008). It provides the most detailed findings concerning approaches to citizenship in schools in England.

WHAT IS RESEARCH IN CITIZENSHIP TELLING US?

Citizenship research and its key findings are not always in a form that is readily accessible to student teachers, tutors and practitioners. They can be contained in long reports, dense research summaries and academic books and conference papers. They are not in a form that easily bridges the gap between research findings and the realities of daily practice. Rather, there is a need for that gap to be bridged if the findings are to succeed in having impact on daily practices. In this spirit, this section of the chapter summarises the key findings from some of the major international and European citizenship research studies referenced above. It is followed in the next section by an example of making the findings from the CELS study accessible to those working in schools.

IEA Civic Education Study (CIVED)

The study has provided a number of critical findings concerning the state of citizenship education in Europe and how to progress it. They include:

Task 16.2 **WHAT IS RESEARCH IN CITIZENSHIP TELLING US?**

Access *one* of the citizenship studies referenced in this chapter. Use the list of questions below to read, review and reflect on the study. Compare your findings with those of other student teachers. How useful were the questions? What other ones would you ask and why?

When reading or reviewing research in citizenship education there are a number of questions that can be used to help sharpen your review and reflection on the research findings. They include:

- How is the research framed? What are its key aims and purposes?
- What key research issues is the research addressing?
- What specific aspects are being addressed – teachers, teaching, schools, pupils or citizenship education programmes, or a mixture of these?
- What is the context for the research? What research methodology is being employed and why?
- How well do the research findings provide answers to the research issues originally addressed?
- To what extent are the research findings applicable to contexts and practices that I know – in my own practice and that of student teachers and tutors in schools?
- How can I use the research findings to help reflect on and improve my own practice and the practice of others with whom I work closely?
- How far do the research findings throw up further research questions and issues? How can I take these issues forward in my own practice?

- *Citizenship education is a complex enterprise*, which involves a variety of citizenship dimensions (knowledge, skills, concepts, attitudes, engagement and participation) and a range of educational approaches and opportunities for young people, both in and out of school.
- *Pupils with higher levels of civic knowledge are more likely to expect to participate in political and civic activities as adults*, and schools have an important role to play in shaping future participation by teaching about topics such as elections and voting.
- *Schools that model democratic values and practices*, through encouraging pupils to discuss issues in the classroom and take an *active role* in the life of school, are *most effective in promoting civic knowledge and engagement*. However, this is not the norm for many pupils.
- *Four out of five pupils indicated that they do not intend to participate in conventional political activities (with the exception of voting) and young people are only moderately interested in politics*. Young people appear to be more open to other forms of civic and political engagement such as charity work or non-violent protest marches.

- *Schools and community organisations have untapped potential to influence positively the civic preparation of young people.* Pupils believe that working with other young people can help to solve problems. The large majority of pupils across countries have had some positive experience with pupils getting together at school, in either formal or informal groups, to solve problems and improve the school. The school environment provides pupils with opportunities to take part in 'real actions' that matter to them.
- *Pupil attitudes may suggest the growth of a 'new civic culture'*, which is characterised by less hierarchy and more individual decision making. Young people appear to be gravitating towards actions linked to more informal social movement groups rather than to more formal conventional political parties and groupings.

The findings have been eagerly picked up by national governments and supranational organisations in Europe and used to inform approaches to policy and practice.

Council of Europe All-European EDC Policy Study

The synthesis and regional studies found that:

- There is a real 'compliance gap' between EDC declarations and what happens in practice; indeed a gulf, in many countries.
- The main 'pillar' for EDC is the formal school curriculum. This is because a curriculum already exists providing a ready-made framework and the possibility of a structured approach, particularly with regard to the transfer of knowledge.
- There is beginning to emerge a more diversified approach to EDC that goes beyond the curriculum. It encompasses whole-school and wider community dimensions as well as formal and non-formal education and training routes.
- There are a number of challenges that remain to be addressed concerning EDC, including: establishing stronger partnerships between stakeholders and practitioners; developing more effective and comprehensive teacher education, at both initial and in-service levels; and introducing a culture of, and suitable measures for monitoring, quality assurance and evaluation.

Above all, the All-European Policy Study confirmed the considerable interest in EDC policy and practices across Europe. It also revealed a growing recognition that the development and growth of effective EDC policy, legislation and practice is not a 'quick fix' policy solution but a long-term process that requires vision, adequate resources and considerable effort and patience.

Eurydice survey Citizenship Education at School in Europe

The Eurydice survey showed the considerable strides made by citizenship education in Europe. The main findings were:

- Most European countries now provide citizenship education in schools. It is more visible and part of ongoing educational reforms in many countries, with agreement among governments about its positive impact on young people and society. Citizenship education is seen as a way of facing up to the challenges of the twenty-first century.
- Though all European countries agree on the need for citizenship education in the school curriculum, there is no single prevailing general approach across countries.
- Citizenship education is not just about importing knowledge but also developing positive civic attitudes and values and the promotion of active participation by pupils at school and in society.
- Support for the importance of a 'democratic school culture' and opportunities for pupil participation.
- Measuring the success of citizenship education remains a challenge, particularly the assessment of pupils and the evaluation of schools.
- There is a need for more teacher education to support successful citizenship on a more formal and systematic basis.
- There is a requirement for the development of a European/international dimension as part of citizenship education in schools.
- More research into teaching methods and outcomes and how they should be evaluated and monitored is needed.

These findings have been taken forward at a national and also at a supranational level by organisations such as the European Commission (EC) and Council of Europe.

Task 16.3 WHAT CAN WE LEARN FROM RESEARCH IN CITIZENSHIP?

Review the citizenship research studies referenced in this chapter. Then compile and compare two lists:

- What can England learn from research about citizenship policy and practice in other countries?
- What can research about England contribute to citizenship policy and practice in other countries?
  Discuss your conclusions with other student teachers and tutors.

HOW CAN YOU MAKE USE OF CITIZENSHIP RESEARCH FINDINGS?

As noted in the previous section, citizenship research and its findings can be impenetrable to all bar researchers. However, there are growing attempts to make research findings accessible to, and usable by, a wide range of audiences, including those working in schools and young people. The following is an example of an attempt to synthesise and make more accessible the latest findings from the groundbreaking CELS study about citizenship in schools in England (Lopes and Kerr 2005).

Key findings from the CELS study

To date, the CELS study has improved our understanding of citizenship by:

- identifying the main drivers of citizenship provision in schools in England;
- determining the factors, at management, institution and learning context levels, that underlie successful citizenship provision in schools and colleges;
- ascertaining the views of young people about their citizenship experiences in schools and colleges and about wider citizenship issues.

WHAT ARE THE MAIN APPROACHES TO CITIZENSHIP EDUCATION IN SCHOOLS?

The study has identified four main drivers of school approaches to citizenship: schools that are *citizenship rich driven*, others that are *efficacy driven*, those that are *curriculum driven* and those that are *participation driven* in terms of citizenship (see Figure 16.1).

The main difference in the typology is the relative emphasis that schools give to citizenship in terms of *curriculum* provision and *active citizenship* developments in the school and wider community. *Citizenship rich driven* schools are the most advanced in terms of curriculum provision and active citizenship developments, whereas in *participation driven* schools there is the greatest scope for improvement in both areas.

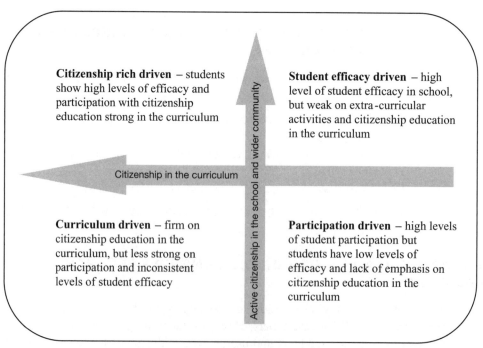

Citizenship rich driven – students show high levels of efficacy and participation with citizenship education strong in the curriculum

Student efficacy driven – high level of student efficacy in school, but weak on extra-curricular activities and citizenship education in the curriculum

Citizenship in the curriculum

Active citizenship in the school and wider community

Curriculum driven – firm on citizenship education in the curriculum, but less strong on participation and inconsistent levels of student efficacy

Participation driven – high levels of student participation but students have low levels of efficacy and lack of emphasis on citizenship education in the curriculum

■ **Figure 16.1** Four drivers of school approaches to citizenship

Student efficacy driven and *curriculum driven* schools each have their own strengths: namely, active citizenship in the former and citizenship in the curriculum in the latter. In a nationally representative sample of schools, about one-third of the schools surveyed fall into the *citizenship rich* category and one-quarter into each of the *student efficacy* and *curriculum driven*. This suggests that though progress has been made citizenship education provision in schools in England, it remains uneven. Many schools are still to develop a holistic approach to citizenship education.

HOW AND WHERE ARE SCHOOLS AND COLLEGES PROVIDING CITIZENSHIP OPPORTUNITIES?

Citizenship is delivered most typically in school and college contexts where:

- citizenship is delivered through PSHE (Personal Social and Health Education) and/or though assemblies;
- school/college is viewed as an institution that is 'moderately democratic' by staff;
- there is a traditional teaching and learning environment, where note taking and listening while the teacher/tutor talks are more prevalent than more active discursive approaches;
- there is a positive classroom climate (that is, pupils feel free to express their opinions and bring up issues for discussion);
- there are a variety of extra-curricular opportunities on offer for pupils;
- there is less of a concentration, according to pupils, on teaching about *political literacy* (that is, political and legal processes and institutions) and more on other citizenship topics.

WHAT FACTORS UNDERPIN THE MOST SUCCESSFUL PROVISION?

There is a series of factors – at management, institution and learning context levels – that underpin the most successful provision of citizenship education in schools and colleges. These include:

At management level

- *senior managers* who actively support and promote citizenship education in the school and college;
- *sufficient resources* allocated to citizenship education, including time (for example, curriculum space and time for planning);
- *an effective and manageable assessment strategy* through which pupils' achievements can be recognised;
- *ongoing planning and reviewing* to sustain the development of citizenship.

At institution level

- *a clear and coherent understanding* of what citizenship education means;
- *high status of citizenship*, promoted by a well-respected coordinator who is 'a citizenship champion';

- *staff training and development* that builds confidence and improves teaching and learning strategies;
- *a participatory school/college ethos* that supports the aims of citizenship education and positive relationships within the school/college community;
- *delivery approaches* that are diverse and effectively link the curriculum, school/college and wider community dimensions of citizenship education;
- *tailoring of citizenship education* to the needs, skills, interests and experiences of young people.

At learning-context level

- *positive relationships between the school/college and the wider community* that enable the school/college to foster opportunities for the pupils to engage with individuals and organisations beyond the school/college;
- *dedicated and enthusiastic staff*, with the skills to facilitate as well as teach;
- *dedicated timeslot for citizenship*, whether as a discrete course, a module within a programme or a specific project;
- *involvement and participation of pupils* in decisions about their learning, and the development of a pupil voice;
- *focus on critically active forms of learning*, including discussion, debate, dialogue and reflection. The best examples are where pupils are helped to think, reflect and take action.

WHAT FACTORS IMPACT ON PUPILS' DEVELOPMENT OF CITIZENSHIP KNOWLEDGE, UNDERSTANDING, SKILLS AND ATTITUDES?

Broadly, these influencing factors can be divided into two groups:

- *school/college factors*: citizenship (education) experiences offered by schools and colleges;
- *pupil background factors*: personal, family and community characteristics (for example, home literacy resources, age, ethnicity, gender).

The following are important and influential factors:

- *school/college experiences of citizenship* – pupils currently define citizenship as more to do with rights and responsibilities and issues of identity and equality than with political literacy and formal political processes;
- *home literacy resources* – the more books pupils have at home, the higher their civic knowledge and the greater their intended future political engagement;
- *age/year group* – pupils' sense of belonging to the school community increases with age in comparison to attachment to other communities;
- *ethnicity* – Asian and black pupils have the most positive views about volunteering compared to other groups;
- *gender* – compared to boys, girls think that volunteering has fewer costs and more benefits.

This suggests that young people's development of citizenship-related dimensions is influenced not only by their experiences in school and college (both in the curriculum and in the school/college community) but also by their wider experiences beyond school.

The CELS study findings suggest a number of key considerations for reviewing citizenship in schools and colleges (see Box 16.1 below).

Box 16.1 **KEY CONSIDERATIONS FOR REVIEWING CITIZENSHIP EDUCATION IN SCHOOLS AND COLLEGES**

1   What is the status of citizenship in the school/college?
2   How is citizenship education provision approached in the school/college?
3   What citizenship opportunities are provided for pupils?
4   What is the impact of school and other factors on pupils' citizenship experiences and development?
5   What factors underpin citizenship developments in the school/college?
6   How can the school/college move its citizenship provision and practice forward?

Task 16.4 **MAKING RESEARCH IN CITIZENSHIP MORE ACCESSIBLE**

1   Read the CELS study synthesis above:
   • In what ways and how well does the review succeed in linking research to practice?
   • To which audiences is the review accessible and why?

Use the synthesis to prepare a CPD session on the outcomes from the CELS study in relation to a school with which you are familiar. Discuss the session with tutors and fellow student teachers.

2   Choose a piece of research with which you are familiar and write a synthesis for fellow student teachers or tutors. Show the outcome to these audiences and discuss its usefulness. What did you learn from the process?

If you are feeling brave write the synthesis so that it is accessible to young people.

SUMMARY AND KEY POINTS

This chapter has underlined the increase in the volume and availability of research in citizenship over the past decade. This has taken place at all levels from international and European to national and local. The increased activity has been driven by rapid developments in policy and practice in citizenship. This has whetted the appetite of policy makers and practitioners to construct a strong evidence base that they can use to take decisions in moving this new area forward. There have been a series of major international and European studies that have established comparative base-lines about citizenship within and across countries. These have been supported by increasing national research that focuses in more detail on the processes, practices and outcomes of citizenship in and beyond schools.

One of the challenges is keeping up with current research in citizenship and making the findings relevant and usable by a wide range of audiences, including student teachers, tutors, school leaders, teachers and even young people. Though gaps in our knowledge and understanding about citizenship are rapidly being filled in, there is still much that we do not know about. There remains, therefore, a considerable research agenda still to tackle for this area.

Some of the main ongoing developments in citizenship research that you should be aware of and attempt to follow include:

International

- *IEA International Civic and Citizenship Education Study (ICCS)*. This study builds on the previous CIVED study. It currently involves nearly 40 countries, including England. Its main aim is to investigate the ways in which young people are prepared to undertake their roles as citizens in a range of countries in the twenty-first century. It also includes regional modules for Europe, Latin America and Asia. The ICCS study will report in 2010 (IEA 2008).

European

- Ongoing research by the European Commission on measuring civic competence and active citizenship in Europe. This is working towards reporting on the 2010 Lisbon Process and will include analysis of the latest data from European countries participating in ICCS (Hoskins *et al*. 2008).
- Research on pupil assessment in citizenship across European countries. A report on a cross-European project will be published in spring 2009 (Kerr *et al*. 2009). Pupil assessment remains an under-researched area.

National

- The *CELS study* has one more annual report to come, looking at change in citizenship in schools over time. There will also be final outcomes summing up the short-term and long-term effects of introducing citizenship into schools in England. The final outcomes will be published in 2010.

FURTHER READING

Citizenship research at NFER

The NFER website contains details about current and previous citizenship research studies, involving NFER, at international, European and international levels. There is also a bibliography of key texts and direct access to key research findings. The site includes: the latest findings from the Citizenship Education Longitudinal Study (CELS), as well as previous annual reports and literature reviews; details about the IEA CIVED study (England and international); and information about the new IEA ICCS study. Information can be accessed at: www.nfer.ac.uk/research-areas/citizenship/.

CitizED Project

CitizED project is funded by the Training and Development Agency (TDA) and focuses on citizenship teacher education. The website provides useful links to citizenship developments at primary, secondary, post-16, cross-curricular and community levels. There are also direct links to: EPPI literature reviews; research commissioned by CitizED; useful bibliography; and the e-journal *International Journal of Citizenship Teaching and Learning*. Information can be accessed at: www.citized.info/.

IEA International Civic and Citizenship Education Study (ICCS)

The ICCS website provides up-to-date information about the new IEA International Civic and Citizenship Education Study (ICCS). It includes details about the study's research questions and framework as well as details about the international consortium partners and participating countries. There are also direct links to papers and publications relating both to ICCS as well as the earlier IEA CIVED study. Information can be accessed at: http://iccs.acer.edu.au/index.php?page=home.

The SAGE Handbook of Education for Citizenship and Democracy (2008)

The SAGE Handbook (edited by Arthur, Davies and Hahn) provides the most comprehensive overview of developments in citizenship education currently available. It brings together leading researchers, practitioners and policy makers involved in education for citizenship and democracy. The five sections of the handbook cover: key ideas about citizenship education; geographical-based national case study overviews involving comparative research; key perspectives such as anti-racism and gender; different characterisations of citizenship and the pedagogy of citizenship. The breadth of coverage of issues and scope of the handbook is unparalleled: to be dipped in and out for reference and information. Details available at: www.sagepub.co.uk/refbooks ProdDesc.nav?prodId=Book230964.

APPENDIX 1

Useful websites and organisational links

Rather than present extensive lists of websites, provided here are a number of key hubs that will provide further useful links to organisation resources for teaching and learning citizenship.

Association for Citizenship Teaching (ACT)

ACT is the leading professional association for teachers of citizenship education in England, and provides much useful support for new entrants to the profession as well as experienced practitioners, visit www.teachingcitizenship.org.uk.

British Educational Research Association (BERA)

The BERA website contains downloadable reviews of citizenship research, including Gearon (2003) *How Do We Learn to Become Good Citizens?: a professional user review of UK research* and Osler and Starkey (2006) *Education and Democratic Citizenship* 1995–2005, visit www.bera.ac.uk (and follow links).

CitizED

www.citized.info (and follow links) provides a major source of current information on citizenship for schools and universities, including links to the Citizenship Foundation and Institute for Citizenship, and other agencies responsible for promoting citizenship education.

Citizenship Foundation

The Citizenship Foundation is a well-established and important resource for citizenship education, and a major hub for teaching and learning resources and organisational links, www.citizenshipfoundation.org.uk.

Community Service Volunteers (CSV)

CSV is a useful resource for learning beyond the classroom and active participation, visit www.csv.org.uk.

Council of Europe

The Council of Europe is a human rights-focused organisation of over 50 member state countries of Europe. The Council of Europe dedicated 2005 as the European Year of Citizenship through Education and its website provides a Europe-wide resource of recent research in Education for Democratic Citizenship, www.coe.org.

Department for Children, Schools and Families (DCSF)

The DCSF is the government department responsible for all aspects of education in England, and its website includes many links to citizenship education, www.dcsf. gov.uk.

Education Resources Information Center (ERIC)

ERIC is reputed to be the world's largest digital library and an invaluable research tool in education, including citizenship, visit www.eric.ed.gov (and follow links).

Equality and Human Rights Commission

The Equality and Human Rights Commission is an important source of legal and related information about all aspects of equality and human rights within the UK, www. equalityhumanrights.com.

European Union

The newly expanded European Union has, like the Council of Europe a considerable interest in harmonising notions of European identity, and thus prioritising notions of citizenship across its member states, visit http://europa.eu.int (and follow links).

Eurydice

This hub provides excellent empirical resources for education and, in particular, citizenship across Europe, visit www.eurydice.org (and follow links).

Evidence for Policy and Practice Information and Co-ordinating Centre

EPPI is based at the Institute of Education. It has undertaken systematic reviews of empirical research in citizenship education. It is a most useful hub for research; visit http://eppi.ioe.ac.uk (and follow links).

IEA

The International Association for the Evaluation of Educational Achievement (IEA 2004) *Civic Knowledge and Engagement at Age 14 in 28 Countries: results from the IEA Civic Education Study*, visit www.indiana.edu and www.iea.nl (and follow links).

Institute for Citizenship

The Institute for Citizenship is a well-established and important resource for citizenship education, and like the Citizenship Foundation a major hub for teaching and learning resources and organisational links, www.instituteforcitizenship.org.org.

Learning and Skills Development Agency (LSDA)

The LSDA is a generic education site but has especially useful support for post-16 citizenship, visit www.post16citizenship.org.

National Foundation for Educational Research (NFER)

This is a major funder of educational research generally with a considerable interest and track record in empirical research in citizenship, visit www.nfer.ac.uk (and follow links).

Office for Standards in Education (Ofsted)

A general rather than citizenship-specific resource, Ofsted nevertheless provide critical material on all aspects of the inspection of standards across education, including initial teacher education, as well as reports on citizenship www.ofsted.gov.uk.

Office of Public Sector Information (OPSI) and the UK Parliament

OPSI (www.opsi.gov.uk/acts.htm) is an invaluable source for general, including education-specific, legislation, in particular Acts of Parliament, with links to UK Parliament General Acts (from 1988 onwards), and between 1837–1987 more selective sources for UK Parliament General Acts. It also includes links through the UK Parliament to Bills currently before Parliament (www.parliament.uk).

Qualifications and Curriculum Authority (QCA, UK)

Contains links to curriculum material, including the National Curriculum Citizenship, visit www.qca.org.uk (and follow links).

The Commonwealth

The Commonwealth (www.thecommonwealth.org) is an inheritance from the days of British Empire, the Commonwealth is a diverse and rich association of independent states, representing both developed and developing nations.

Teachernet

This site contains a diverse range of educational resources, including many on teaching, learning and assessment in citizenship, http://publications.teachernet.gov.uk.

The Training and Development Agency (TDA)

With a broad remit for the development of professional standards in the teaching profession, the TDA is an essential general resource for new entrants to the profession as well as experienced practitioners, visit www.tda.gov.org.

Teacher Training Resource Bank (TTRB)

This is an invaluable generic resource for all aspects of initial teacher education, with links to Curriculum, Key Stage and Age Range, QTS Standards, Teaching and Learning, Tutors, Mentors and Trainers, Type of Resource, and Whole School. The site (www.ttrb.ac.uk) contains a Glossary and E-librarian Service. Other sources on the site include: Professor Peter Tymms on *Evidence Based Education*; Professor Kit Field on the new *Masters in Teaching and Learning*; Dr Jonathan Savage on Using the *TTRB in Teacher Education*; Professor Richard Andrews on *What counts as evidence in education*; Professor David Lambert on *The TTRB – from a subject specialist perspective*.

United Nations (UN)

The UN offers a wealth of sources on all issues in citizenship, including economics, environment, global terrorism and human rights, *www.un.org* (and follow links).

United Nations Educational, Scientific and Cultural Organisation (UNESCO)

UNESCO is a highly useable resource, with much specific work on citizenship education research www.unesco.org (and follow links).

APPENDIX 2

Citizenship and special educational needs: key resources and guidance

Citizenship as a concept and as a subject places a value on each individual member of a community and the wider society. The inclusive principles behind special educational needs are thus closely cognisant with the sociopolitical principles of citizenship.

The following is a selective list of useful resources:

Directgov

Directgov (www.direct.gov.org) is a public services website, including educational and special educational needs-specific pages. Follow links, for example, to the publication *Special Educational Needs: a step-by-step approach.*

Equality and Human Rights Commission

www.equalityhumanrights.com is an excellent general source, including on disability, with definitions and an authoritative overview of disability rights, with useful lists of addresses for specific aspects of disability.

House of Commons

The House of Commons Education and Skills Select Committee has produced a number of reports on Special Educational Needs – visit www.publication.parliament and follow links.

SEN Teacher

SEN Teacher (www.senteacher.org) provides cost-free teaching and learning resources for pupils with special needs and learning disabilities.

Special Education Needs: Code of Practice (and relevant, related Annexes).

Teachernet SEN

Teachernet SEN provides a wide range of guidance on teaching special educational needs.

Training and Development Agency (TDA)

The TDA provide wide-ranging guidance for teachers at all stages of their career, but especially relevant is *Special Educational Needs in Mainstream Schools: a guide for the beginning teacher*.

REFERENCES

Ajegbo, K., Kiwan, D. and Sharma, S. (2007) *Diversity and Citizenship Curriculum Review*, London: DfES.

Alexander, C. (1996) *The Art of Being Black: The creation of Black British youth identities*, Oxford: Clarendon Press.

Amor, A. (2001) 'The role of religious education in the pursuit of tolerance and non-discrimination', study prepared under the guidance of Prof. Abdelfattah Amor, Special Rapporteur on Freedom of Religion of Belief, for the International Consultative Conference on School Education in Relation with Freedom of Religion and Belief, Tolerance and Non-Discrimination, Madrid, 23–25 November 2001). Retrieved 1 August 2005 from the UN website: www.un.org and links through to http://ap.ohchr.org/documents/dpage_e.aspx?m=86.

Anderson, B. (1991) *Imagined Communities*, London: Verso.

Andreotti, V. and Warwick, P. (2007) 'Engaging students with controversial issues through a dialogue based approach'. Available online at www.citized.info/pdf/commarticles/Post-16%20Paul%20Warwick.doc.

Annette, J. (2003) 'Community, politics and citizenship education', in A. Lockyer, B. Crick and J. Annette (eds) *Education for Democratic Citizenship: Issues of theory and practice*, London: Ashgate, pp. 139–48.

AQA (2008) *GCSE English Specification A (3702) GCSE English Literature Specification (3712) 2009 Examination Information for Teacher Autumn 2008*, Manchester: QCA.

Arendt, H. (2004) [1951] *The Origins of Totalitarianism*, New York: Schocken Books.

Arnon, S. and Reichel, N. (2007) 'Who is the ideal teacher? Am I? Similarity and difference in perception of students of education regarding the qualities of a good teacher and of their own qualities as teachers', *Teachers and Teaching*, 13(5): 441–64.

Arnot, M. (2008) *Educating the Gendered Citizen*, London: Routledge.

Arnot, M. and Dillabough, J.-A. (2002) *Challenging Democracy: International perspectives on gender, education and citizenship*, London: Routledge.

Arthur, J. and Davison, J. (2003) 'Active citizenship and the development of social literacy: a case for experiential learning', www.citized.info/pdf/commarticles/Arthur_Davison.pdf.

Arthur, J., Davies, I. and Hahn, C. (2008) *The SAGE Handbook of Education for Citizenship and Democracy*, London: SAGE.

Arthur, J., Davies, I., Wrenn, A., Haydn, T. and Kerr, D. (2001) *Citizenship through Secondary History*, London: RoutledgeFalmer.

Assessment Reform Group (2002) 'Assessment for learning: 10 principles', www.assessment-reform-group.org.

Association for Citizenship Teaching (2007) 'Identity, diversity and citizenship – a critical review of educational resources', www.teachingcitizenship.org.uk.

Audigier, F. (1998) *Basic Concepts and Core Competencies of Education for Democratic Citizenship*, Strasbourg: Council of Europe.

Ayers, W. (2006) 'The hope and practice of teaching', *Journal of Teacher Education*, 57: 269–77.

Ayton-Shenker, D. (1995) 'The challenge of human rights and cultural diversity', Geneva: United Nations Department of Public Information.

Bagley, J. J. (1965) *Historical Interpretation I: Sources of English medieval history 1066–1540*, Harmondsworth: Penguin.

Bailey, R. (2000) *Education in the Open Society: Karl Popper and schooling*, Aldershot: Ashgate.

Banton, M. (1997) *Ethnic and Racial Consciousness*, 2nd edition, London: Longman.

Barnes, P., Wright, A. and Brandom, A.-M. (eds) (2008) *Learning to Teach Citizenship in the Secondary School*, London: Routledge.

Bennett, M.N. and Finnemore, M. (2004) *Rules for the World: International organizations in global politics*, Ithaca, NY: Cornell University Press.

Benton, T., Cleaver, E., Featherstone, G., Kerr, D., Lopes, J. and Whitby, K. (2008) *Citizenship Education Longitudinal Study (CELS): Sixth annual report. Young people's civic participation in and beyond school: Attitudes, intentions and influences* (DCSF Research Report 052), London: DCSF.

Berger, P., Davie, G. and Fokas, E. (2008) *Religious America, Secular Europe? A theme and variations*, Aldershot: Ashgate.

Bezzina, C. (2006) 'Views from the trenches: beginning teachers' perceptions about their professional development', *Journal of In-Service Education*, 32(4): 411–30.

Bhavnani, R. (2001) *Rethinking Interventions in Racism*, Stoke on Trent: Trentham Books.

Biggs, J. (1996) 'Enhancing teaching through constructive alignment', *Higher Education*, 32: 342–64.

Birzea, C., Kerr, D., Mikkelsen, R., Pol, M., Froumin, I., Losito, B. and Sardoc, M. (2004) *All-European Study on Education for Democratic Citizenship Policies*, Strasbourg: Council of Europe.

Black, P. and Wiliam, D. (1998) *Inside the Black Box: Raising standards through classroom assessment*, London: King's College School of Education.

Black, P., Harrison, C., Lee, C., Marshall, B. and William, D. (2003) *Assessment for Learning: Putting it into practice*, Maidenhead: Open University Press.

Bowles, N.R. (2004) *The Diplomacy of Hope: The United Nations since the Cold War*, London: I.B. Tauris.

Brecht, B. and Willett, J. (1978) *On Theatre*, London: Methuen.

Brentano, F. (1995) *Psychology from an Empirical Standpoint*, edited by L. McAlister, London: Routledge.

Brett, M. (2005) *The Tempest: AS/A-Level student text guide*, Deddington: Philip Allan Updates.

Brett, P. (2002) 'Citizenship through history: what is good practice?', www.citized.info/pdf/commarticles/PB_Citizenship_through_History.doc.

Burleigh, M. (2006) *Earthly Powers: Religion and politics in Europe from the Enlightenment to the Great War*, London: Harper Perennial.

Burleigh, M. (2007) *Sacred Causes: The clash of religion and politics from the Great War to the War on Terror*, New York: HarperCollins.

Burn, K., Hagger, H., Mutton, T. and Everton, T. (2000) 'Beyond concerns with self: the sophisticated thinking of beginning student teachers', *Journal of Education for Teaching*, 26(3): 259–78.

Burns, J.H. (1951) 'The political ideas of George Buchanan', *Scottish History Review*, 30.

Cairns, P. (2008) 'Children being failed by progressive teaching, say Tories', *Guardian*, 9 May.

Casanova, J. (1994) *Religion and Public Governance*, Chicago, IL: Chicago University Press.

Chadwick, O. (1990) *The Reformation*, Harmondsworth: Penguin.

Cleaver, E., Ireland, E., Kerr, D. and Lopes, J. (2005) 'Citizenship Education Longitudinal Study: second cross-sectional survey 2004. Listening to Young People: Citizenship Education in England', DfES Research Report 626, London: DfES.

Clemitshaw, G. (2002) 'Have we got the question right? Engaging future citizens in local historical enquiry', *Teaching History* 106: 20–7.

Copley, T. (2005) *Indoctrination, Education and God: The struggle for the mind*, London: SPCK.

Copley, T. (2009) *Teaching Religion*, second edition, Exeter University Press.

Counsell, C. (2002) 'Editorial', *Teaching History*, 106: 2.

CRE (2005) *After 7/7: Sleepwalking to segregation* (Report on the speech by Sir Trevor Phillips CRE Chair at Manchester Town Hall September 2005). Available online at http://83.137.212.42/sitearchive/cre/Default.aspx.LocID-0hgnew07r.RefLocID-0hg00900c001001.Lang-EN.htm (accessed 9 March 2008).

Cremin, H. and Warwick, P. (2007) 'Subject knowledge in citizenship', in L. Gearon (ed.) *A Practical Guide to Teaching Citizenship in the Secondary School*, London: Routledge.

Crick, B. (1978) 'An explanatory paper', in B. Crick and A. Porter (eds) *Political Education and Political Literacy*, London: Longman.

Crick, B. (1998) *Education for Citizenship and the Teaching of Democracy in Schools: Final report of the Advisory Group on Citizenship*, London: QCA, QCA/98/245.

Crick, B. (2000) *Essays on Citizenship*, London: Continuum.

Crick, B. (2001) 'Foreword', in J. Arthur, I. Davies, A. Wrenn, T. Haydn and D. Kerr (eds) *Citizenship Through Secondary History*, London: RoutledgeFalmer, pp. xvii–xix.

Crick, B. (2004) 'Foreword', in D. Heater (ed.) *Citizenship: The civic ideal in world history, politics and education*, Manchester: Manchester University Press.

Crick, B. (2007) 'Foreword', in D. Kiwan (ed.) *Inclusive Citizenship*, London: Routledge.

Crick, B. and Porter, A. (1978) *Political Education and Political Literacy*, London: Longman.

Darder, A., Baltodano, M.P. and Torres, R. (2008) *The Critical Pedagogy Reader*, 2nd edition, London: Routledge.

Davies, B. and Harré, R. (1990) Positioning: the discursive production of selves, *Journal of the Theory of Social Behaviour*, 20: 43–65.

Davies, I. (1995) 'Education for European citizenship and the teaching and learning of history', in A. Osler, H.F. Rathenow and H. Starkey (eds) *Teaching for Citizenship in Europe*, London: Trentham, pp. 149–60.

Davies, I. (2000) 'Citizenship and the teaching and learning of history', in J. Arthur and R. Phillips (eds) *Issues in History Teaching*, London: Routledge, pp. 137–47.

Davies, I. (2004) 'Science and citizenship education', *International Journal of Science Education*, 26(14): 1751–64.

Davies, I. (2007) 'What is citizenship?', in L. Gearon (ed.) *A Practical Guide to Teaching Citizenship in the Secondary School*, London and New York: Routledge, pp. 1–8.

Davies, I. and John, P. (1995) 'Using history to develop citizenship education in the National Curriculum', *Teaching History*, 78: 5–7.

Davies, I., Hatch, G., Martin, G. and Thorpe, T. (2002) 'What is good citizenship education in history classrooms?', *Teaching History*, 106: 37–43.

Davis, C., Milbank, J. and Zizek, S. (eds) (2005) *Theology and the Political: The new debate*. Durham, NC: Duke University Press.

Davison, J. and Moss, J. (eds) (2000) *Issues in English Teaching*, London: Routledge.

DCSF (2007) *Guidance on the Duty to Promote Community Cohesion*, London: DCSF.

DCSF (2008) *The Assessment for Learning Strategy*, London: DCSF.

DCSF (2008) 'Every Child Matters Framework' (update), http://publications.everychildmatters.gov.uk/eOrderingDownload/DCSF-00331-2008.pdf.

DCSF Standards Site 'Citizenship at Key Stage 3. Getting involved: extending opportunities for pupil participation', www.standards.dcsf.gov.uk/schemes2/citizenship/takingpart?view=get.

DCSF/QCA (2007) *The National Curriculum: Statutory requirements for Key Stages 3 and 4*, London: DCSF.

Deakin Crick, R., Coates, M., Taylor, M. and Ritchie, S. (2004a) *A Systematic Review of the Impact of Citizenship Education on the Provision of Schooling*, London: EPPI – Centre, University of London.

Deakin Crick, R., Coates, M., Taylor, M. and Ritchie, S. (2004b) *Developing Citizenship in Schools: Implications for teachers and students arising from the EPPI Review of the Impact of Citizenship Education on the Provision of Schooling*, Bristol: University of Bristol.

DES (1989) *English for Ages 5–16*, London: DES.

De Souza, M., Engebretson, K., Jackson, R. and McGrady, A. (eds) (2006) *International Handbook of the Religious, Spiritual and Moral Dimensions of Education*, Netherlands: Springer Academic Publishers.

De Souza, M., Durka, G., Engebretson, K. and Gearon, L. (eds) (2010, forthcoming) *International Handbook of Religious Education and the Global Community*, Netherlands: Springer Academic Publishers.

De Vries, H. and Sullivan, L.E. (eds) (2006) *Political Theologies: Public religions in a postsecular world*, New York: Fordham.

DfEE (1998) *The Health and Safety of Pupils on Educational Visits*, London: DfEE.

DfEE (1999) *National Curriculum for England: Citizenship*, London: DfEE.

DfEE/QCA (1999) *The National Curriculum for England: Programmes of study in citizenship*, London: DfEE and QCA.

DfES (2002) *K53 Strategy Training Materials for Foundation Subjects Module 3*, London: DfES.

DfES (2004) 'The school self evaluation tool for citizenship education'. Available at www.citizenshipfoundation.org.uk/lib_res_pdf/0732.pdf.

DfES (2006) *Making Sense of Citizenship: A continuing professional development handbook*, London: Hodder.

DfES (2007) *Diversity and Citizenship Curriculum Review* (the Ajegbo Report), London: DfES. Available at www.teachernet.gov.uk/publications.

Dewey, J. (1966) *Democracy and Education*, London: Macmillan Free Press. Available online at: www.ilt.columbia.edu/Publications/Projects/digitexts/dewy/ (retrieved 9 November 2007).

Dickinson, H. T. (1977) *Liberty and Property: Political ideology in eighteenth century Britain*, London: Methuen.

Douglas, A. (2003) 'Educating for change in the political culture?', *Teaching Citizenship*, Issue 5, Spring: 8–17.

Duffy, C. (2006) 'Education for leisure', in *Selected Poems*, London: Penguin.

Earl, L. (2003) *Assessment as Learning: Using classroom assessment to maximize student learning*, Thousand Oaks, CA: Corwin.

Eco-schools website www.eco-schools.org.uk/.

Elton, G. (1991) *Return to Essentials: Some reflections on the present state of historical study*, Cambridge: Cambridge University Press.

EPPI (2005) *An International Review of Citizenship Education Research*, The Evidence for Policy and Practice Information and Co-ordinating Centre, London: EPPI.

Essed, P. (1991) *Understanding Everyday Racism: An interdisciplinary theory*, London: SAGE.

Eurydice (2005) *Citizenship Education at School in Europe*, Brussels: Eurydice.

Figueroa, P. (2000) 'Citizenship education for a plural society', in A. Osler (ed.) *Citizenship and Democracy in Schools: Diversity, identity, equality*, Trentham: Stoke-on-Trent.

Forsythe, D. P. (2000) *Human Rights in International Relations*, 3rd edition, Cambridge: Cambridge University Press.

Fox, J. and Sandler, S. (eds) (2006) *Religion in World Conflict*, London: Routledge.

Freire, P. (1972) *The Pedagogy of the Oppressed*, London: Penguin.

Freire, P. (1975) *Education: The practice of freedom*, London: Writers and Readers Cooperative.

Froumin, I. (2004) *All-European Study on Policies for EDC: Regional study Eastern European Region*. Strasbourg: Council of Europe.

Furedi, F. (1997) *Culture of Fear: Risk-taking and the morality of low expectation*, London: Cassell.

Gardner, J. (2006) 'Assessment and learning: an introduction', in J. Gardner (ed.) *Assessment and Learning*, London: SAGE.

Gearon, L. (ed.) (2002) *Religion and Human Rights: A reader*, Brighton and Portland: Sussex Academic Press.

Gearon, L. (2003) *How Do We Learn to Become Good Citizens? A professional user review of UK research*, London: British Educational Research Association.

Gearon, L. (ed.) (2003a) *Learning to Teach Citizenship in the Secondary School*, London: Routledge.

Gearon, L. (2004) *Citizenship through Religious Education*, London and New York: Routledge.

Gearon, L. (Guest Editor) (2006) 'Children's spirituality and children's rights', Special Issue, *International Journal of Children's Spirituality*, 11(2): 193–8.

Gearon, L. (2007) *A Practical Guide to Teaching Citizenship in the Secondary School*, London and New York: Routledge.

Gearon, L. (2007a) 'Researching Citizenship', in L. Gearon (ed.) *A Practical Guide to Teaching Citizenship in the Secondary School*, London and New York: Routledge, pp. 98–111.

Gearon, L. (Guest Editor) (2008) 'Religion, human rights and citizenship', Special Issue, *British Journal of Religious Education*, 30 (2).

Gearon, L. (2008a) in P. Barnes, A. Wright and A.-M. Brandom (eds) *Learning to Teach Religious Education in the Secondary School*, London and New York: Routledge.

Gilroy, P. (1997) 'Detours of identity', in S. Hall and K. Woodward (eds) *Identity and Difference*, London: SAGE.

Gilroy, P. (2006) *After Empire: Melancholia or convivial culture?* London: Routledge.

Goldie, P. (2000) *The Emotions: A philosophical exploration*, Oxford: Clarendon Press.

Gray, J. (2007) *Black Mass*, London: Penguin.

Griffin, C. (1997) 'Representations of the young', in J. Rocher and S. Tucker (eds) *Youth in Society: Contemporary theory, policy and practice*, London: SAGE.

Grimmitt, M. (2000) *Pedagogies of Religious Education*, Great Wakering: McCrimmons.

Habermas, J. (1996) *Between Facts and Norms*, London: Polity.

Hall, S. (2000) 'Multicultural citizens, monocultural citizenship?', in N. Pearce and J. Hallgarten (eds) *Tomorrow's Citizens: Critical debates in citizenship and education*, London: Institute for Public Policy Research.

Halstead, J.M. and Pike, M.A. (2006) *Citizenship and Moral Education: Values in action*, London: Routledge.

Hancock, W.K. and Latham, R.T.E. (1937) *Survey of British Commonwealth Affairs: Vol.1. Problems of nationality, 1918–1936*, London: Allen & Unwin.

Hanson, E.O. (2006) *Religion and Politics in the International System Today*, Cambridge: Cambridge University Press.

Hargreaves, A. (1998) 'The emotional practice of teaching', *Teaching and Teacher Education*, 14(8): 835–54.

Hargreaves, A. (2001) 'The emotional geographies of teaching', *Teachers College Record*, 103: 1056–80.

Harlen, W. (2006) 'On the relationship between assessment for formative and summative purposes', in J. Gardner (ed.) *Assessment and Learning*, London: SAGE.

Harlow, B. and Carter, M. (eds) (1999) *Imperialism and Orientalism: A documentary sourcebook*, Oxford: Blackwell.

Harpviken, K.B. and Roislien, H.E. (2005) *Mapping the Terrain: The role of religion in peacemaking*, Oslo: International Peace Research Institute, for the Norwegian Ministry of Foreign Affairs.

Hayes, D. (2003) 'Emotional preparation for teaching: a case study about trainee teachers in England', *Teacher Development* 7(2): 153–71.

Haynes, J. (ed.) (2006) *The Politics of Religion: A survey*, London and New York: Routledge.

Hayward, J. (2007) 'Values, beliefs and the citizenship teacher', in L. Gearon (ed.) *Starting to Teach Citizenship in the Secondary School*, Oxford: RoutledgeFalmer.

Heater, D. (1974) *History and Political Education*, Occasional Pamphlet No. 1, Manchester: Politics Association.

Heater, D. (1997) 'The reality of multiple citizenship', in I. Davies and A. Sobisch (eds) *Developing European Citizens*, Sheffield: Sheffield Hallam University Press.

Heater, D. (1999) *What is Citizenship?*, Cambridge: Polity Press.

Heater, D. (2004) *Citizenship: The civic ideal in world history, politics and education*, Manchester: Manchester University Press.

Held, D. (1995) 'Democracy and the new international order', in D. Archibugi and D. Held (eds) *Cosmopolitan Democracy*, Cambridge: Polity Press.

Held, D. (1996) *Models of Democracy*, 2nd edition, Cambridge: Polity Press.

Held, D. (2001) 'Violence and justice in a global age', paper published at www.opendemocracy.net/forum/strands_home.asp on 14 September 2001.

Hess, D. and Avery, P. (2008) 'The discussion of controversial issues as a form and goal of democratic education', in J. Arthur, I. Davies and C. Hahn (eds) *The SAGE International Handbook on Democracy and Citizenship Education*, London: SAGE.

Himmelfarb, G. (2004) *The Roads to Modernity: The British, French and American Enlightenments*, New York: Alfred A. Knopf.

HMI (2006) 'Towards consensus: citizenship in secondary schools', report no. HMI 2666 from www.ofsted.gov.uk.

Hobbes, T. [1647] (1998) *On the Citizen*, Cambridge: Cambridge University Press.

Hoelzl, M. and Ward, G. (eds) (2006) *Religion and Political Thought*, London: Continuum.

Home Office (2001) *Community Cohesion: A report of the independent review team (Cantle Report)*, London: HMSO.

Hoskins, B. (2006) *Framework for the Development of Indicators on Active Citizenship and Education and Training for Active Citizenship*, Ispra: Joint Research Centre/CRELL.

Hoskins, B. Villalba, E., Van Nijlen, D. and Barber, C. (2008) *Measuring Civic Competence in Europe: A composite indicator based on the IEA Civic Education Study 1999 for 14 year olds in school*, Ispra: Joint Research Centre/CRELL.

Hoskins, B., Jesinghaus, J., Mascherini, M., Munda, G., Nardo, M., Saisana, M., Van Nijlen, D. and Villalba, E. (2006) *Measuring Active Citizenship in Europe*, CRELL Research Paper 4, Ispra: Joint Research Centre/CRELL.

House of Commons (2007) *House of Commons Education and Skills Committee Citizenship Education: Second report of Sessions 2006–07*, London: HMSO.

Huddleston, T. and Kerr, D. (2006) *Making Sense of Citizenship: A continuing professional development handbook*, London: Hodder.

Hume, D. (2000) *A Treatise of Human Nature*, D. Norton and M. Norton (eds), Oxford: Clarendon Press.

Huntington, S. (2002) *The Clash of Civilizations*, London and New York: Free Press.

Hutchings, K. and Dannreuter, R. (eds) (1999) *Cosmopolitan Citizenship*, Basingstoke: Macmillan.

IEA (2004) *Civic Knowledge and Engagement at Age 14 in 28 Countries: Results from the IEA Civic Education Study*, The International Association for the Evaluation of Educational Achievement, www.indiana.edu and www.iea.nl (and follow links).

IEA (2008) *International Civic and Citizenship Education Study: Assessment framework*, Amsterdam: IEA.

Illich, I. (1970) *Deschooling Society*, New York: Harper Row.

Ireland, E., Kerr, D., Lopes, J., Nelson, J. and Cleaver, E. (2006) *Active Citizenship and Young People: Opportunities, experiences and challenges in and beyond school*, DfES Research Report 732, London: DfES.

Isin, E. F. and Wood, P.K. (1999) *Citizenship and Identity*, London: SAGE.

Jackson, R. (2002) *International Perspectives on Citizenship, Education and Religious Diversity*, London: Routledge.

Jackson, R. (2004) *Rethinking Religious Education and Plurality: Issues in diversity and pedagogy*, London: Routledge.

Jackson, R., Miedema, S., Weisse, W. and Willaime, J.-F. (2007) (eds) *Religion and Education in Europe: Developments, contexts and debates*, Munster: Waxmann.

James, H. (ed.) (2006) *Civil Society, Religion and Global Governance: Paradigms of power and persuasion*, London: Routledge.

Jeffrey, B. and Woods, P. (1996) 'Feeling deprofessionalized: The social construction of emotions during an OFSTED inspection', *Cambridge Journal of Education*, 26(3): 325–45.

Jenkins, R. (1996) *Social Identity*, London: Routledge.

Jerome, L. (2008) 'Assessing citizenship education', in J. Arthur, I. Davies and C. Hahn (eds) *The SAGE International Handbook of Democracy and Citizenship Education*, London: SAGE.

Johnson, L. and Reiman, A. (2007) 'Beginning teacher disposition: examining the moral/ethical domain', *Teaching and Teacher Education*, 23(5): 676–87.

Juergensmeyer, M. (ed.) (2005) *Religion in Global Civil Society*, Oxford and New York: Oxford University Press.

Kendal, S., Murfield, J., Dillon, J. and Wilkin, A. (2006) *Education Outside the Classroom: Research to identify what training is offered by initial teacher training institutions*, London: DfES and National Foundation for Educational Research.

Kerr, D. (1993) 'History', in J. Edwards and K. Fogelman (eds) *Developing Citizenship in the Curriculum*, London: David Fulton.

Kerr, D. (1999) *Re-examining Citizenship Education: The case of England*, Slough: NFER.

Kerr, D. (2003) 'Citizenship education in international perspective', in L. Gearon (ed.) *Learning to Teach Citizenship in the Secondary School*, London: Routledge, pp. 5–27.

Kerr, D. (2004a) *All-European Study on Policies for EDC: Regional study Western Europe Region*, Strasbourg: Council of Europe.

Kerr, D. (2004b) 'How to develop citizenship education in schools: England's results from the IEA Citizenship Education Study', *Topic*, Issue 31, Item 3.

Kerr, D. and Cleaver, E. (2004) *Citizenship Education Longitudinal Study: Literature review – citizenship education one year on – what does it mean? Emerging definitions and approaches in the first year of national curriculum citizenship in England*, DfES Research Report 532, London: DfES.

Kerr, D., Keating, A. and Ireland, E. (2009) *Pupil Assessment in Citizenship Education in Europe: Purposes, practices and possibilities*, Slough: NFER/CIDREE.

Kerr, D., Lines, A., Blenkinsop, S. and Schagen, I. (2002) *What Citizenship and Education Mean to 14-year-olds: England's results from the IEA Citizenship Education Study*, London: DfES/NFER.

Kerr, D., Cleaver, E., Ireland, E. and Blenkinsop, S. (2003) *Citizenship Education Longitudinal Study: First cross-sectional survey, 2001–2002*, DfES Research Report 416, London: DfES.

Kerr, D., Ireland, E., Lopes, J. and Craig, R. with Cleaver, E. (2004) *Making Citizenship Real. Citizenship education longitudinal study: Second annual report. First longitudinal survey*, DfES Research Report 531, London: DfES.

Kerr, D., Lopas, J., Nelson, J., White, K., Cleaver, E. and Benton, T. (2007) 'Vision versus pragmatism: citizenship in the secondary school curriculum in England', available from www.dfes.gov.uk/research/data/uploadfiles/RR845.pdf.

Kincheloe, J.L. (2004) *Critical Pedagogy Primer*, Oxford: Peter Lang.

Kinloch, N. (1998) 'Learning about the Holocaust: moral or historical question?', *Teaching History*, 93: 44–6.

Kohlberg, L. (1981) *Essays on Moral Development, Vol. I: The philosophy of moral development*, San Francisco, CA: Harper & Row.

Kolb, D. (1984) *Experiential Learning*, New Jersey: Prentice Hall.

Kotze, G. (2004) 'Outcomes-based assessment strategies', in J.G. Maree and W.J. Fraser (eds) *Outcomes-Based Assessment*, Sandown: Heinemann.

Krasno, J.E. (ed.) (2004) *The United Nations: Confronting the challenges of a global society*, Boulder, CO and London: Lynne Rienner Publishers.

Kymlicka, W. (2001) *Politics in the Vernacular: Nationalism, multiculturalism and citizenship*, Oxford: Oxford University Press.

Kyriacou, C. (1998) *Essential Teaching Skills*, Cheltenham: Nelson Thornes, p. 113.

Kyriacou, C. (2001) *Effective Teaching in Schools: Theory and practice*, 2nd edition, Cheltenham: Nelson Thornes.

Kyriacou, C. and Kunc, R. (2007) 'Beginning teachers' expectations of teaching', *Teaching and Teacher Education*, 23(8): 1246–57.

Lacey, C. (1977) *The Socialization of Teachers*, London: Methuen.

Lankshear, C. (1997) 'Critical social literacy for the classroom: an approach using conventional texts across the curriculum', in C. Lankshear, J.P. MGee, M. Knobel and C. Searle *Changing Literacies*, Buckingham: Open University Press, pp. 41–62.

Lee, P. and Shemilt, D. (2007) 'New alchemy or fatal attraction? History and citizenship 14–19', *Teaching History*, 129: 14–19.

Leighton, R. (2004) 'Trainees, mentors and citizenship: fair conflict resolution begins here', *Teaching Citizenship*, 9: 26–31.

Leonard, T. (1984) 'This is thi six a clock news', *Intimate Voices*, Newcastle: Galloping Dog Press.

Lerner, N. (2000) *Religion, Beliefs, and Human Rights*, Maryknoll, NY: Orbis.

LINC (1992) *Language in the National Curriculum: Materials for professional development*, LINC.

Lindholm, T., Durham, W.C. and Tahzib-Lies, B.G. (eds) (2003) *Facilitating Freedom of Religion or Belief*, The Hague: Kluwer.

Lockyer, A. (2003) *Introduction and Review*, in A. Lockyer, B. Crick and J. Annette (eds) *Education for Democratic Citizenship: Issues of theory and practice*, London: Ashgate, pp. 1–14.

Lopes, J. and Kerr, D. (2005) 'Moving citizenship education forward: key considerations for schools and colleges', *Topic*, 34: 50–6.

Losito, B. (2004) *All-European Study on Policies for EDC: Regional study Southern Europe Region*, Strasbourg: Council of Europe.

Lundeen, C. (2004) 'Teacher development: the struggle of beginning teachers in creating moral (caring) classroom environments', *Early Child Development and Care*, 174(6): 549–64.

Lyotard, J.-F. (1984) *The Postmodern Condition: A report on knowledge*, Manchester: Manchester University Press.

MacCulloch, D. (2005) *The Reformation*, London: Penguin.

McLaughlin, T. (1992) 'Citizenship, diversity and education: a philosophical perspective', *Journal of Moral Education*, 21(3): 235–50.

McLaughlin, T. (2000) 'Citizenship education in England: the Crick Report and beyond', *Journal of Philosophy of Education*, 34(4): 541–70.

McLaughlin, T. (2005) 'The educative importance of ethos', *British Journal of Educational Studies*, 53(3): 306–25.

Macpherson, W. (1999) *The Stephen Lawrence Inquiry*, London: HMSO.

Magee, B. (1985) *Popper*, London: Fontana.

Marshall, P. (ed.) (2000) *Religious Freedom in the World: A global report on freedom and persecution*, London: Broadman & Holman.

Marshall, T.H. (1950) *Social Class and Citizenship*, Cambridge: Cambridge University Press.

Marshall, T.H. and Bottomore, T. (1992) *Citizenship and Social Class*, London: Pluto.

Marwick, A. (1970) *The Nature of History*, London: Macmillan.

Maylor, U., Read, B., Mendick, H., Ross, A. and Pollack, N. (2007) *Diversity and Citizenship in the Curriculum: Research review*, London: DfES.

Mikkelsen, R. (2004) *All-European Study on Policies for EDC: Regional study Northern European Region*, Strasbourg: Council of Europe.

Mill, J. S. (2003) [1859; 1861] *Utilitarianism; On Liberty: Including Mill's Essay on Bentham, and Selections from the Writings of Jeremy Bentham and John Austin*, edited with an introduction by Mary Warnock, 2nd edition, Malden, MA and Oxford: Blackwell.

Miller, D. (1999) 'Bounded citizenship', in K. Hutchings and R. Dannreuther (eds) *Cosmopolitan Citizenship*, London: Macmillan.

Morgan, M.L. (ed.) (2005) *Classics of Moral and Political Theory*, 4th edition, Cambridge: Hackett.

National Advisory Committee on Creative and Cultural Education (1999) *All Our Futures: Creativity, culture and education*. Report to the Secretary of State for Education and Employment and the Secretary of State for Culture, Media and Sport, May 1999, London: NACCCE.

Neelands, J. (2004) *Beginning Drama 11–14*, London: David Fulton.

Neill, A.S. (1953) *The Free Child*, London: Herbert Jenkins.

NFER (2007) *Vision Versus Pragmatism: Citizenship in the secondary school*, Slough: National Foundation for Educational Research.

Nias, J. (1996) 'Thinking about feeling: the emotions in teaching', *Cambridge Journal of Education*, (26)3: 293–306.

Oakshott, M. (1956) 'Political education', in P. Laslett (ed.) *Philosophy, Politics and Society*, Oxford: Basil Blackwell.

Ofsted (2006) *Towards Consensus? Citizenship in secondary schools*, London: Ofsted.

Ofsted (2007) *Making Sense of Religion*, London: Ofsted.

Oliver, D. and Heater, D. (1994) *The Foundations of Citizenship*, Hemel Hempstead: Harvester Wheatsheaf.

Orsmond, C. (2004) 'Assessment in social science education', in J.G. Maree and W.J. Fraser (eds) *Outcomes-Based Assessment*, Sandown: Heinemann.

OSDE (2006a) 'Critical literacy, independent thinking, global citizenship, global issues and perspectives', available online at www.osdemethodology.org.uk (accessed 4 January 2008).

OSDE (2006b) *Critical Literacy in Global Citizenship Education: Professional development resource pack*, Derby: Global Education Derby.

Osler, A. (1997) *The Education and Careers of Black Teachers: Changing identities, changing lives*, Buckingham: Open University Press.

Osler, A. (2000) 'The Crick Report: difference, equality and racial difference', *Curriculum Journal*, 11(1): 25–37.

Osler, A. (2007) *Faith Schools and Community Cohesion: Observations on community consultations*, Runnymead Trust Interim report.

Osler, A. and Starkey, H. (1996) *Teacher Education and Human Rights*, London: Fulton.

Osler, A. and Starkey, H. (2000) 'Citizenship, human rights and cultural diversity', in A. Osler (ed.) *Citizenship and Democracy in Schools: Diversity, identity, equality*, Stoke-on-Trent: Trentham.

Osler, A. and Starkey, H. (2001a) Young people in Leicester (UK): community, identity and citizenship, *Interdialogos*, 2(1): 48–9.

Osler, A. and Starkey, H. (2001b) 'Citizenship education and national identities in France and England: inclusive or exclusive?', *Oxford Review of Education*, 27(2): 287–305.

Osler, A. and Vincent, K. (2002) *Citizenship and the Challenge of Global Education*, Stoke: Trentham.

Osler, A. and Vincent, K. (2003) *Girls and Exclusion: Rethinking the agenda*, London: RoutledgeFalmer.

Osler, A. and Starkey, H. (2005) *Changing Citizenship: Democracy and inclusion in education*, Maidenhead: Open University Press.

Osler, A. and Starkey, H. (2006) *Education for Democratic Citizenship: Research policy and practice 1995–2005*, London: British Educational Research Association.

Osmer, R.R. (2003) *Religious Education between Modernization and Globalization: New perspectives on the United States and Germany*, Grand Rapids, MI: W.B. Eerdmans.

Paine, T. 1985 [1791/2] *Rights of Man*, Harmondsworth: Penguin.

Palmer, J. and Garratt, D. (2003) 'Active citizenship reconsidered – the challenge for initial teacher training', www.citized.info/pdf/commarticles/Dean_Garratt_Janet_Palmer.pdf.

Parekh, B. (2000) *The Future of Multi-Ethnic Britain*, London: The Runnymede Trust.

Peterson, A. (2008) 'The civic republican tradition and citizenship education', unpublished PhD thesis, University of Kent.

Peterson, A. and Knowles, C. (2007) 'PGCE citizenship student teacher understandings of active citizenship', www.citized.info/pdf/commarticles/ActiveProjectReport.pdf.

Phillips, R. (2002) 'Historical significance – the forgotten key elements?', *Teaching History*, 106: 14–19.

Phillips, R. (2003) 'History, citizenship and identity', *Past Forward* (Historical Association), 37–41.

Pol, M. (2004) *All-European Study on Policies for EDC: Regional study Central European Region*, Strasbourg: Council of Europe.

Popper, K. (1946) *The Open Society and its Enemies*, London: Routledge.

Powell, A. (2007) 'Practical learning, lifelong learning – why it matters and the role of Edge', in M. Yarnit (ed.) *Advancing Opportunities: New models of schooling*, London: The Smith Institute, pp. 24–37.

Putnam, R. (2000) *Bowling Alone: The collapse and revival of American community*, London: Simon & Schuster.

QCA (1998) *Education for Citizenship and the Teaching of Democracy in Schools: Final report of the Advisory Group on Citizenship* (The Crick Report), London: QCA. Available online at www.qca.org.uk/downloads/6123_crick_report_1998.pdf.

QCA (2004) *Play Your Part: Post-16 citizenship*, London: QCA.

QCA (2006) *Assessing Citizenship Education*, London: QCA.

QCA (2006) *Assessing Citizenship: Example assessment activities for Key Stage 3*, London: QCA.

QCA (2007) *Citizenship Programme of Study for Key Stage 3 and Attainment Target*, http://curriculum.qca.org.uk/key-stages-3-and-4/subjects/index.aspx.

QCA (2007) *National Curriculum*, http://curriculum.qca.org.uk.

QCA (2007) *The National Curriculum: Statutory requirements for Key Stages 3 and 4*, London: QCA.

QCA (2008) *Assessing Pupils' Progress: Assessment at the heart of learning*, London: QCA.

QCA (2008) *Big Picture*, www.qca.org.uk/libraryAssets/media/Big_Picture_2008.pdf.

QCA (undated) *Bigger Picture of the Curriculum*, www.qcda.gov.uk/curriculum.

QCA (undated) *National Curriculum: Peer assessment and self-assessment*, www.curriculum. qca.org.uk.

QCA (undated) *Citizenship at Key Stage 4 Staying Involved: Extending opportunities for pupil participation*, www.standards.dcsf.gov.uk/schemes2/ks4citizenship/takingpart?view=get.

QCA (undated) *Citizenship at KS3 Subject Leaflets*, www.standards.dcsf.gov.uk/schemes2/ citizenship/566646?view=get.

QCA (undated) *Citizenship at KS4 Scheme of Work Teachers Guide*, www.standards.dcsf. gov.uk/schemes2/citizenship/teachersguide?view=get.

QCA (undated) *Citizenship and PSHE: Working with external contributors – guidance for schools*, www.qca.org.uk/libraryAssets/media/6144_pshe_working_with_external_ contributors.pdf.

QCA/DfES (2004) *The Non-Statutory National Framework for Religious Education*, London: QCA/DfES.

QCA/DfES (2007) *Programme of Study (Non-Statutory) for Religious Education*, London: QCA/DfES.

Queensland, The State of (2004) *The New Basics Project*, Department of Education, Training and the Arts (http://education.qld.gov.au/corporate/newbasics).

Rea, T. (in progress) *Understanding Children's Experiences at a Residential Outdoor Education Centre: Discourses, identity and positioning*, unpublished PhD, University of Plymouth, Plymouth.

Rea, T. and Rutter, O. (2003) 'Learning from them learning from us', *Pastoral Care in Education*, 21(4): 22–6).

Ria, L., Seve, C., Saury, J., Theureau, J. and Durand, M. (2003) 'Beginning teachers' situated emotions: a study of first classroom experiences', *Journal of Education for Teaching*, 29(3): 219–34.

Rickinson, M., Dillon, J., Teamey, K., Morris, M., Choi, M.Y., Sanders, D. (2004). *A Review of Research on Outdoor Learning*. Shrewsbury: NFER/Field Studies Council.

Robson, W.A. (1967) *Politics and Government at Home and Abroad*, London: Allen & Unwin.

Roker, D., Player, K. and Coleman, J. (1999) 'Young people's voluntary and campaigning activities as sources of political action', *Oxford Review of Education*, 25(1/2): 185–98.

Rousseau, J.J. (1968) [1762] *The Social Contract*, translated by Maurice Cranston, London: Penguin.

Rousseau, J.J. (2007) [1762] *Emile, or on Education*, Sioux Falls, SD: NuVision.

Ruddock, J. (2003) 'Pupil voice and citizenship education – a report for the QCA Citizenship and PSHE Team'. Available online at www.qca.org.uk/libraryAssets/media/6236_pupil_voice.pdf.

Runzo, J., Martin, N.M. and Sharma, A. (eds) (2004) *Human Rights and Responsibilities in the World's Religions*, Oxford: Oneworld.

Rushton, R. (2004) *Human Rights and the Image of God*, London: SCM.

Rutter, J. (2003) *Supporting Refugee Children in 21st Century Britain*, Stoke-on-Trent: Trentham Books.

Ryan, J. (1999) *Race and Ethnicity in Multi-Ethnic Schools*, Clevedon: Multilingual Matters.

Schlesinger, S.C. (2003) *Act of Creation: The founding of the United Nations*, Boulder, CO: Westview Press.

Searle, C. (1998) *None but Our Words*, Buckingham: Open University Press.

Seely Brown, J., Collins, A. and Duguid, P. (1989) 'Situated learning and the culture of learning', *Education Researcher*, 18(1): 32–42.

Shattuck, J. (2003) 'Religion, rights and terrorism', Harvard University conference on Religion, Democracy and Human Rights, www.law.harvard.edu (and follow links).

Smart, N. (1969) *The Religious Experience of Mankind*, Toronto: Collier Macmillan.

Smart, N. (1989) *The World's Religions*, 2nd edition, Cambridge: Cambridge University Press.

Smith, A. (2008) 'Teachit staffroom roundup – hot topics', *Classroom*, 6: 49, Sheffield: NATE.

Sordi, M. (1998) *The Christians and the Roman Empire*, London and New York: Routledge.

Stables, A. (2005) *Semiotic Engagement: A new theory of education*, Lewiston, NY: Mellen Press.

Stanulis, R., Campbell, P. and Hicks, J. (2002) 'Finding her way: a beginning teacher's story of learning to honour her own voice in teaching', *Educational Action Research*, 10(1): 45–66.

Starkey, H. (2000) 'Citizenship education in France and Britain: evolving theories and practices', *The Curriculum Journal*, 11(1): 39–54.

Steiner-Khamsi, G., Torney-Purta, J. and Schwille, J. (eds) (2003) *New Paradigms and Recurring Paradoxes in Education for Citizenship: An international comparison*, International Perspectives on Education and Society, Vol. 5, Amsterdam: Elsevier Science.

Stern, J. (2006) *Teaching Religious Education*, London and New York: Continuum.

Storkey, A. (2005) *Jesus and Politics: Confronting the powers*, Grand Rapids, MI: Baker Academic.

Sutton, R. and Wheatley, K. (2003) 'Teachers' emotions and teaching: a review of the literature and directions for future research', *Educational Psychology Review*, 15(4): 327–58.

Swaine, L. (2006) *The Liberal Conscience: Politics and principle in a world of religious pluralism*, New York: Columbia University Press.

Talmon, J. L. 1961 [1952] *The Origins of Totalitarian Democracy*, Mercury Books.

Taylor, M. (1998) *Values Education and Values in Education*, London: ATL.

TDA (2007) *Professional Standards for Teachers: Qualified teacher status*, London: TDA.

Tocqueville, A. de (2003) [1836] *Democracy in America*, translated by G.E. Bevan, introduction and notes I. Kramnick, London: Penguin.

Tomlinson, S. (2008) *Race and Education: Policy and politics in Britain*, Maidenhead: Open University Press.

Torney-Purta, J., Schwille, J. and Amadeo, J.-A. (eds) (1999) *Civic Education across Countries: Twenty-four national case studies from the IEA Civic Education Project*, Amsterdam: International Association for the Evaluation of Educational Achievement (IEA).

Torney-Purta, J., Lehmann, R., Oswald, H. and Schulz, W. (2001) *Citizenship and Education in Twenty-Eight Countries: Civic knowledge and participation at age fourteen*, Amsterdam: International Association for the Evaluation of Educational Achievement (IEA).

Trigg, R. (2007) *Religion in Public Life: Must faith be privatized?*, Oxford: Oxford University Press.

Turner, B. (1993) 'Contemporary problems in the theory of citizenship', in B.S. Turner (ed.) *Citizenship and Social Theory*, London: SAGE, pp. 1–18.

UN (2008) 'Alliance of civilizations', www.unaoc.org/content/view/39/187/lang,english/ (accessed 29 May 2008).

UNESCO (1995) *Integrated Framework of Action on Education for Peace, Human Rights and Democracy*, Paris: UNESCO.

UNESCO (2006) *Guidelines on Intercultural Education*, Paris: UNESCO.

UNESCO (2006a) 'Expert meeting on intercultural education', Report, Paris: UNESCO.

Upton, J. (2004) 'Facing history and ourselves', *Teaching Citizenship*, 8: 35–7.

Urban-Smith, J. and Crawford, N. (2005) *Assessing Citizenship. Making it manageable and meaningful*, Gloucestershire: Gloucestershire County Council.

Verhellen, E. (2000) 'Children's rights and education', in A. Osler (ed.) *Citizenship and Democracy in Schools: Diversity, identity, equality*, Stoke-on-Trent: Trentham.

Ward, G. (2003) *True Religion*, Oxford: Blackwell.

Warwick, P. (2008a) 'The development of apt citizenship education through listening to young people's voices', *Educational Action Research*, 16(3): 321–35.

Warwick, P. (2008b) Talking through global issues: a dialogue based approach to CE and its potential contribution to community cohesion', available online at www. citized.info/ ?strand=2&r_menu=res.

Wellman, C. (2000) *The Proliferation of Rights: Moral progress or empty rhetoric?* Oxford: Westview.

Wenger, E. (1998) *Communities of Practice: Learning, meaning and identity*, Cambridge: Cambridge University Press.

Wenger, E. (2008) 'Communities of practice: a new discipline of learning', unpublished seminar paper, Exeter University.

West, L. (2007) 'Developing subject knowledge', in L. Gearon (ed.) *A Practical Guide to Teaching Citizenship in the Secondary School*, London: Routledge.

Whiteley, P. (2005) *Citizenship Education Longitudinal Study: Second literature review. Citizenship education: The political science perspective* (DfES Research Report 631), London: DfES.

Whitty, G. (2002) *Making Sense of Education Policy*, London: Paul Chapman.

Winch, C., Roberts, M. and Lambert, D. (2005) *Civic Education for the 14–19 Age Group: How subject might contribute*, available online at www.nuffield14–19review.org.uk/files/documents96–1.pdf.

Wineburg, S. (2001) *Historical Thinking and Other Unnatural Acts: Charting the future of teaching the past*, Philadelphia: Temple University Press.

Wolin, S.S. (2008) *Democracy Inc: Managed democracy and the specter of inverted totalitarianism*, Princeton, NJ: Princeton University Press.

Woodhead, L., Fletcher, P. and Kawanami, H. (eds) (2002) *Religions in the Modern World*, London: Routledge.

Wootton, D. (1986) *Divine Right and Democracy*, Harmondsworth: Penguin.

Wrenn, A. (1999) 'Build it in, don't bolt it on: history's opportunity to support critical citizenship', *Teaching History*, 96: 6–7.

Wright, C. (1986) 'School processes – an ethnographic study', in J. Eggleston, D. Dunn and M. Anjali (eds) *Education for Some: The educational and vocational experiences of 15–18-year-old members of ethnic minority groups*, Stoke-on-Trent: Trentham.

Wright, C. (1992) *Race Relations in the Primary School*, London: David Fulton.

Young, H. (1988) 'Citizens! The cure-all rallying cry', *Guardian*, 1 September.

Zembylas, M. (2004) 'Emotional issues in teaching science: a case study of a teacher's views', *Research in Science Education*, 34: 343–64.

INDEX

Unless otherwise stated, topics relate to citizenship education in the UK, primarily England.